New Era, New Church?

New Era,
New Church?

THE NEW MILLENNIUM
CHALLENGE TO THE CHURCHES

Steve Chalke and Sue Radford

HarperCollins*Publishers*

HarperCollins*Religious*
Part of HarperCollins*Publishers*
77–85 Fulham Palace Road, London W6 8JB

First published in Great Britain in 1999 by HarperCollins*Religious*

1 3 5 7 9 10 8 6 4 2

The Scripture quotations contained herein are from the New Revised Standard Version Bible,
copyright © 1989, by the Division of Christian Education of the National Council of the
Churches of Christ in the USA, and are used by permission. All rights reserved.

Extract from *Common Worship: Initiation Services* on p. 36 copyright © The Central
Board of Finance of the Church of England 1980. Reproduced by permission.

Extracts on pp. 63 and 118 from the *Oxford English Dictionary*, 2nd edition,
1989, are quoted by permission of Oxford University Press.

Extract on p. 69 from the *Book of Common Prayer* reproduced by kind
permission of Cambridge University Press.

The Preface to Chapter 10 is extracted from a Homily given by Cardinal Basil Hume at
the Gathering Meeting at Aylesford Priory, 27 June 1998. Used with kind permission.

A catalogue record for this book is available from the British Library

ISBN 000 274026 5

Printed and bound in Great Britain by
Caledonian International Book Manufacturing Ltd, Glasgow

Contents

■ Acknowledgements

Thank you to all those who have helped us produce the book, especially Andrew Carey, Paul Hansford, Gill Harper, James Catford, Kathy Dyke and the team at HarperCollins.

Many thanks also to: Archbishop George Carey, Cardinal Basil Hume and Charles Wookey (Archbishop's House), Roger and Faith Forster, Rev. Vera Hunt, Rev. Preb. Richard Bewes (All Souls, Langham Place), Ron Allison, Robert Stent, David Rennie, Sir Cliff Richard, Gill Snow and the Cliff Richard Organisation, Erica Youngman (March for Jesus), Martin Robinson (Bible Society), Joel Edwards, Colin Saunders and Diane Toothill (Evangelical Alliance), Stephen Lynas (The Archbishops' Millennium Advisory Group), Anne Hibbert and Alan Dixon (Churches Together in England), Pam Glover and Sheena Gillies (All Souls, Langham Place), Ruth Hansford, and all those connected with Fanfare for a New Generation and Oasis Media.

Introduction:
New Era, New Church

Some years before the privatization of the rail network, or so the story goes, British Rail appointed a new Chief Executive. The company's reputation was on a par with the reputation of its legendary sandwiches ... which is to say that people used it because they felt they *needed* to, rather than out of choice. One of the new Chief Executive's first tasks, therefore, was to turn around this wave of negative publicity and give the company a more positive image and a zippy new slogan, attracting people off the roads and onto the trains. To achieve this, he turned to the professionals, employing a major advertising agency.

A few weeks later, after they'd done extensive market research and opinion polling and thought long and hard about how best to revamp BR's image, the agency invited him to come to their offices to hear their ideas. As he walked into the smart lobby of their plush London premises, he was greeted by the sight of the receptionist calmly filing her nails. He approached the reception desk and waited for her to look up. After a few seconds, when she still didn't seem to have noticed his presence, he cleared his throat.

'Hmmm?' she intoned, still engrossed in her nails.

'I'm here to see the director,' he announced. 'I have an appointment. My name is...'

'Wait there, love,' she interrupted him, pointing to a large sofa in the reception area. He walked over to the sofa, sat down, glanced at the day-old newspaper and the empty coffee cup lying on the low table in front of him, and waited. Five long minutes passed. The receptionist stopped filing her nails, reached into her bag, drew out a small pot of varnish, and started to paint them a dazzling shade of pink. Concerned that she didn't seem to have notified anyone of his arrival, the BR Chief Executive stood up and walked over to the desk to remind her that he was still waiting to be seen.

'Excuse me, but I've been waiting for over five minutes now. I have an appointment with the director of the company. If you could tell him that I'm on a rather tight schedule. My name is...'

'Yeah, alright love,' she replied, cutting him off again but otherwise showing no interest whatsoever in what he was saying. 'Keep your hair on. Be with you in a minute.'

Unsure what to make of such an apparently unbusinesslike attitude, he returned to the sofa, looked at his watch and waited. Still she made no move to inform anyone that he was waiting in the lobby. Still no one came to greet him, or explain why things were seemingly running late. As the minutes rolled by, he grew more and more infuriated. When nothing further had happened after another five minutes, he got up, strode over to the receptionist and slammed the day-old newspaper down on her desk.

'I'm the Chief Executive of British Rail, and you can tell your boss that you've just lost our account,' he said, barely containing his anger. 'I've never been treated so shabbily in my life.' With that, he turned and began to storm out of the building. Just as he reached the entrance, however, a door opened and the agency's director stepped into the lobby, smartly dressed and immaculately turned out.

'It's too late,' the British Rail boss cried out, shaking his head and holding up his hand. 'There's no excuse for this kind of treatment. It's unprofessional.'

'But that's just BR's problem,' the agency director replied. 'You see, millions of your customers feel exactly how you do every single day. They're not only disappointed by the service you're offering, they're also angry at the kind of treatment they're getting. We've done a lot of research in the last few weeks and we've come to one inescapable conclusion – you need more than just a better image and a slogan. You need a substantially improved service.'

We're getting there...
Subsequent British Rail advertising slogan

The Truth Is Out There

Like so much in life, we laugh at this story because it's funny, and we laugh because it's true. But in case we're tempted to laugh a little too loudly, we would do well to remember that our own position as the Church isn't much better. Seventy per cent of the UK population still claim to have some kind of faith in God, and two in five adults want to explore answers to the big questions in life, yet over the past 20 years church membership has dwindled by one-fifth. People simply aren't looking to the churches for answers any more.

The vast majority of people in the country, whilst unashamedly 'spiritual', have largely written off the Church as being boring, irrelevant and well past its sell-by date. Church is perceived as being out of touch with both reality and society's needs, and whilst it's true that some churches are growing almost exponentially, the vast number are spiralling into decline. The word is out there, and people are voting with their feet: church, as Winston Churchill might have put it, has 'nothing to offer but blood, toil, tears and sweat', with the possible exception of terminal boredom. Most people don't consider it worth the effort.

So what can we do to stem the tide? How can we attract people back to church – and, more to the point, back to the gospel? Well, the first thing to do, as the advertising agency prompted British

Rail to do, is to take a hard, honest look at ourselves to see how much we are to blame for the state of disrepair. There may be nothing wrong with our 'product' as such: the gospel has hardly dulled or tarnished with age. It's just as vibrant, dynamic and life changing now as it was when Peter preached the first 'gospel sermon' on the day of Pentecost almost two thousand years ago. But we may well have obscured it under a mound of seemingly irrelevant traditions and veiled it with archaic language and culture.

Since the arrival of Christianity in Britain – first from Ireland, then from the European mainland – in the second half of the sixth century, Christians have had a big impact on our society. Our laws are founded on Christian ideas of morality and freedom, our political system is rooted in the Judaeo-Christian view that all people are inherently equal, our social fabric and infrastructure remain grounded in the Christian notion of the family unit, and even the science so often hailed as the Church's archenemy was in its infancy a decidedly Christian endeavour. It hasn't all been plain sailing, of course: along the way the Church has given its backing to unjust wars (including the Crusades), witch-hunts, inquisitions and burnings. But it has also pioneered universal education and health-care provision, social welfare, charitable action, workplace rights, the abolition of slavery, the peace movement and even the institution of the weekend!

But in some ways, this truly astonishing list of achievements has been our undoing. Like a political party on the brink of electoral disaster, we have displayed a tendency to remind people loudly and proudly of our accomplishments rather than investigating our 'policies' to see if we might not have lost touch with people's needs and expectations. Confident that we're right, to the exclusion of anyone else, and that we know what's best for people, we often appear to those outside the Church as being arrogant, opinionated ... and just plain wrong. And tragically, we have stopped listening to people's complaints.

Winston Churchill is credited with having said that we should always listen to our best friends *and* our worst enemies, as they both tell us the truth, but from different angles. By ignoring criticisms made of us by people whose point of view we disagree with, or whose motives we suspect, we have effectively insulated ourselves from the very world we want to reach with the gospel. We have consoled ourselves by distorting Paul and convincing ourselves that, when people don't agree with us, it's because 'the god of this world has blinded the minds of the unbelievers, to keep them from seeing the light of the gospel of the glory of Christ, who is the image of God', and not because we have failed to make our 'statement of the truth' quite 'open' and understandable enough (2 Corinthians 4:2–4). As a result, we have often been more concerned with 'speaking the truth' than with finding out if we're speaking it in comprehensible language.

> **Christians are a dim, ego-tripping minority which is dead set on telling everybody why they ought to become Christians, instead of finding out why they aren't.**
> *Australian journalist Max Harris*

A Master of Disguise

Some Christians are wary about *adapting* our presentation of the gospel to make sure it's relevant to the culture of those around us. 'Isn't it our job just to *present* the truth of the gospel?' they ask. Well yes, it is. But that isn't as easy as it might first seem, because whilst the *content* of the gospel hasn't changed in two thousand years, the *context* in which we are called to present it has changed beyond all recognition. Not only are fewer and fewer people coming to church, but fewer and fewer of those who *do* come have anything like the same level of knowledge of Christianity and the Bible as they might have had a century or so ago. What's more, the way they take in information is radically different.

A hundred years ago, for example, the sermons of the famous Baptist preacher Charles Spurgeon were hugely popular amongst ordinary men and women in south London. Yet today, few ordinary churchgoers – let alone people who don't often go to church – would find it easy, or even possible, to get to grips with his sermons. Most of us would find them too wordy and difficult to fathom; perhaps even pretentious. We'd call for a simultaneous translation into English. Or we'd vote with our feet.

Take the following example, picked at random from his 1860 New Park Street Pulpit. Whether it's 'gospel truth' or not makes very little difference. Even accounting for the fact that it's been lifted out of context, for most of us it's just plain incomprehensible:

> Do we call that man an infidel who should teach that some things of the old creation were of man? What name shall I give to the being who will dare to say that anything in the new creation of grace is of man? Surely if the first be an heresy, the second must be an heresy equally damnable, and perhaps more so. For one doth but touch the external works of God, while the other thrusts its sacrilegious hand into the internal works of his grace, plucks the brightest jewel from his crown, and treads it in the dust.

We may be preaching the same gospel as Spurgeon, but it doesn't take Einstein to work out that we're using a very different style to do so. And that style is set by the culture and concerns of the people around us.

In fact, of course, we're following in the best footsteps by adapting the way we present our message to suit our surrounding culture. When the 'Word' became 'flesh', he became a particular kind of 'flesh': an olive-skinned, Aramaic-speaking, first-century Jew. He was made incarnate at a very specific moment in time, speaking to people in ways they could easily understand, using cultural references with which they would readily have identified. No one listening to Jesus tell his rather unsavoury story about a nobleman who had to travel abroad to be appointed king (Luke 19:11–27), for example, would have failed to spot the similarities between the nobleman and Herod Archelaus, who was forced to go to Rome to have his authority rubber-stamped after the death of his father, Herod the Great, in 4 BC. Herod suffered the humiliation of having a delegation of his subjects follow him out to petition Rome not to make him king – an action for which he exacted revenge when he got back home, just as in the story. Gospel stories don't come more culturally relevant than this, though in the mists of time we've lost our understanding of it as a piece of biting political satire and have tended to see it, instead, as just an allegorical fairy tale.

Similarly, Paul's sermon to the Athenians in Acts 17 is a brilliant example of cultural adaptation. Not only did Paul manage to weave in a reference to an altar dedicated 'to an unknown god' that he had seen in the city, and support his argument that this 'unknown god' was really the Judaeo-Christian God by quoting from two pagan Greek poets, but as a man who 'decided to know nothing among you except Jesus Christ, and him crucified' when he was with the church in Corinth (1 Corinthians 2:2), he preached a sermon to the people of Athens that explicitly mentioned neither Jesus Christ nor the crucifixion! In fact, some of the resident philosophers there accused him of being a 'babbler' – basically a kind of guttersnipe: a charlatan who picked up little titbits of information and stored them away like a magpie, liberally peppering his conversation with them later on in order to give the illusion of being well informed!

But Paul's skill in adapting his presentation of the gospel to suit his audience – proving that the Athenian philosophers were wrong to suggest his understanding and use of their culture was only skin deep – becomes even more apparent when we compare his sermon to Gentile intellectuals in Acts 17 with that to the Jews of Pisidian Antioch in Acts 13. These two sermons, to very different people in very different cultures, are so unlike each other in tone and style that some scholars have even suggested that Paul couldn't possibly have given them both! Far more likely, however, is that it points to the seriousness with which Paul took his responsibility to 'become all things to all people, that I might by all means save some' (1 Corinthians 9:22).

Two thousand years later, the world is moving into a new era. And as we mark what the government has called an 'extremely important Christian anniversary', we need to work hard to make sure that our understanding and presentation of the gospel is just as relevant to life at the dawn of the third millennium as Paul's was to life at the dawn of the first.

> **Christianity was born in Palestine.**
> **They took it to Greece and they made it into a philosophy.**
> **They took it to Rome and they made it into an institution.**
> **They took it to America and they made it into a business enterprise.**
> **They took it to England and they made it into a tourist attraction.**
> *American sociology professor Tony Campolo*

New Era, New Church

In preparation for the year 2000, Christian charity Fanfare for a New Generation launched its *New Millennium Challenge to the Churches* in April 1998. Backed by Archbishop George Carey, Cardinal Basil Hume, Baroness Kathleen Richardson and church leaders from a host of other denominations and groupings, it sets out 10 practical goals aimed at helping us be more welcoming, relevant and challenging in our churches and communities.

1 We will make you welcome
2 We will be family friendly
3 We will make sure you can hear clearly

4 We will be practical and relevant
5 We will help you explore answers to your deepest questions
6 We will offer you time to stop and think in a busy life
7 We will help you make sense of the Bible and who Jesus is
8 We will make sure your visit will be helpful and challenging
9 We will help you discover for yourself God's love, acceptance and forgiveness
10 We will offer you the chance to make a new start

Of course, some of these statements will already be true for many churches. But we can all review, evaluate and improve our standard of performance and service, constantly moving forward to meet people's spiritual and practical needs in our churches and communities.

Midnight (Greenwich Mean Time) on 31 December 1999 will capture a significant moment in our history. Celebrations the like of which we've never seen before and will probably never see again will help the world roll into a new era. For some, it will be a time of great fear and anxiety, accompanied by the Four Horsemen of the Apocalypse! But for most people, it will be a real combination of parties, questions and uncertainty about the future. We can't afford to let two thousand years of Christianity pass by in insignificance. Our churches need to be ready to help nourish the spiritual hunger that will undoubtedly arise in our local communities in the run-up to 1 January 2000 and beyond.

In many ways, the preparations for the turn of the millennium are like the preparations for a wedding. The Greenwich marquee is already going up, and some of the entertainers have already been booked. Cases of 'Millennium Champagne' have been ordered, and the guests are starting to think about the big day itself. Yet somehow, in the midst of all these preparations, the identity of the bridegroom – Jesus – has been virtually overlooked. And so has the need for marriage preparation classes. The practical side of the festivities is being planned down to the last detail, both in central government and in towns and villages across the country. But the spiritual heart of the big event is in danger of being neglected.

And that's where the churches come in. Because if 1 January 2000 is going to be a real 'new start', rather than another 'false start', we're all going to have to do some serious thinking about the future. No responsible pastor or priest lets a couple get married in their church without some form of marriage preparation, letting them know what to expect and how to cope not only on their wedding day, but on every single day of their married lives. Just a walk-through rehearsal of the service itself is hardly enough, given the seriousness of the vows the bride and groom will make to one another!

In the same way, churches need to prepare – and help their local communities prepare – for more than just New Year's Day 2000. They also need to prepare for Sunday 2 January 2000, the first Sunday of the third millennium, and Tuesday 4 January 2000, the first working day of the third millennium … and beyond! The preparations that your church will make in the run-up to 31 December 1999 will ensure that it is well focused and able to cope with any influx of visitors on 2 January 2000, and on into the first full decade of the new millennium.

As friends of the bridegroom, it's our task – and our challenge – to be ready when the big day comes. That means some hard thinking and reviewing if we're not going to be caught out unawares by the groom's sudden arrival (cf. Matthew 25:1–13). And it means some real attention to how we demonstrate God's love through our service, services and basic customer care.

The English think incompetence is the same thing as sincerity.
English-born New York writer Quentin Crisp

The Challenge Ahead

The *New Millennium Challenge* is a call for churches to pledge themselves to work at being practical, relevant and challenging as we meet the practical and spiritual needs of the people in our churches and local communities. If thousands of churches pledge themselves to take on board the *Challenge* and put into practice the 10 goals by 2 January 2000, the nation will hear a positive message that the Christian faith is as relevant today, in our pick-'n'-mix postmodern culture, as it was two thousand years ago ... and that rather than being dull and depressing, churches are welcoming and relevant.

New Era, New Church? explores each of the 10 *Challenge* goals, examining the biblical perspective behind them and offering a wealth of practical ideas and suggestions as to how we can respond within our churches and communities. Each chapter will:

- look at some of the issues facing our churches in relation to a specific goal, illustrated by real-life stories;
- examine the kinds of things the Bible has to say about each issue and goal;
- offer ideas and suggestions for practical ways to implement each goal within our local churches and communities.

At the end of each chapter there's a list of suggested resources, relevant agencies and further reading, designed not so much to be exhaustive, but to act as a starting point.

1 We Will Make You Welcome

Preface by Archbishop George Carey

George Carey became Archbishop of Canterbury in 1991. Under his leadership as Vicar of St Nicholas in the centre of Durham (1975–82), the church experienced rapid growth. He went on to become Principal of Trinity College, Bristol, and Bishop of Bath and Wells, before being appointed Archbishop of Canterbury.

'First impressions matter.' Try thinking of your church as your 'home', which in a way it is. But what kind of home would it be if it's unwelcoming, cold, drab and dreary? And yet many churches are like that.

When I became Vicar of St Nicholas, Durham, I was challenged to put my theories into practice. The church is at the heart of the city but was shut six days a week and, frankly, was a depressing building – cold and very wet (literally!) when it rained because the rain poured through the roof in six places. In my book *The Church in the Market Place* (Kingsway) I tell the story of the renewal of our church people and the church building (the two MUST go together).

So now, as an inveterate church visitor, I am always looking out for those tell-tale signs that the church I'm visiting is actually interested in being a Christian church! What do the signs outside tell me of the church and its place in the community? As I enter it, does it exude a friendly welcome? Is it clean and tidy? Is it really a place of prayer and does the atmosphere express that? Is it 'beautiful for God'? Yes, I do believe that there should be elements that lead us up to God, so colour and inviting symbols of faith should be considered as part of the aesthetic quality of the building.

But perhaps what matters more than anything is a warm and friendly but unthreatening welcome from people. Strangers who come to church want several things: they want to be welcomed and put at ease, but they don't want too much attention paid to them, and they don't want anyone hissing 'Jesus loves you!' and 'Praise God you're here!' Both may be right, but there's a right moment for everything!

However, making your church welcoming, friendly, warm and worshipful is only part of what it is to be a 'missionary' congregation. We must go out to them and in this the ordained person is vital.

To those of you ordained and set aside to be priests and ministers I say: 'Don't neglect visiting.' If I were in a parish ministry today, I would without hesitation set aside time daily to visit. Visiting falls into three categories: knocking on doors of homes in parts of the neighbourhood that you haven't visited before; (crisis) visiting of those who are sick and in need; and visits to those who are new to the church or the area. Each category is important. Don't be fobbed off by the view that 'people are never at home these days' and 'people don't want you to visit'. There will, of course, be many disappointments when you 'door-knock', but there will be unexpected joys too. So don't leave visiting to the Mormons and JWs!

In addition, get known in the community by joining in – and get members of your congregation to see that being local councillors, or members of the Rotary, Lions, Women's Guild, etc., are important Christian ministries and potential bridges for God to use.

We Will Make You Welcome

A church official decided to drop in on one of the churches in his area unannounced one Sunday. The service had already started and the doors were closed, so he hammered on the main door – but to no avail. As he was leaving, he saw that the noticeboard outside the building proclaimed, 'Seek the Lord while He may be found.' He resisted the temptation to scrawl underneath, 'Well, I did try!'

On his way home he passed a scruffy old church building with wide-open doors ... and dived in. Immediately he realized his mistake. It was no longer a church, but a place of worship for a new Indian sect. But what a difference! Though the service had started, he was given a warm welcome. A young Asian sidesman sat down next to him, explained what was going on and handed him some leaflets in English that explained their beliefs and practices. It made him think, 'What kind of welcome would that young man get if he wandered into a church halfway through next Sunday's service? Would someone offer to sit with him and explain the service? Would there be leaflets about our faith to offer him in his own language?'

The Anglican Church Welcomes You.
The Premises are Protected by Guard Dogs.
Two signs on the gates of Winnipeg Cathedral

Members Only?

The great Archbishop of Canterbury William Temple famously observed that the Church is the only society in the world that exists purely for the benefit of its non-members. But in the 1980s a member of the Church of England's governing body, General Synod, lamented that the opposite had now often become the case: 'We have become involved in a public enactment of heresy. We believe and proclaim a gospel of grace available to all, but we operate a structure which takes the form of a club with limited membership.'

In 1998 a small group of members of the Marylebone Cricket Club were defeated in their first attempt to open the membership of the MCC – the home of cricket – to women. With the door shut firmly in their faces, many women retorted that they weren't that interested in cricket anyway. Yet the attempts persisted because the administrators of the game knew that if they couldn't attract a new generation of cricket lovers – if they appeared totally out of touch to younger people, who wouldn't tolerate such blatant sexism whatever its motives – then the England team's chances of ever shining at the game again would ultimately die. In September 1998 women were finally accepted into membership of the MCC.

Sadly, the Church is often perceived as exactly this kind of exclusive club. Members pay their dues, follow the rules and enjoy the benefits of membership. Some even have their own privileged club seats! And like most clubs, the Church has been guilty of imposing its own set of regulations. It has adopted its own jargon, unwritten rules, ritual – a steep learning curve for newcomers! Wittingly or unwittingly, it has restricted its membership.

Phil was completely lost when he went to church for the first time. He was worried about when to stand up, when to sit down, when to speak and when to be silent. It was an alien culture to his world of cyberspace, techno-babble, virtual reality and websurfing.

He was puzzled by the strangeness of the words and ideas. The only link to his 'normal world' was Ray, the youth worker. Ray was aware that Phil felt uncomfortable. And as he looked at the ritual afresh through Phil's eyes, church appeared strange and unreal. He realized that Phil would no more listen to organ music at home than he would sit still for an hour. 'I couldn't help wondering whether the church was expecting Phil to do all the adjusting,' he said, 'and whether there wasn't something more that we could do as a church.'

John Smith, who gave up his respectable job as a teacher to work amongst Melbourne's bikers and outcasts, remembers the first time he took one of his new friends to church. Dressed in leathers (whilst the rest of the congregation was in 'Sunday best'), they sat to one side and tried to blend in. John could tell his friend was having problems following the service and adjusting to the differences in culture, but he was encouraged by the fact that he hadn't walked out. And then came the part of the service that included the communion. As they went up to the communion rail, John turned to reassure his friend. 'Just do exactly what I do, okay?' He nodded, and knelt down beside John at the rail. But after taking a sip of the wine, he got up and, without waiting for John, angrily marched straight to the back of the church building … and right out of the door! Trying not to draw attention to himself, John followed him out. He found his friend outside, fuming and upset.

'What's the matter?' John asked. 'Why did you suddenly storm out?'

'I didn't understand most of what was going on in there,' his friend replied, 'but that communion thing was the last straw! You really care about Jesus, right? And communion is all about his last meal? So what's with the wine? I wouldn't serve wine that bad to my worst enemy, and you people use it for remembering your best friend!'

People come to church from all sorts of backgrounds. For some, who grew up going to church, it's a return to something they once knew. For others, it's entirely virgin territory. They come with their own ways of seeing the world, and their own views about what's important and what's not. Many churches up and down the country bear this in mind when they arrange their services, trying hard to make them as accessible and 'seeker friendly' as possible. Tragically, however, others seem not to have realized that, like an exclusive club, they are going about things in their own way with little or no consideration as to how it all seems to those who've never encountered anything like it before.

The stark challenge facing every local church at the dawn of the third millennium is to take William Temple's words to heart and address the way we do things, giving people a chance to hear the refreshing news of the gospel without it being entirely obscured by all our Christian jargon and theo-babble. We need to take a long, hard look at ourselves to see how we're restricting our membership, both in obvious and in not so obvious ways. The alternative is simply to keep doing what we're doing and fizzle slowly out of existence.

> **The definition of folly is to keep doing what you have been doing ... and expect a different result.**
> *Anonymous*

In the Image of God

We're all part of God's creation, whether we're able bodied or disabled, self-confident or emotionally scarred, physically beautiful or disfigured, smart or dumb, black or white, temperate or alcoholic, well heeled or homeless, a member of God's family or a visitor to church. Everyone, regardless of their appearance or ability, is made in God's image. That means we need to be welcoming to *everyone* in our church and community.

When Jesus accepted an invitation to a formal dinner at Simon the Pharisee's house, he must have wondered what to expect. On the one hand, his cavalier approach to healing, forgiveness, fasting, Sabbath rules and tax collectors had already landed him in trouble with many of Simon's fellow Pharisees; on the other hand, Simon was taking a big risk just by inviting him for a meal. Perhaps that's why, hedging his bets, Simon deliberately failed to extend to Jesus the usual courtesy of kissing him in greeting and giving him water for his feet and olive oil for his head (Luke 7:36–50).

But Simon's lukewarm welcome stood in marked contrast to the reception given to Jesus by the party's notorious gatecrasher – a city prostitute – who washed his feet with her tears, dried them with her hair, smothered them with her kisses and anointed them with perfume (a tool of her trade). What's more, it stood in marked contrast also to the reception Jesus gave the prostitute in return: rather than sending her away and chastizing her for daring to contaminate him with her ritual impurity, as any self-respecting Pharisee would have done, he announced that her sins (which defined her standing in the community) were forgiven.

The challenge that faces our churches at the start of the new millennium is to emulate the welcome this unnamed woman gave Jesus and he in turn gave her, rather than the lack of welcome Simon the Pharisee extended to them both. We need to find ways to include people in our church family, demonstrating the overwhelming and unconditional love God shows them, rather than letting or even making them feel inadequate or alienated.

You're Welcome!

Businesses go to great lengths to pick the best marketing strategy and the highest quality public relations staff. They generally pay them well, too, because they know that as the 'public face' of the company – the one most people see first – they're a vital component in guaranteeing the success of their product. Millions of people around the world can testify to the 'success' of *our* 'product' – Christianity is life changing and ultimately satisfying. But wouldn't it be a terrible disaster if, by not paying enough attention to our 'marketing strategy' (evangelistic approach) and 'public relations staff' (welcome stewards) we put people off at the church door?

Andrew and Helen moved into a new area. They had both been committed churchgoers in the past. Now in their mid-thirties, they were considering starting a family and wanted to see their children grow up – as they had both done – in the larger family of the Church. The first Sunday after they finished unpacking, they decided to check out their nearest church. They were greeted at the door by an unsmiling steward who handed them a hymn book, a thick prayer book and a notice sheet. A congregation of 150 were scattered in small, isolated pockets around the large, sparsely decorated Victorian building. No one sat anywhere near Andrew and Helen. No one said a word to them. When it came to the 'Peace', no one was even close enough to shake their hands. As they left at the end of the service, the vicar – locked in a conversation with a regular member of the congregation – rather limply shook their hands and thanked them for coming.

What was their impression? 'A take-it-or-leave-it attitude, coupled with a culture shock of baffling new liturgies, unfamiliar words and unannounced page numbers, which made it virtually impossible for us to join in. At least we had the benefit of anonymity!'

The following Sunday, Andrew and Helen tried another church about 100 yards further on. It was a small congregation of about 25 in a renovated hall. Here they were greeted effusively by the steward and the minister came to talk to them even before the service began. When she discovered that Andrew and Helen were new to the area, her face lit up. She took down their names and address and made enthusiastic conversation, telling them all about the church. But after the first hymn, Helen's and Andrew's hearts sank as she pointed them out to the whole congregation and remarked on how much she hoped they would soon become members. Andrew, the only man there, felt particularly unsure about this church. As they left, they had to walk the gauntlet of smiling faces, encounter a barrage of questions, a plethora of outstretched hands – and even hugs!

Their impression? 'The welcome was a little too enthusiastic for us. As newcomers, we were a rare commodity and were snapped up in an almost stifling way.'

The welcome people receive is one of the main reasons why they return to a church, or get involved and become new members. Simple things such as smiling, saying hello, seeing people to a seat if appropriate, recognizing and helping if they're having trouble making sense of the service, offering them tea or coffee, talking to them afterwards, encouraging them to fill in a simple 'welcome card', and even remembering their names if they come again the next week: all these things can make the difference between people coming back or not. They suggest that, rather than seeing new people as extra 'pew fodder', we are genuinely interested and care about them.

There's no one way to greet people and make them feel welcome, of course. It's a delicate balance of being friendly while not intruding. It depends entirely on the personality of the person doing the welcome. For example, at one church in south London, newcomers are greeted by a large, glowing West Indian woman called Daphne. Her enthusiasm and exuberance are infectious. She has the natural ability to put people at ease with her beaming smile and words of welcome, and the undeniable gift of building relationships very quickly.

By contrast, Angela is almost a shrinking violet. When she noticed a woman sitting in a pew after the service, quietly sobbing, she sat down close by, not wishing to intrude. After a while, she moved closer and asked if there was anything she could do. Well past the point of self-containment, the woman explained that her husband of 40 years had died suddenly during the week.

She hadn't been to church for years, but had wanted to come today even though it was difficult and painful because she felt she had to be somewhere spiritual. She'd thought of this church because her daughter had sung in the choir here when she was a girl. The service had been difficult for her emotionally and, by the end, it had just become too much. Angela just sat and listened. Having lost her husband six years earlier, she knew something of the pain and trauma that the woman was going through. From that initial point of contact, they formed a friendship. And as the woman came back to church over the following weeks and months, she discovered a caring, supportive community that would, over time, help her through those early days of grief.

> **The most important element of *being* a more welcoming church is a commitment from the whole congregation to *be* more welcoming. Although welcoming procedures are important, a welcoming attitude is vital.**
> **Rob Norman, Executive Director of Administry**

Access and Attitude

Nancy and Andrew are wheelchair users. When their son was five years old, they wanted to take him to their local church. Access into the church wasn't easy, since it was situated on a hill and there were four steps to get into the building. But the people were welcoming and friendly, and a special ramp was soon made for them. Unfortunately, it took such a lot of effort to get the ramp out each week, and caused so much hassle, that Nancy and Andrew wondered if it was really worth the effort. But they persevered because the church members were so friendly and they didn't want to hurt their feelings.

The church leaders eventually agreed to make another door accessible so that Nancy and Andrew wouldn't have to bother with the ramp any more. At the same time, they decided to take out a block of chairs in the church so that anyone with a wheelchair could be part of the congregation, rather than having to sit apart at the side. In addition, a couple in the congregation who were about to celebrate their silver wedding anniversary decided that instead of having presents, they would ask their friends and relatives for enough money to build a small patio in front of the church hall, giving Nancy and Andrew access for coffee there after the service. The terrain had previously been too rocky and infirm.

The results have surprised everyone. Nancy and Andrew are committed church members who now regularly take part in the services, leading prayers or reading the lessons. But the improvements in access didn't only help them. Elderly people find the hall an ideal venue for their lunch club now that they don't have to negotiate the stairs, and the accessibility to buggies and pushchairs means that it's used as a pre-school nursery. And the church has recently installed a specially adapted unisex toilet for use by anyone in the community who is part of RADAR's National Key Scheme.

'Access is a welcoming attitude,' says John Pierce, an Anglican priest and former co-ordinator of Church Action on Disability (CHAD). But the first thing some disabled people encounter when coming to church is a stark reminder of the *dis*similarity between them and a non-disabled person: restricted access. There is essentially no difference between the locked door encountered by the church official at the start of this chapter and the inaccessible door encountered by a wheelchair-bound person when they try to go to a church that hasn't thought through the issue of disabled access.

It's essential to give everyone who wants it easy access into church buildings, church halls, meeting rooms and anywhere else that church activities take place. What's more, from 2004 it will be a *legal requirement* for 'service providers' – including churches whose buildings are used for worship and other community services – to make 'reasonable adjustments' to buildings and premises so that they are physically accessible to disabled people (though what counts as 'reasonable' will depend on the size and available resources of the service provider, and may exclude certain historical buildings).

But the biggest 'handicap' many disabled people face according to Terry Thompson, an ordained Baptist minister who has been involved with disabled people for nearly 30 years, is the 'Does-he-take-sugar?' attitude towards them of many *non*-disabled people. In its mission statement, Church Action on Disability (CHAD) states, 'Disability is part of an individual person's make up. It does not make him or her a different type of person, and as an individual he or she will share the same (and different) feelings and have similar (and special) needs and characteristics to those of anyone else.'

'Disabled people and non-disabled people have the same right to be treated with dignity, respect, honour and courtesy,' says Paul Dicken of Through the Roof, a UK organization committed to making the gospel accessible to all, especially through the disability outreach of Joni Eareckson Tada.

Around 10 per cent of people in Britain have some form of disability. Some are obvious; others – partial sight, hearing problems, asthma, dyslexia, osteoporosis, angina, learning difficulties – may be hidden. If our churches are to be truly welcoming places, we need to consider our attitude to those who have disabilities. Do we accept everyone who comes into our church and lives in our community as equal in God's sight? Is there whole-hearted acceptance of the *whole* person? Or do we just see people with disabilities as being in need of our help and support, forgetting to ask, 'What opportunities are there for us to work together in mutual service in our church and in our community?'

We need to stop assuming that we know how best to help people with disabilities, and *ask* them.
Paul Dicken, Through the Roof

Caring Is Not Enough

Care and support are vital to enable many people with disabilities to share in the life of the community. Equally important, however, is the recognition of skills, abilities and talents, and the contribution that disabled – as well as non-disabled – people can make. 'There is a real hunger for full membership of the church among disabled people,' says Father Michael Garvey. 'They want to take part in the prayer and companionship and responsibilities of the Christian community. This hunger is largely unsatisfied.'

Geoffrey was training to be a minister. It just happened that he was blind. He knew there would be certain limitations: he knew, for example, that he would never be able to serve three or four rural parishes spread over several miles, no matter how athletic his guide dog was! But walking his dog through the community gave him the chance to make personal contact with the local people and spend time talking to them. His ability instantly to recall names and conversations gave those he talked to a real sense of being valued. The fact that he couldn't see the people he counselled often proved to be advantageous, as they felt less intimidated and more secure. And his well-developed memory made his preaching fluent and open to spontaneity. Though he had experienced prejudice, fear and discrimination in his life, he found that most church people encouraged him with loving, supportive, realistic and positive attitudes.

Margaret was disabled and attended a small rural church. Six months after she started to do a part-time course in theology, she was asked to consider becoming a member of her Parochial Church Council (PCC). She agreed and, a couple of years later, was asked if she would sit on the Deanery Synod. Although she didn't know how the Church of England worked at local and regional level, she soon found her way around and worked out how to get things done. From Deanery Synod she was appointed to the Diocesan Synod, slowly getting to grips with the numerous papers that landed on her doorstep. Two years later, she was asked to be on the Diocesan Board for Social Responsibility. Through that group, not only was she able to use her considerable gifts, she was also able to speak up on behalf of other people with disabilities throughout the diocese.

The truth is, we all have gifts and we all have areas of weakness and disability. Without wishing to divert attention from the vital need to think about *all* people when we consider things like access to buildings, we need to realize that the only real difference between those people who are considered 'disabled' and those who aren't is that 'disabled' people are constantly reminded of what they *can't* do and rarely given the chance to contribute what they *can* do. If our churches are to be truly welcoming places, we are going to have to work a lot harder at ensuring that *everyone* belongs and *no one* is left on the sidelines as a pure spectator. Caring for everyone, whether they have a recognized disability or not, is simply not enough. We need to give people the chance to play an active role, well suited to their unique gifts and abilities, in the life of our churches and local communities.

> **For a person who is disabled, the important thing is what we *can* do and not what we *cannot* do.**
> **Michael Barker, lay minister**

First Impressions

We live in a gullible and fickle society. Our opinions are often based on first impressions. When someone walks into a room, we notice their attitude, their looks, the clothes they wear and how they behave. On the basis of this, we form an impression – often a lasting impression – of what they are like. Sometimes this impression is wrong. Sometimes it's right. Most of the time, however, it's only *partly* right. We need to be careful we don't fall into the trap of forming opinions of people based on what they look like, what they're wearing, what habits or attitudes they display. Rather we need to demonstrate God's unconditional love.

Even before a person walks through the door of a church, they will already have built an impression of what to expect from what little they know about church and Christians and from the outside of the building. The noticeboard, garden or burial ground, entrance, first greeting: like it or not, all these things contribute to a person's opinion not only of the church, but also of the Christian gospel itself. A drab building, peeling paint, litter on the ground, faded notices on a decaying board, or stained coffee cups or mugs don't communicate a welcoming environment.

It can be immensely hard just walking through the door of a church. Sophie had been a core member of her last church, but when she moved to a new area and had to start again from scratch in a new church, she was nervous about the kind of reception she would get. She was helped by the fact that the building was often used during the week by local groups and organizations, and she managed to sneak in and have a look at the inside of the building in the week leading up to her first Sunday there. It gave her an idea of what to expect, and helped diffuse some of her anxiety. Nevertheless, simply walking through the door took a lot of courage.

If it was hard for Sophie, who was used to church, think what it must feel like for people who've hardly ever been to church before, and for whom the whole experience is a new one from start to finish. The first thing they'll notice, of course, is the outside of your building. If it's bright and cheerful, or even architecturally beautiful and well decorated, this will make a good first impression. On the other hand, if it looks bleak and dismal, with cracked or faded paintwork, dark and forbidding doors, menacing spiked railings, and cold granite exteriors, then making that first contact will seem about as appealing as entering one of Her Majesty's prisons.

Have a look at the outside of your building, trying to imagine what it must seem like to someone who's not used to coming to church, and for whom the experience of coming through the door for the first time will be an intimidating one. Even if you think your building looks more like something out of *The Addams Family* or *Frankenstein* than a place of worship, there are things you can do to make it less forbidding ... and they needn't cost the earth.

> **The best instrument for spreading the news of God's love is a congregation which shows it.**
> *Nigel McCulloch,* **Treasures in the Field**

A Foot in the Door

The best way to help people overcome their anxiety over going to church is to find a non-threatening way for them to come into the building long before they attend a Sunday service. Of course the architecture and layout of some churches may prove to be unsuitable and inadequate even for your own church uses in the twenty-first century. There's a limit to what you can realistically *do* to a small Norman or Saxon building. But more than ever we need flexible worship spaces, along with quiet rooms, play rooms, small group rooms, offices, kitchens, storage space and proper toilet facilities. Your church may not be able to provide all of these things, but it can provide *some*, even if they're 'off site'. So start thinking and saving now, because if you don't you'll only be putting off the inevitable. Besides, you *don't* have to change everything all at once. It's far more sensible to devise a realistic Fifty-Year Plan than an overly optimistic Five-Year one. And you'll be surprised what you *can* do without spending that much money, provided you're prepared to invest the time and imagination.

We need to make sure we're not over protective about our buildings. Certainly we need to care for them, but we shouldn't allow ourselves to become a club whose clubhouse is out of bounds for non-members. Rather than appreciating your distinctiveness, people outside the church may come to see you as aloof and unconcerned with the strains and stresses of everyday life. Rather than reinforcing the church's uniqueness, your approach may unwittingly serve to reinforce the age-old 'them-and-us' stereotype in which people assume that church people aren't concerned with the everyday problems in life.

Throughout the Gospels, Jesus had major run-ins with the Pharisees. At times it seems there was no love lost between them. At one point, Jesus even compared them to masked play-actors ('hypocrites') and well-kept tombs, nicely presented on the outside but inside 'full of the bones of the dead and of all kinds of filth' (Matthew 23:27). At heart this was a dispute over holiness and evangelism. The Pharisees felt strongly that the way to attract 'the nations' to God was to live such pure, clean, uncontaminated lives that they would be an example to everyone around – a 'light to the Gentiles'. Keeping the Jewish Law was so important to them that they adopted a 'belt-and-braces' approach, adding a whole tier of extra rules and regulations to make sure that they never even came close to breaking the Law itself. They were, in essence, squeaky clean.

And that, of course, is why they had a problem with Jesus. They felt that his associations with the 'wrong kind of people' muddied the 'clear blue water' they had tried so hard to establish between themselves and everyone else in Palestine. They doubted his ability to make friends with 'tax collectors and sinners' without having some of that sin rub off on himself and his disciples, and were especially concerned that onlookers would be confused as to precisely what it was about God's 'chosen people' that made them special, distinct and worth joining.

By contrast, Jesus – fully aware of what made him and his followers distinct – felt that the Pharisees' strategy was backfiring disastrously. Though they were popular with most ordinary Jews, they came across as being 'holier than thou' to everyone else. Instead of role-modelling a clear, easy-to-copy 'holy' lifestyle, they made God seem unapproachable to those who most needed to come close to him. That's why Jesus deliberately sought out the people on the fringes of Judaism who didn't quite make the moral grade. He wanted them to know that a new life and a right relationship with God was theirs for the asking. What's more, he knew that the best way to demonstrate the appeal of that new life was to live it in and amongst the people who needed it the most, letting them see at close quarters what a difference it could make.

By getting involved in our society – perhaps through letting other organizations such as Alcoholics Anonymous, Scouts, Guides, women's groups, residents' associations, play schemes, dance classes and evening classes use our premises – we send people in our local area the message that we're interested and involved. At the same time, we give people an opportunity to become familiar with the inside of our building – even to the point where they begin to feel like they belong – making it that much easier for them to come to a service later on.

When one south London church, in the heart of the inner city, opened up its main 'sanctuary' area for use by a local fitness instructor, some church members were far from convinced that it was the right thing to do. A few even felt that there was something a bit disrespectful to God about holding a step aerobics class in the 'church' part of the building (there was no other space large enough). But, after prompting from the minister, several church members started going along to support the activity. After a while, not only did they find themselves enjoying it, they found that it gave them unprecedented opportunities to make friends with people who wouldn't otherwise dream of setting foot inside a church building. And the result? One or two have started coming to church on a regular basis, and asking serious questions about the Christian faith, and they've all come to see the church in a new, far more positive light.

**God is not Christian. God has never been Christian.
I wonder if Christians are godly.**
Palestinian Melkite Priest Elias Chacour

IDEAS

People want to feel they are welcomed in their local church, that they are not entering some exclusive club. A welcoming attitude is crucial, but as we've already seen, we need to be careful how we do it – neither overwhelming nor too cold. Our welcome will manifest itself in the way we look after the *church building*, in the way we encourage *people* into our church, and our *attitude*. Some of the ideas that follow are very simple to implement, others are more long term and ambitious. The most important element of *being* a welcoming church is a commitment from the whole congregation to *be* more welcoming.

A welcoming building

- The litmus test! Imagine you are a visitor and you are coming to your church for the first time. What first impression do you have of the outside of the building? Does it seem welcoming? Walk into the church, look around and see what impression it gives. You may find the *Visitor-friendly survey* (Appendix 1, page 28) a good way of doing this.
- Is there someone who can keep a regular check on the church grounds for litter, moss on steps, general appearance, etc? Do you provide a bin for litter? Do exterior noticeboards need updating, or a coat of paint? Are there unsightly railings which could be removed?
- How accessible is the church to pushchairs, buggies and wheelchairs? Would a ramp be feasible? If there are steps, is there a handrail for support, guidance and safety? Is the path uneven?

- Do the Car Test! Drive past your church. Are the times of the church services visible from the road, or even the path?
- Liven up your interior noticeboard with photos of recent church family events, or photos of some of your church members (including children, young people, leadership team, older members, etc.). Display a list of the times of church services; the other services your church may provide, such as lunch club, crèche, youth club, hostel, aerobics, etc. It's also helpful to display 'useful numbers' (doctor, hospital, social services, etc.). What information would help both newcomers and regular churchgoers? Try to think of creative ways of displaying the notices. If the board is scruffy, re-cover it with felt material or buy an inexpensive cork board. Is there someone in your church whose job it could be to look after the noticeboard or entrance area? Check to make sure your noticeboard isn't too high for wheelchair users. Is it well lit? (You may need to upgrade your light bulbs!)
- Do you have welcome cards available for people to fill in? Try making it relevant to the people in your community. For example, if you have a lot of students in the area, you may want to find out which college they attend; whether they would like to be invited to a home for Sunday lunch; whether they would like to join a home group, etc. Make sure you follow up anyone who has filled in a card – don't leave it longer than a fortnight. One follow-up call is generally enough – you don't want to intimidate people. There's a balance between being friendly and being intrusive.
- An 'information point' or 'welcome desk' can be helpful, with details of church activities, welcome packs, collection point for welcome cards, etc., available and preferably manned before and after services.
- Encourage feedback. Have a suggestions/feedback box where people can drop in ideas for improving the welcome. (Comments should be anonymous!)

- Some churches are freezing in winter, in spite of efforts to heat the building! This can be a real turn-off for elderly people in particular. Travel rugs, cushions for pews, etc., could make it more comfortable.
- Ensure someone is at church well before people arrive for the service to make sure the lights are on, the building is tidy – and the doors are open!
- Is there an area for wheelchair users, so they are *part* of the service and not sitting apart? If you use chairs, perhaps you could remove a block.
- Is the lighting bright enough? Although it's often atmospheric to have dim lighting or candles, it isn't very helpful for people with poor vision or who need to rely on lip reading.
- Loos! Have you got any? If so, are they clearly signed? What condition are they in? Make sure the towels are clean, the soap isn't on its last legs, there's enough loo paper, and the toilet itself is clean! Apply the 'home standard' test.
- Brainstorm! Forget the money issue. Think what you would do to improve the building if money were no object. (By forgetting the money issue, you may come up with more creative ideas for making the building user friendly. And you may decide on some longer-term goals.)
- Vision! You may want to dream dreams for undertaking a building project. Thousands of churches have seen the benefits from altering and improving their buildings. Yes, there are problems associated with improving Norman, Saxon, Victorian and other older buildings – but they're not insurmountable with some creative thinking and may require a longer-term strategy. Although projects cost money, churchgoers have found creative ways and means of raising funds and have seen their faith grow in the process! It's hard work, and can cause friction, but the ultimate benefits outweigh the shorter-term effort and problems.

- Think of ways in which you can open up your church to the community. People may need to feel they belong *before* they believe. Ideas include: flower festivals, concerts, drama, music and reading presentations, fashion shows, chat shows, aerobics, crèche, youth zone, lunch club, kids club, history tours, after-school homework centre, art gallery, coffee shop, drop-in and advice centre.
- Banners, kneelers, a fresh coat of paint, dried flowers, fresh flowers, etc., can all help to give the interior a feel of welcome.

A welcoming attitude

- Do a health check on your church. Find out whether it's meeting the physical and spiritual needs of its churchgoers and visitors. (See *Making Sunday Best* resource.)
- Put yourself into a newcomer's shoes and ask: if this were my first time here, would I feel welcomed? Would I know what page the service was on, or the hymns and songs? Is there any explanation as to what's going on at various stages in the service? Would I know why we repeat songs several times, or break into songs 'in tongues', or why people make the sign of the cross and genuflect? (See Appendix 2 for *The visitor-friendly survey!*)
- How truly welcoming are we in our individual and corporate attitudes? Do we accept people regardless of what they look like, whether they have a disability, their social standing? Do we really see each other as part of God's family?
- Visit another church where you aren't known to understand what it feels like to walk into a 'strange church'.
- Make sure there's someone at church to greet and welcome people as they arrive. Look out for newcomers and visitors and make them feel at home. Most people return to church because of the welcome they receive. Try to rotate your welcome team.

- Is there a crèche, Sunday school, kids club, youth group, etc. for young people? Make sure young people feel at home, too.
- Invite people to stay on after the service for a cup of coffee. Rather than charging for coffee, why not leave a basket for contributions? Or, better still, make it free! Encourage churchgoers to look out for visitors and offer them coffee.
- Food! As Alpha has proved, food is a great way of encouraging people to the church. Are you able to provide after-service lunches (occasional or regular), picnics, barbeques, etc? Why not try an after-service Sunday lunch on the first Sunday of each month which could be done on a rota basis by one or two families? (People should only have to do it once a year!) People generally find it difficult to resist food.
- Saturdays and Sundays are often the loneliest days of the week for people who are on their own. Perhaps you could invite people to join you for lunch.
- Chapter 2 offers more ideas on being welcoming to families. Chapter 3 gives suggestions and ideas for people who have hearing difficulties.
- It can be very helpful to have a few copies of your service available in large print for people who are visually impaired.
- Encourage people to get involved – in offering their time and gifts. Allow people to take part.
- Check out your church's attitude to money! If your church wants to draw people in and help them feel welcome, you may have to spend some money. But when people feel they *belong*, they are far more likely to give cheerfully.
- Brainstorm ideas for ways in which the church can be more welcoming to both the churchgoers and the wider community. Think creatively – and pray!

RESOURCES

Resources

Making Sunday Best. Health check for churches. A free resource pack, including: three surveys, Sunday service material, house group material, audio tape and more! Produced by Fanfare for a New Generation.

Is your church worth joining? A practical resource produced by the Bible Society.

Service with a smile! and *We came, we saw, we joined!* Two of a number of resource papers available from Administry.

Welcome to our church! and *Come and join us!* Two training events which look at issues related to welcoming and integrating newcomers. Organized by Administry.

Preparing a welcome pack. A mini-guide produced by Administry.

How Friendly to Strangers is Your Church? A booklet produced by Rev. Symon Beesley. You can send for the booklet by writing to: 8 Shales Road, Southampton SO18 6NR (please enclose £2). Or you can download the text via the CPAS website (http://www.cpas.org.uk).

Unchurched People Welcome Here. A practical resource book published by CPAS.

Willow Creek Association have a number of useful materials and resources to help churches find ways of being welcoming as they reach out to people who aren't Christians.

Church Action on Disability Access Pack. Produced by CHAD, an ecumenical campaign addressing attitudes in the churches to disability.

Hand in Hand. Study pack exploring biblical and social aspects of disability. Produced by Christian Impact.

Beautiful or What? Adrian Snell and Phil Thomson looking at disability. Available in CD or cassette form. Published by Word UK (1993).

Visually impaired people in church. Information for clergy and church workers. Available from Royal National Institute for the Blind.

The Christian Enquiry Agency produces material for people who prefer to enquire anonymously about the Christian faith by sending for information through the post.

Agencies

Administry, PO Box 57, St Albans, AL1 3DT. Tel: 01727 856370.

Age Concern England, Astral House, 1268 London Road, London SW16 4ER. Tel: 0181 679 8000.

Age Concern Northern Ireland, 3 Lower Crescent, Belfast BT7 1NR. Tel: 01232 245729.

Age Concern Cymru, 4th Floor, 1 Cathedral Road, Cardiff CF1 9SD. Tel: 01222 371566.

Age Concern Scotland, 113 Rose Street, Edinburgh EH2 3DT. Tel: 0131 220 3345.

Association of Blind Catholics, Paul Questier, 58 Oakwood Road, Horley, Surrey RH6 7BU. Tel: 01293 772104.

Bible Society, Stonehill Green, Westlea, Swindon SN5 7DG. Tel: 01793 418100.

The Christian Enquiry Agency (CEA), Inter-Church House, 35–41 Lower Marsh, London SE1 7RL. Tel: 0171 523 2123.

Christian Impact, St Peter's Church, Vere Street, London W1M 9HP. Tel: 0171 629 3615.

Church Action on Disability (CHAD), 50 Scrutton Street, London EC2A 4PH. Tel: 0171 452 2085.

Church Pastoral Aid Society (CPAS), Athena Drive, Tachbrook Park, Warwick CV34 6NG. Tel: 01926 334242.

Fanfare for a New Generation, 115 Southwark Bridge Road, London SE1 0AX. Tel: 0171 450 9070/1.
E-mail: fanfare@btconnect.com

Guild of Church Braillists, c/o 321 Feltham Hill Road, Ashford, Middlesex TW15 1LP. Tel: 01784 258040.

John Grooms Association for Disabled People, 50 Scrutton
   Street, London EC2A 4PH. Tel: 0171 452 2000.
Kingdom Trust, 30a Musters Road, West Bridgford, Nottingham
   NG2 7PL. Tel: 0115 945 5542. Researching into the
   relationship between Christianity and disability.
Royal Association for Disability and Rehabilitation, Unit 12, City
   Forum, 250 City Road, London EC1V 8AF. Tel: 0171 250
   3222. Information line: 0345 622 644.
Royal National Institute for the Blind (RNIB), 224 Great
   Portland Street, London W1N 6AA. Tel: 0171 388 1266.
Through the Roof, PO Box 178, Cobham, Surrey KT11 1YN.
   Tel/fax/Minicom: 01932 866333. The UK branch of the
   disability outreach of Joni Eareckson Tada.
Willow Creek Association, PO Box 622, Maidenhead, SL6 0YX.
   Tel: 01628 620602.

Books

David Beer, *Growing a Healthy Church* (Kingsway, 1999)
George Carey, *The Church in the Market Place* (Kingsway,
   1995 ed.)
Elias Chacour, *Blood Brothers* (Kingsway, 1985)
Elias Chacour, *We Belong to the Land* (Harper & Row, 1991)
Steve Chalke, *I Believe in Taking Action* (Hodder & Stoughton,
   1996)
David Cohen and Stephen Gaukroger, *How to Close your Church
   in a Decade* (Scripture Union, 1992)
David Evans and Mike Fearon, *From Strangers to Neighbours*
   (Hodder & Stoughton, 1998)
Michael Fanstone, *The Sheep that Got Away* (Monarch, 1993)
Rob Frost, *Which Way for the Church?* (Kingsway, 1997)
David Gillett and Michael Scott-Joynt (eds), *Treasures in the Field:
   The Archbishop's Companion for the Decade of Evangelism*
   (HarperCollins, 1993)

Simon Jones, *Struggling to Belong. What is the church for anyway?* (IVP, 1998)

James Mitchell-Innes, *God's Special People: Ministry with the 'Handicapped'* (Grove booklet, 1995)

P. Nunnerly and R. Wood, *Making and Using Banners* (Gazelle Books, 1998)

Philip Richter and Leslie J. Francis, *Gone But Not Forgotten* (DLT, 1998) – explores the problem of church leavers and why people drop out of church

APPENDIX 1

Welcome to our church!

You're on the church council at St Lukewarm's. You want to make services more welcoming for newcomers and can think of 20 possibilities. If money is no problem, which five would you choose as priorities for immediate action, and what would you add at No. 20?

1 A couple or family to shake hands as people arrive.
2 Facilities such as wheelchair access, induction loop system.
3 An attractive 'welcome pack' of information for visitors.
4 Adequate heating and good lighting in the church building.
5 Clear information on notice sheets, hymn boards, external signboards.
6 Good quality coffee and tea after the service.
7 Regular training for your sidespeople.
8 A 'beginners' group or 'newcomers' supper on offer.
9 Glass doors into the church to break down the entrance barrier.
10 An attractive 'welcome card' in the pews/seats.
11 A sermon series to encourage everyone to see themselves as welcomers.
12 Clear name badges for all sidespeople.

13 A well-designed photographic display of church leaders and activities.

14 Flowers, carpet, welcome sign at the entrance and a tidy church.

15 A well-run children's programme, crèche, etc.

16 A staffed 'welcome desk' after the service.

17 A personal visit/letter to every visitor within 48 hours.

18 Clear directions from service leader on how to follow the service.

19 Visitors being shown to seats by sidespeople.

20

Reproduced by kind permission of Administry and *Celebrate* magazine. Administry is an organization whose work includes looking at issues related to welcoming and integrating newcomers.

APPENDIX 2

The visitor-friendly survey!

The best way to do this exercise is to invite a couple of non-churchgoers or newcomers to visit your church and take part in the survey. They should complete the survey sometime after leaving the church (preferably on the same day) and return it to the church.

Most questions require a brief, written answer, or a score on the following scale:

0 – non-existent
1 – poor
2 – below average
3 – average
4 – good
5 – excellent

1 How does the church advertise its services, organizations, etc.?

   a. posters around the district
   b. posters outside the building
   c. noticeboard(s)
   d. leaflets
   e. other…

2 How visible from the road is the church and how attractive are the grounds and buildings?

   a. visibility
   b. attractiveness of the grounds
   c. attractiveness of the buildings

3 How accessible is the church?

   a. by car
   b. on foot
   c. for the disabled

4 How are newcomers welcomed?

   a. on arrival
   b. during the service, at any stage
   c. after the service

5 a. How does a newcomer know where to go and what to do on entering the building?
   b. How do parents know what is available for children?
   c. What does the church offer for children? (Sunday school, crèche, toy bags, books)

6 How easy is the service to follow?

a. Notice sheets – do they list hymns, page numbers, paragraph numbers, etc.?
b. Hymn or song books – is mention made of the book to be used and is the number announced?
c. Service books – are page and/or paragraph numbers announced?
d. Are service sheets used?

7 How audible and visible are the service leaders?

a. audibility
b. visibility

8 How welcoming to newcomers are the members of the church?

9 How welcoming are the sidespersons?

10 Is there an informal opportunity to meet church members after the service (e.g. over coffee)?

11 What type of bookstall or library is there?

12 Is there an information table/stand?

Reproduced by kind permission of Rev. Symon Beesley. From *How Friendly to Strangers is Your Church?*

2 We Will Be Family Friendly

Preface by Joel Edwards

Joel Edwards was born in Jamaica and came to Britain at the age of eight. He was a Probation Officer for 10 years, a former General Secretary of the African and Caribbean Evangelical Alliance, and is currently the General Director of the Evangelical Alliance UK. He is married with two teenage children and is also a New Testament Church of God Associate Pastor.

Identity, belonging and care. That is still what most people in our fragmented world are crying out for. People still want to know they are valued and belong. The Church as the family of God is supremely placed to offer that sense of belonging.

That was certainly true for me as a black youngster growing up in Britain. As a member of a lone-parent family I have no recollection of what it meant to walk with two parents at the same time, or to sit in the back of the car with a Mum and Dad in the front. It was the church that supplemented my mother's caring, giving identity, security and an awareness that I was a person of value, made in God's image.

In a broken community, people still want to hear that they too can belong to other people. Church leaders who realize how much the church has to offer to the socially homeless in society will bend our structures and programmes to meet the real needs of real people. This kind of church offers challenging love, genuine care and the opportunity to care for others. A real family.

We Will Be Family Friendly

Carolyn quietly broke down in tears. Her four-year-old son had been boisterous and noisy throughout the Family Service. A woman sitting in the pew in front had turned round and given them withering looks several times. It had been an effort for Carolyn even to get her son and newborn daughter to church on time in the first place, and she had been looking forward to recharging her flagging spiritual batteries. As a single mother, prone to a short fuse and plenty of self-doubt, she felt a failure both as a parent and as a Christian. And somehow, the piercing eyes and disapproving frown of the woman in front just served to reinforce her feelings of inadequacy. Rather than feeling recharged and prepared for the long week ahead, she left the service running on empty.

She's not alone. 'My 25-year-old single daughter will no longer attend church because of the sense of exclusion she has felt,' wrote Norma in a letter to the *Church Times*. And the reason for this sense of exclusion? 'The over-concentration of "Family Services" which is excluding a huge section of society.'

It's ironic, isn't it? Carolyn takes her kids to a church Family Service and feels excluded because they're not well-behaved 'little angels'. Norma's daughter refuses even to go to a church Family Service because she doesn't have any 'little angels' to take with her, well behaved or not. Both feel totally excluded in a service designed to be the most inclusive, welcoming one the Church has – the one that shows the Church to be one big family itself!

One hundred years ago, families were the backbone of both Church and society. Unlike today's 'nuclear family' – mum, dad, two-point-four children and the dog – they often had three or even four generations living under the same roof. In poorer families, this had as much to do with economic necessity as social convention. Nevertheless, going to church, dressed in one's 'Sunday best', was very much a family affair. Few went to church alone.

Today, not only this 'extended family' but also the 'nuclear family' is a dying breed. We no longer consider it a duty to look after ageing relatives, who are encouraged to remain independent in their own homes for as long as possible … and then often consigned to an old people's home. There's been a huge rise in the number of younger single people living on their own, too – whether out of choice or through circumstances. Over the last 30 years, there's been a marked increase in the number of one-parent families, caused by separation, divorce, death, design or accident. Over a third of all marriages end in court and the number of people getting married in the first place is declining. We seem to live in an increasingly dysfunctional, isolationist society. Never before have so many lived alone.

In the midst of this, many churches appear to be stuck in a no-win scenario. If they cater for families, they risk alienating single people. But if they *don't* cater for families, they risk losing them either to another church that *does*, or else altogether.

Home is the place where, when you have to go there, they have to take you in.
American poet Robert Frost

'Our Father…'

There is a way forward, however. The Church has an opportunity, and a responsibility, to model a very different way of being 'family', drawing its inspiration from the Bible where families were even bigger than families in the Victorian Era.

Families in the Bible were even bigger than families in the Victorian era. In fact, the biblical writers would not have understood the idea of the 'nuclear family'. At the time of Abraham, for instance, a family would have meant a man, his wives and concubines, his sons, their wives and concubines, *their* sons and unmarried daughters, everyone's servants, and any widows, foreigners and assorted others picked up along the way. By the time of Jesus, monogamy was more common than polygamy, concubines were rare and servants were only for the wealthy. However, families still lived together in extended units of up to five generations in what might be called 'family compounds', as they still do in parts of Africa, the East and the Middle East.

Not only was the family the basic unit of society, it was also the basic unit of religion. The family, for instance, was where Jews celebrated the Sabbath, which was marked by a festive meal and study of the Torah, the first five books of the Old Testament. The key Jewish practice of the whole community meeting together on the Sabbath in the synagogue to study the Torah developed after, and in some ways in addition to, the family meeting. The family was also the place where the festival of Passover (Exodus 12) was celebrated.

But among the many radical reinterpretations of Judaism performed by Jesus was his extension of the idea of family to include the entire Church. When he was told that his mother and brothers had come to see him in Galilee (Matthew 12:46–50), Jesus asked his hearers, 'Who is my mother, and who are my brothers?' This was not so much a snub of his blood relatives as an inclusion of all his followers under the title of 'family'. The synagogue had provided faithful Jews with a powerful symbol of their membership in the one family of Israel; Jesus made that symbolism as explicit and in-your-face as he could by suggesting that 'whoever does the will of my Father in heaven is my brother and sister and mother'.

This notion of family was clearly taken to heart by the disciples. John's first letters insist that we are all brothers. Paul similarly exhorts Timothy to treat older members of the Ephesian church as parents and younger members as children (1 Timothy 5:1–2). He seems to have considered Timothy as a son, and we can only assume that Timothy saw Paul as a kind of surrogate father, similar to the relationship between Elijah and Elisha (2 Kings 2:12).

The ultimate father figure, of course, is God. Again, we tend to associate this idea with Jesus when it's actually Jewish. Jesus' characteristic term '*Abba*' – used just once, in Mark 14:36, but undoubtedly the image behind his use of the word 'Father' in the Lord's Prayer – was a common Aramaic way of referring to a dad with respect and intimacy. Most of his Jewish contemporaries would have seen God this way, even if there's no evidence that they ever addressed him as '*Abba*'. Nevertheless, God is said to be 'like a father' in Deuteronomy 1:31, and is *specifically* called 'Father' (using a more formal Hebrew word) in Psalm 2:7, Psalm 89:26, Isaiah 63:16 and 64:8, Jeremiah 3:4,19, and in Malachi 2:10. The father image is alluded to particularly strongly when Isaiah's own children are used as a sign of the worsening relationship between God and his people (Isaiah 7–9), though the author also compares God's love with that of a mother (Isaiah 49:15; 66:13).

So, regardless of whether you're an exhausted parent, newborn baby, lively toddler, bored teenager, single young professional, or manic depressive; married, widowed, divorced or disabled; as a 'child of the same heavenly Father', you're part of the Christian family, like it or not.

But do we make people feel a part of our church family? How friendly are we to elderly people, disabled people, single people, divorced people, homeless people, young people, children, couples, single parents … anyone who walks through the doors of our buildings? Are we *ex*clusive or *in*clusive?

Being part of the Church family should be a positive, inclusive experience. As one lady put it, responding to Norma's letter in the

Church Times by quoting from the New King James Version of Psalm 68:6, '"God sets the solitary in families," and, as a single, retired woman, I enjoy being part of my church family. Occasionally a preacher may make insensitive remarks which assume that all the hearers are parents, particularly on Mothering Sunday; but I consider that a family service includes me as much as the toddlers, and would not allow myself to feel excluded. So, please ... claim your place in the extended church family.'

Our churches, then, must surely offer the care, welcome, love, friendship and support that Jesus personified as God incarnate to *all*.

> **We welcome you into the Lord's Family; we are members together of the Body of Christ; we are children of the same heavenly Father; we are inheritors together of the kingdom of God. We welcome you.**
> *Words of the congregation to a newly baptized person from* **Common Worship: Initiation Services**

Happy Families?

The problem with families, of course, is that we didn't ask to be born into them! We didn't choose our older sister or younger brother. There was no selection process to allow us to choose our mum and dad. We arrived and – bingo! – we were 'one of the family'. Let's be honest: it's the same with our church family. We don't actually choose who is part of our congregation or community.

Our experiences of home and family life will vary. Some of us will have grown up in a loving, caring, safe family unit. Others will have been sexually, physically or emotionally abused, and will either have been rejected or else prompted for some reason or other to reject their own family. Similarly, we all have different experiences in our church families. We have different interests, backgrounds, incomes, opinions, skills and political beliefs. We have different lifestyles and languages. One person's idea of relaxing may be a quiet night in, curled up watching *Coronation Street* with a take-away, whilst another's will be to go out clubbing or wander round an art exhibition.

Given these kinds of differences, it can be as hard to show Christian love in our churches as it is within our families. 'Mummy,' cried seven-year-old Amy, after her brother Sam had locked her and her sister Emily in the shed. 'I believe everyone has a "love" *and* a "like". I love *and* like Emily. I love and *don't* like Sam.' As with our families, we don't necessarily *like* everyone in our church all of the time – but we're called to love them, warts and all!

In fact, *liking* everyone in our church – even a relatively small church – may be more than just unnecessary. It may be downright impossible. Judith was the first person Elliot met when he turned up at church one day ... and very nearly the last! Having just moved into the area, he was trying it out to see if he would fit in. Judith wasn't a good start. She was a bit of a mother hen, and her 'gushing' personality made the hackles on Elliot's back start to rise. He knew immediately that they were never going to hit it off, but he let her usher him to a seat anyway. After the service, she introduced him to a number of other people, and the next week he came back. He was soon a regular member of the church, involved in many of its activities.

In fact, Judith didn't like Elliot any more than Elliot liked Judith. It's not that they hated one another. It's just that their personalities were so different they had virtually nothing in common except for their faith. They only had to talk to each other for a couple of minutes before sparks began to fly. In a small church, such a dramatic personality clash couldn't stay hidden for long, but the other members were struck by the fact that neither of them ever said a bad word about the other.

Elliot learned to see that the things about Judith that made him squirm were the very things that made her so valuable to the church. If she hadn't clucked about him at the end of that first service, for example, introducing him to all and sundry, he would have found it much harder to come back the next week. And she was like that with everyone, especially the single people in the church: she always had time for them and always made sure they were OK. Elliot found it claustrophobic, but everyone else in the church got on fine with her. In the same way, Judith came to see that Elliot's skills and up-front personality were an asset to the church ... even if all she wanted to do was throttle him sometimes!

> **It's pretty difficult to like some people. Like is sentimental and it is pretty difficult to like somebody bombing your home. It is pretty difficult to like somebody threatening your children. It is pretty difficult to like congressmen who spend all of their time trying to defeat civil rights. But Jesus says love them, and love is greater than like.**
> *Martin Luther King, Jr*

Horses for Courses

Paul often compared the Church to a body, in which all the different parts played a vital role and none was superior to another. 'If all were a single member, where would the body be?' he asked. 'As it is, there are many members, yet one body. The eye cannot say to the hand, "I have no need of you," nor again the head to the feet, "I have no need of you." On the contrary, the members of the body that seem to be weaker are indispensable.' He even compared some parts of the Church to a body's genitalia, 'those members of the body that we think less honourable' and in need of covering up! We can't choose which bits of the body we have, and those we *wouldn't* choose are often the ones we need the most. 'If one member suffers, all suffer together with it,' he concluded; 'if one member is honoured, all rejoice together with it' (1 Corinthians 12:19–26).

When Adrian arrived as the new minister of a church, he found a loyal ally in Charles, the church secretary. A lawyer by training, Charles had just the kind of analytical mind that Adrian lacked, and he looked forward to what he thought would be a most 'interesting' working relationship. But the problems started almost immediately. Charles began to find Adrian's haphazard approach to paperwork irritating, and came to resent the way he put off every administrative duty until the last possible moment. But every time he tried to talk to Adrian about it, the two of them got into an argument and things just got worse. In the end, Charles felt he had to talk to Brenda, one of the other church leaders, about it.

When Brenda talked to Adrian, she found that he knew he was the world's worst when it came to paperwork, and had been pleased to hear that the church had such a competent secretary in Charles. But he soon discovered that the efficiency came with a price tag. Charles wanted prompt, written responses to his queries and Adrian – who preferred to settle things over the phone or in person, and didn't see the point of all the 'i's Charles wanted dotting and the 't's he wanted crossing – had neither the time nor the inclination to provide them. When Charles had 'pestered' him, he'd misinterpreted the lawyer's dogged insistence as a personal attack and had reacted badly.

Brenda finally decided that a face-to-face meeting was called for. She sat Charles and Adrian down and told each of them what the other had said. 'You're like that film, *The Odd Couple*,' she concluded. 'If you shared an apartment, you'd drive each other up the wall. Charles, you'd feel as if you were living in a bomb site, surrounded by the debris of half-finished tasks. And Adrian, you'd feel you were living in museum, where you couldn't touch anything unless you put it back in the right place immediately afterwards.

'You both have gifts this church needs. We'd be in debt up to our eyeballs, hopelessly double-booked and completely disorganized if it weren't for your efficiency and analytical skills, Charles. Adrian, you're going to have to meet him halfway and give him prompter, written replies. But Charles, you've also got to cut Adrian some slack, because we'd be a soulless, aimless, dying congregation if it weren't for his spirituality and people skills. The truth is, the church needs both of you, and you're going to have to learn to do more than just *tolerate* each other's differences. You're going to have to start *treasuring* them.'

Learning to accept all the different members of our churches, and everyone who walks through the door, is not easy. Learning to appreciate them for who and what they are, and to see them as indispensable parts of the Body of Christ, is even harder. We're all different, and we'd all arrange things a little bit differently if we had the chance. Some don't like the way children are allowed to make lots of noise during services; others resent having to gag their kids when they're at church. Some old people find many young people's approach to church disrespectful, whilst the younger people themselves may despair of the 'stuffy' and strait-jacketed atmosphere many of their elders seem to prefer. But this variety is more than just inevitable; as the saying goes, it's the spice of life.

We're not perfect, and we're often quick to judge people and write them off when they do things in a way we don't like. But as Gerald Coates is fond of saying, 'Everyone is winnable. We must never write them off!' We're designed to be dependent on God and on one another. As members of the Christian family, we're called to share the burdens of life through 'mutual burdensome-ness'. Being part of the Body of Christ means not merely *tolerat-ing* many of the things we don't like about other Christians – and others who come to church – but learning to see these differences as being good for the Body as a whole. As opposed to judging things on the level of what we personally find acceptable or desirable, we need to learn our own and other people's place in the whole Body.

Do people weigh you down?
Don't carry them on your shoulders.
Take them into your heart.
Former Brazilian Archbishop Helder Câmara

Children Have a Place Here Too!

Children are *part* of the Body of Christ. 'The place for children is in the Sunday school' is the cry (or unspoken thought) we so often hear from people in church who prefer *not* to 'suffer the little children' to come unto Jesus. In fact, they'd prefer not to suffer the little children at all – either the noise levels or the disruptive behaviour!

But children *belong* to the body of Christ just as much as adults do. And though some denominations symbolize the reality of this belonging through the practice of infant baptism, *all* denominations – whether they believe in infant baptism or not – are prone to treating children as second-class Christians. Although many churches up and down the country run inventive, creative and spiritually rich activities for children, many more still see children's work as secondary to the 'real' task of adult Christian teaching and worship at best, and as just giving them something to do to shut them up at worst. But as members, children must feel they have a place in the main body of the church.

Christina and her family had recently moved to their little village, and though she'd been to the monthly Family Service a few times herself, the church building was still an alien and uncomfortable environment to her three-year-old son, James. He didn't know what was going on and was intensely bored. As a result he kept on making a noise, and every time she told him to be quiet he simply raked up the decibel level. Painfully aware that she was making a spectacle of herself and spoiling the service for everyone else, she didn't know what else to do. By the end of the service, she was on the verge of tears.

Afterwards, over coffee, Elsie went over to her to see what the matter was. Elsie had met Christina through the Wives' Group, which she led and Christina had just joined, and had noticed the younger woman's distress during the service. When she heard what the problem was, she remembered her own experience as a young mum trying to entertain two children during the service. She thought about it for a week or two, and then came up with the idea of a 'Pram Service' – a special service during the week for pre-school children and their mums and/or dads. It was held once a month, and older brothers and sisters were allowed to join the service 'by invitation only' during the holidays.

It was a whole service for 'little people'. They sang, played musical instruments, and sat on cushions in the aisle listening to a Bible story. They had a short time of talking to God and praying for their families, including praying for any family member with a need (a sister with exams, a brother having his tonsils out, a granny unwell, a new baby brother). Babies could sleep in their prams or buggies, which were dotted around the church. And it didn't matter if they ran around, or threw a tantrum, or cried. No one there would turn round to give withering looks to either them or their mum or dad. After the service they played in the church hall as their parents chatted over a cup of coffee.

Christina took James along. As time went by, he started to feel more comfortable in church, which became a familiar and comfortable place to him. He was part of it now. It was his building and his community as much as anyone else's. James grew up used to churchgoing, and with a solid grounding in the Christian faith. And like many toddlers, he went on to Sunday school, later joining the music group and eventually the youth group. And Christina went on to become a church warden.

'Too often we have found ourselves unable to include the young in our liturgies, affirm their enthusiasms or find a way of expressing the Gospel in youth culture,' writes George Carey in *Treasures in the Field*. 'It has been less a failure of nerve than a failure of imagination. And imagination is usually lacking where there is fear. Often we are fearful of noise, spontaneity and colour in the controlled environment of our church life. We have often deprived ourselves of the fun to be had in expressing faith. We rob ourselves, as well as the young, of the chance to encounter the richness of liturgy and the wider contacts which faith can make with culture.'

We mustn't just tolerate children – we must *treasure* them and *involve* them in our church services, and look for opportunities where they can really contribute.

> **Families can still offer children their earliest and most deep-seated experience of Christian community and church going ... The foundations of church going – or church leaving – are laid in a person's childhood, during his or her most formative years. Where parents are successful in transmitting faith to their children and are themselves good churchgoing role models, there is much less likelihood that their offspring will drop out of church.**
> *Philip Richter and Leslie J. Francis,* **Gone But Not Forgotten**

Youth Matters

'Never has a generation had so much opportunity and yet been so lost,' said Tony Blair at the 1995 Labour Party Conference. As we move into the twenty-first century, we find a generation of young people living in a world full of opportunity, yet desperately searching for meaning. Theirs is an isolated culture, frequently balkanized into a bewildering variety of different youth *sub*-cultures.

Young people want to belong. They need to feel that their voice counts and they have a role in bringing about change. They're looking to be part of something, whether it's a community or a shared experience. In that respect, they're just like their elders. But for many young people, belonging is hard work. They're used to a culture in which the rights of the individual are paramount, and in which about the only heresy left is to suggest that a value or belief can and should be shared by everyone across the board. In a sense, if most of the church is better at handling unity than diversity, young people are better at handling diversity than unity.

The Church – more than any other group – has to grasp the opportunity to show young people what 'belonging' means. That will include welcoming them, trusting them, giving them responsibility and empowering them. They'll need to know they matter, which will involve taking risks and giving them as much say as anyone else in the church's decision-making process.

When Michael's church set up a working party to investigate the possibility of starting a church-based youth group, their meetings seemed to be getting nowhere. Michael and the other members could never agree on the best course of action. They couldn't even agree on whether the group should be exclusively for church youth or 'open' to other young people from the local area. Suddenly, Michael realized what the problem was: he and the other members of the working party, drawn from the church leadership, were over 40 years old.

When he pointed this out, they opted to draft two new members onto the group – Tom, in his early twenties, and Tina, in her late teens. Things improved ... but they didn't exactly go smoothly. Tom and Tina wholeheartedly approved of the idea of a youth group with its own times of worship and Bible study, but insisted there also had to be a weekly social evening not restricted just to church kids. This made some members of the working party nervous. The church teenagers were rowdy enough, they thought. What would it be like with outside kids as well? Vandalism? Drugs?

And as if that weren't bad enough, Tom and Tina were adamant that the church would have to do more than just set up a youth group if it was serious about keeping its young people. Things were going to have to change in the main services, too, or the teenagers weren't going to touch them with a bargepole. If they didn't learn to be integrated into the main services, they'd never stick with church, so some compromises were going to have to be made to accommodate the young people's way of doing things.

Some churches have tried to tackle the 'youth problem' by setting up alternative youth services. The most famous – or infamous – of these was the *Nine O'Clock Service* at St Thomas' Crookes, in Sheffield. There is a definite place for these, just as there is a place for 1662 Prayer Book services for those who like their worship more traditional than a family-based Sunday morning service will allow. But there are also considerable dangers. The 'autopsy' report on NOS suggested that the service had been allowed to become too independent and unaccountable to the rest of the church. But the problem was bigger than that: NOS had evolved to the point where there was little crossover or cross-fertilization between it and the parent church. The culture shock had become so great that they were essentially two entirely different churches with entirely different congregations.

For most local churches, this is neither a desirable nor a realistic option. The place for separate worship is in a more informal youth group meeting after the main Sunday service, for example. But if we stop at that, and make no changes to our main worship services, then we'll unwittingly have opted to remove young people from our church body. Rather than welcoming them and *allowing* them influence to change the way we do things, we'll be hiding in a safe, controlled environment. It's the worst of two worlds, because young and old ultimately belong together.

Young people need to know they *belong* in church. In fact, they're more concerned about the way adults in the church often expect them to fit in and become miniature clones than about the way the service might feel alien to their own culture. So as well as some healthy compromise when it comes to the service, the keys to making young people feel welcome and involved are dialogue, friendship, mutual respect and building relationships.

For the older people to share their spirituality and their worship as equals would be welcomed by many young people. The difficulties and divisions occur when young people are expected to assent to others' viewpoints and ideologies without question.
Phil Moon

Age Matters

'I sometimes get fed up with all this emphasis on young people,' moaned one elderly lady. 'What about us pensioners? We matter too!' It's predicted that the next 20 years will see a shift in terms of the population towards the elderly. The pendulum is beginning to swing back away from the young. Improvements in health-care technology and the ageing of the baby-boom generation mean that 'grey power' will increasingly become a force to be reckoned with.

Older people have a wealth of experience and expertise to offer. In the business world, senior managers are sometimes asked to 'mentor' younger managers. Mentoring doesn't mean they take over control. Rather it's about nurturing, encouraging, offering advice and the wisdom of experience, and giving less experienced people the freedom to make their own mistakes within a relatively safe environment.

We need to create frameworks for *valuing* one another, whatever our age or marital status. We form part of a web of relationships woven at local, national and international levels, because we're part of God's family. And these relationships stretch beyond the limitations of the 'nuclear family'. We're all part of God's family, God's children – so we're always somebody's child, and often somebody's parent.

Arthur's smile was as broad as he was tall. Welcoming people into church, he always had a friendly word for visitors and regulars alike. A man in his seventies, he loved the company of young people, making time for them, finding out about their world and encouraging them and praying for them through their exams, driving tests, job interviews and relationships. And he always had a twinkle in his eye for the ladies! When he died, at the age of 81, he was sorely missed by everyone who knew him, from his contemporaries right down to the children. Arthur had a very special place in the church.

Older members have two particularly valuable assets: *time* and *experience*. As we get older, and sometimes less active, we tend to become much better at making the most of the time we have left. Experience and old age teach us the relative importance of things, prompting us to make more time for people, building relationships, thinking, studying, listening and praying.

Mrs Wilding, well into her nineties, was the oldest member of her church. Her slight, frail body belied a very active brain. A tremendous 'prayer warrior', she'd pray daily for her friends, political situations, the church and the local community. If one of her friends or someone else she knew wasn't at church, she'd always be on the phone to them – just to make sure they weren't ill or in need of help. She always had a kind word to say to and about people, and no one could remember her ever saying anything negative. She used her time to encourage and support many of the church members, and people of all ages felt that they really mattered to her and that she genuinely cared. And she did.

That elderly lady sitting at the back of your church; she has a ministry and your church is deficient if her ministry isn't exercised.
Dr Roy Pointer

The Single Life

'If we really mean it when we sing things like, "You alone are my heart's desire",' asked a Spring Harvest speaker a few years ago, 'then why are so many single people looking for a marriage partner, and why do so many married people in the church assume that you're not really complete unless you've found one?' Single people form a sizeable portion of the Church, but are often made to feel one vital appendage short: a partner.

Especially for those who haven't chosen to be single for life, church Family Services can be an uncomfortable reminder of what they feel they're missing. Yet single people have time and talents vital to the Church – which is why Paul once longed that everyone could be single, as he was (1 Corinthians 7:7). The problem is, when churches see themselves as 'family friendly' only in the sense of accommodating young families with children – rather than helping *everyone* to feel part of the wider church family – single people begin to feel more like 'servants' than 'sons'. They do much of the work, but never feel that either they or their contributions are adequately recognized.

It can be similar for married couples who, by choice or circumstance, have no children. When Greg and Maggie got married, they already knew they didn't want kids. They saw what a massive investment having children could be, and though friends and relatives kept telling them that the 'returns' on the investment easily outweighed its 'costs', they felt it wasn't for them. It would be better for them to use their time and talents in other areas. But whenever they told people they didn't *want* children, they were met with an initial wall of disbelief, slowly giving way to something more closely resembling hostility, as though not having kids were selfish and 'un-Christian'. Those who made them feel fully accepted as a childless couple – such as the priest who married them, and reminded them they were a *real* family, even if they never had children – were the exceptions rather than the rule.

To combat this, some churches make active efforts to include single people – and those couples without children – in some of the more blatantly family-oriented services. When the children are invited to give their mothers flowers or small gifts on Mothering Sunday, for example, some churches organize it in such a way that every adult member of the congregation is included in the distribution. It's a double-edged sword: it reminds them that they're one of the family, but it also reminds them that, like it or not, they're role models – surrogate 'uncles' and 'aunts', to the children in the church family.

Every church, and especially every church service, is an exercise in compromise. Exactly like a large family gathering, some accommodation has to be made to a wide range of ages and tastes. Everyone has to feel welcome. It's a bit like a fruit salad. The trick is to make all the separate flavours work together whilst remaining distinct. You don't collect all the fruit together and whizz it in a blender to create one big, homogenous mass of blended fruit. Instead, you allow the different bits of fruit, cut up into manageable chunks, to retain their distinctive flavour. At the same time, you try to keep as balanced a mix as possible, so that no flavour is allowed to drown out the others.

IDEAS

The Church offers a unique opportunity to provide a caring community where people feel valued and involved. A loving church family is one where people feel they *belong* – regardless of age, sex, relationship status, or where they feel they are in their journey of faith. Our churches can offer *practical support* to those in our church family, while reaching out to those in the *wider community*, showing practical faith in action.

Test how family friendly you are at the moment by filling in the short questionnaire in Appendix 3. Here are some ideas and suggestions to help you find ways of encouraging your church to be more family friendly.

People of all ages want to belong and to be included

- Involve people as you plan services, activities, Family Fun days, etc. The more you encourage people to help in the planning and consult them, the more likely you are to avoid areas of conflict within the various family groupings.

- Encourage people of all ages to take part in the service. Some eight-year-olds and 80-year-olds are excellent readers. Families may like to lead the prayers. Young and old can take up the collection or the bread and wine. Some churches find a monthly 'Parade Service' a good way of encouraging the local Brownies, Guides, Scouts, Beavers, or Boys' and Girls' Brigade groups to come along and be a part of the service.

- There are many ways children can be involved in church services. Look for opportunities where they can really contribute. These may include: reading the Bible passage, taking up the collection, singing, playing instruments, helping to lead prayers, drama, helping to make a video or audio-tape recording, leading competitions, acting as 'servers', bell-ringing, interviewing someone from the congregation ... and plenty more!

- Special Focus Services offer the opportunity of recognizing and celebrating our different groups. You could celebrate age, for example, with a Sunday service dedicated to giving thanks for your older members. They could take an active part in the service, followed by a special lunch served by the younger members. Members of a Methodist church found a similar type of service affirming single people very supportive. Services could also celebrate families or young people.

- Set up your own Pram Service or similar weekday service for the babies and toddlers in your church.

- You may have members of the youth group who have leadership skills. Involve them in your leadership team. The minimum age for a Parochial Church Council member, for example, is 16. Not only will they represent the opinions and views of the youth and young people in your community, but you'll be acknowledging and encouraging their leadership skills and empowering them.

- Do you have a room in your church building that young people could use, which they feel is theirs? Equipment such as a pool table, TV, video, easy chairs, computer, or music system help to create an environment where they feel comfortable and relaxed. If a group member has artistic skills, they could paint murals. Make sure the young people are included in the decision and consultation process.

- Some churches employ a youth pastor or youth worker to work permanently and exclusively with young people. Building relationships is an important part of the role, equipping young people and helping them to feel valued and empowered. Some churches in the same vicinity have jointly funded a youth worker for the area.

- Put on a fun event which encourages the different age groups to mix. A volleyball or rounders match between the young people and the Twenties/Thirties group, for example, encourages the groups to mix, while retaining their own age group identity. It also gets very competitive!

- A Church Family day/weekend/week away is a great way of building relationships and discovering what it means to be a community. Try to include fun, all-age activities. Events like 'It's a Knockout' are usually popular and very messy!

Offering practical support

- The one thing every parent wants to know is how to be a better parent. Why not run a parenting course? You don't need to be an expert to set one up! You simply need to get hold of material such as *Parentalk*. Designed as an eight-session course for up to 10 people, the *Parentalk* pack includes a video, expert advice from Rob Parsons, Steve Chalke and Dr Caroline Dickinson, course guide, suggestions for practical activities, course material and OHP masters. Family Caring Trust also runs a number of parenting skills programmes. (See Resources section for details.)

- A baby-sitting service is a practical way of supporting families. Some churches operate a system whereby everyone who requires a baby-sitter forms part of the baby-sitting rota and receives a number of tokens. They pay a token each time they use someone on the rota, and receive one each time they baby-sit. Some teenagers, students and older members enjoy looking after children and are happy to baby-sit. If payment is involved, a contingency fund could be available for anyone who can't afford to pay.

- Pastoring plays an important role in supporting members of the church family. Keeping an eye on older members, new mums, those who are struggling financially, who've been bereaved … many people need a listening ear, support, advice, a chat over a cup of tea. We can't expect a busy pastor or minister to do everything. Support systems are vital to keep the wheels of the family well oiled. As elderly people become more housebound, for example, home visits and communion at home become increasingly important. And there may be one or two practical tasks that need doing, such as groceries to pick up, letters to post, pensions to get, light bulbs to change.

- Transport. Not all areas are well served by public transport, particularly on Sundays. Some churches have a transport rota where people with cars pick up those who need lifts to church. We need to be particularly sensitive to people with disabilities and elderly members, allowing them extra time to get in and out of cars. Some churches have their own minibuses which can be used for youth groups, day trips, church holidays, etc. Many people without cars appreciate the opportunity of getting out of the area.

- Prayer. A prayer chain for families has proved invaluable to many. The 'chain' is a group of people who will contact each other by phone and pray for family needs as they emerge.

When baby Cameron was taken into hospital with suspected meningitis, members of the prayer chain quickly got on the phone to alert each other and they all started praying for Cameron and his family. Older members often find they have more time to pray and fewer illusions as to what they can do without it. They could be encouraged to pray regularly for the church, the needs in your community, church members, etc. They could pray individually, as part of a prayer group or prayer chain. The Lydia Fellowship, a voluntary prayer fellowship mainly for women, encourages regular prayer for governments and political situations, as well as church and home life.

- The church building may need checking to see if improvements can be made to make it more family friendly. Access and ramps for wheelchair users and prams/buggies are discussed in Chapter 1. Nappy-changing facilities may be possible in your church or hall toilets. Parents at a church in New Malden agreed that putting a table in the loo would be perfectly adequate for changing nappies. The same church has also put several orthopaedic-type chairs in an alcove area near the front of the church, as they have a number of elderly people and others with back problems who find it difficult to stand up and sit down. A list of useful phone numbers (doctor, local hospital, minister or priest, dentist, chiropodist, Citizens' Advice Bureau, solicitor, police station, etc.) could be helpfully displayed in the entrance or on the church noticeboard.

Reaching into the community

- Under-Fives group. Many churches have found running these groups a great way of serving the local community and inviting non-churchgoers to use church premises. These can be good ways of offering practical support and building relationships in the community.

- A parenting course could be offered to people in the community (see above). Parenting skills form a common ground for Christians and non-churchgoers.
- A weekly lunch club in the church hall provides a caring, supportive and social forum for older members. Transport may need to be provided. Hairdressing, laundry and chiropody services could also be provided. Outings are also popular events for older members.
- Youth work is another way of encouraging the church to reach into the community. Social action projects can help raise awareness, while empowering young people in the area. The young people in Croydon, for example, have been challenged to raise £500,000 by the year 2000 to help build and run a special centre for young homeless people. It will provide accommodation, employment skills training and advice for 16–25-year-olds. The project is a joint initiative between the churches of Croydon, the Oasis Trust and Croydon Council.

RESOURCES

Resources

The Open Book. All-age worship material and children's activities, opening up the Bible in a fresh way. Produced by the Bible Society. (There are a number of Christian organizations producing all-age worship resources and specific-age materials for Sunday schools and kids clubs, e.g. Scripture Union, CPAS, Scripture Press, The Bible Society.)

Parentalk. An eight-session course for up to 10 people. The pack includes a video, expert advice from Rob Parsons and Steve Chalke, course guide, suggestions for practical activities, course material, OHP masters.

The Parent Assertiveness Programme, *The Noughts to Sixes Parenting Programme*, *The Teen Parenting Programme*, *The Parent and Sex*

Programme. Just some of a number of programmes to provide support at all stages of the family life cycle. Easy-to-run, flexible, self-help courses for groups of 8–12 participants. Developed by Family Caring. (The basic parenting programme is also available in Welsh.)

The Sixty Minute Marriage and *The Sixty Minute Parent*. Punchy, practical advice from Rob Parsons (Executive Director of Care for the Family). Two resources dealing with relationship and parenting pressures. Book, video and audio tape format.

Help! I'm a Parent. A multi-format resource for use in church and home groups. Produced by CPAS.

The Family Dinner Game. A game for pre-teen families aimed at communicating, having fun and being supportive – all over a family meal. Produced by Family Caring.

Step-families Programme. Eight-session course exploring situations facing step-parents and offering helpful skills. Produced by Family Caring.

The Young Adult Assertiveness Programme. An eight-week resource programme by Family Caring to help 15+s. The kit includes a video, leaders' guides, handbook, etc.

Youth Alpha Leaders manual. Equips leaders to run Youth Alpha in a variety of settings.

The ActivAge Unit enables older people to make a positive contribution towards their own and other people's lives, as well as the life and structure of local communities. Details from Age Concern.

Agencies

Age Concern England, Astral House, 1268 London Road, London SW16 4ER. Tel: 0181 679 8000.

Age Concern Northern Ireland, 3 Lower Crescent, Belfast BT7 1NR. Tel: 01232 245729.

Age Concern Cymru, 4th Floor, 1 Cathedral Road, Cardiff CF1 9DS. Tel: 01222 371566.

Age Concern Scotland, 113 Rose Street, Edinburgh, EH2 3DT.
Tel: 0131 220 3345.

Alpha, Holy Trinity Brompton, Brompton Road, London
SW7 1JA. Tel: 0171 581 8255. Hotline: 0345 581278.

Bible Society, Stonehill Green, Westlea, Swindon SN5 7DG.
Tel: 01793 418100.

Care for the Family, Garth House, Leon Avenue, Cardiff,
CF4 7RG. Tel: 01222 811733.

Catholic Centre for Healing in Marriage, Penamser Road,
Porthmadog, North Wales LL49 9NY. Tel: 01766 514300.

Churches Together for Families, c/o Wendy Bray, 17 Thornhill
Road, Mammamead, Plymouth PL3 5NF. Tel: 01752 661340.
Set up to look at how churches can be more helpful to families.

Church Pastoral Aid Society (CPAS), Athena Drive, Tachbrook
Park, Warwick CV34 6NG. Tel: 01962 334242.

Family Caring Trust, 44 Rathfriland Road, Newry, Co. Down,
BT34 1LD. Tel: 01693 64174. Fax: 01693 69077.

FLAME (Family Life and Marriage Education network), Robert
Runcie House, 60 Marsham Street, Maidstone, Kent ME14
1EW. Tel: 01622 755014. Fax: 01622 693531.

Help the Aged, St James's Walk, Clerkenwell Green, London
EC1R 0BE. Tel: 0171 253 0253. Fax: 0171 250 4474.

Parentalk, PO Box 23142, London SE1 0ZT. Tel: 0171 450
9072/3. Fax: 0171 450 9060. Provides a wide range of
resources and services for parents.

Pre-School Playgroups Association, 61–3 Kings Cross Road,
London WC1X 9LL. Tel: 0171 833 0991. Fax: 0171 837 4942.

University of the Third Age, 26 Harrison Street, London WC1.
Tel: 0171 837 8838. Runs a wide variety of courses for older
people. For local branches contact their headquarters.

Books and publications

Sheila Bridge, *The Art of Imperfect Parenting* (Hodder & Stoughton, 1995)

Fiona Castle, *Rainbows through the Rain* ((Hodder & Stoughton, 1998)

Steve Chalke, *How to Succeed as a Parent* (Hodder & Stoughton, 1997)

Steve Chalke, *The Parentalk Guide to the Childhood Years* (Hodder & Stoughton, January 1999)

Steve Chalke, *The Parentalk Guide to the Teenage Years* (Hodder & Stoughton, January 1999)

Steve Chalke, *The Parentalk Guide to the Toddler Years* (Hodder & Stoughton, March 1999)

Gary Collins, *I Believe in The Family* (Hodder & Stoughton, 1996)

Faith Gibson, *Reminiscence and Recall: understanding and encouraging people to value themselves by valuing their pasts* (Age Concern, 1998)

David Gillett, Anne Long, Ruth Fowke, *A Place in the Family: The Single Person in the Local Church* (Grove Books, 1981)

David Gillett and Michael Scott-Joynt (eds), *Treasures in the Field: The Archbishop's Companion for the Decade of Evangelism* (HarperCollins, 1993)

Parentwise magazine (available from Herald House, 96 Dominion Road, Worthing, West Sussex BN14 8JP. Tel: 01903 537308)

Rob Parsons, *The Sixty Minute Father* (Hodder & Stoughton, 1995)

Rob Parsons, *The Sixty Minute Marriage* (Hodder & Stoughton, 1997)

Rob and Lloyd Parsons, *What Every Kid Wished Their Parents Knew* (Hodder & Stoughton, June 1999)

Nick Pollard, *Why Do They Do That?* (Lion, 1998)

Steve Scrutton, *Bereavement and Grief* (Age Concern, 1995)

Sue Smith, *Power to Parent* (Hodder & Stoughton, 1998)

Verena Tschudin (ed.), *An Introductory Guide for Older People Counselling Older People* (Age Concern, 1998)

Ann Webber, *Life Later On (Older People and the Church)* (SPCK, 1990)

Age Concern produce a number of other helpful books and leaflets for coping with life in older age.

APPENDIX 3

The family-friendly survey

Ask yourself the following questions to help you assess how family-friendly you are:

- Is our church accessible to pushchairs, buggies and wheelchair users?
- What happens if a parent needs to change a nappy or breastfeed?
- Is there a toddlers' club?
- Has the church considered offering after-school clubs for working parents?
- Have we considered running any parenting courses for the church and community?
- Do our families have the chance to be together in church?
- Do we listen to the views of our young people?
- Do we use older members of the church to help 'mentor' the younger parents and members?

3 We Will Make Sure You Can Hear Clearly

Preface by Vera Hunt

Vera Hunt was born in Stepney in the East End of London and was evacuated to Windsor during the war. She was seven years old when meningitis left her profoundly deaf. She still attended a hearing school where she was made to sit at the back of the class – so as not to disturb the other children. At 11, Vera was sent to an oral school for deaf girls. Signing was forbidden, as it was at the local church. But Vera had a deep faith and found in God her closest companion. Now an ordained minister in the Church of England, Vera is a chaplain among deaf people.

Deafness didn't hit me in the same way as it possibly hit others. In fact, I thought the world had lost its voice – not that I had lost my hearing! I kept telling people to 'speak up'.

Deafness left me feeling very isolated. It was strange to step from a world of sound and music into one of utter silence. But I can still remember some of the sounds and music. The last hymn I heard before going deaf was 'The Holy City'.

I enjoyed going to church as a child. Maybe it was simply a sense of security in my world of turmoil. Perhaps it was out of loyalty to the God I couldn't see, but knew was there. Mine was a simple faith. I hadn't read the Bible, I didn't know who Jesus was, I didn't know he was a Jew, or that he was the Son of God. I just knew God was there.

I first received Religious Education when a chaplain with deaf people came to our school once a month, to prepare some of us for confirmation. Although we attended the local church each week, the services were for hearing people. There was no place for deaf people to participate in the worship, no place for learning. The only place for me within the church was to sit quietly like an ornament and receive the sacrament – without understanding what it was all about. In those days, sign language was regarded with contempt.

Looking back, it's hard to understand why. The Gospels tell us about a unique and beautiful pair of hands – the hands of Jesus. He used his hands to heal, to pray, to proclaim to the world how much he loved us. Hands that had nails cruelly driven into them when fixed to the cross. Why, then, should deaf people be denied the right to use their hands to communicate and serve?

I admit I did resent watching other people singing, participating and serving their God whilst I sat in isolation. My God and their God. Was there more than one God? One for the hearing and another for the deaf? It seemed like it to me in those days. The only enjoyment I had was browsing through hymn books, being present within the house of my God. If the doors of the church seemed to be closed to deaf people, the ears of the hearing were deaf to our needs. Was the eye saying to the ear, 'I don't need you'?

'*Ephphatha*', in the story of the deaf man (Mark 7:31–7), appears to be for both deaf and hearing ears. It's a shout to open up to deaf people's needs. Open up to the understanding that deaf people have equal rights and equal needs to spiritual and communal worship. I want to say, 'Please understand, we are part of the Body of Christ.'

The healing of the deaf man gives us a picture of Jesus' compassion and love for deaf people. It gives us a picture that he considers us equal. There is no other Gospel story where Jesus actually 'spits, touches and looks up to heaven'. It was a physical touch of love and compassion; an acknowledgement that deaf people should be accepted – that deaf people are part of the Family of God.

We Will Make Sure You Can Hear Clearly

The preacher walked up the steps into the pulpit. It was a large church, similar in style and stature to a cathedral. He prayed for God's Spirit to guide him: for wisdom, for clarity, and that people's hearts and minds would be opened. His text, Mark 7:31–7, featured the story of Jesus healing a man who was deaf and hardly able to speak, and he illustrated his sermon with stories from his own experience of working for years among deaf people. It was a passionate, clear and convincing call for churches to pay particular attention to the needs of deaf and hard-of-hearing people both in services and in other activities.

Tragically, unknown to him, the pulpit microphone had developed a fault. As a result, no one sitting further away than the third row back could hear a word. Being very British, no one said anything. Instead, the congregation sat in total silence for 15 minutes, the only noises coming from the occasional elderly lady complaining about how she couldn't hear a word the preacher was saying, and how the Church never seemed to take proper account of people's difficulties in hearing!

Frances waited for Trevor to arrive. Her thick coat kept her warm against the chill of the cold, winter evening. She watched the people around her talking animatedly, catching up with each other's news, discussing the latest gossip and fashion, sharing their agonies and embarrassing moments. The babble of conversation and the music drifting out of the stores was inaudible to Frances, who lived in a silent world. As Trevor came round the corner, Frances' face broke into a broad smile as she ticked him off for being late. Soon they were catching up with each other's news, exchanging the latest gossip, all the while their fingers working ten to the dozen, busily communicating their news by sign language.

> **People talking without speaking,**
> **People listening without hearing,**
> **People writing songs that voices never share.**
> *Paul Simon, 'The Sound of Silence'*

A Precious Sense

For most of us, our world is made up of sounds. We're surrounded by them, many of them so familiar that we don't actually hear them. We depend on sounds to get us through each day. Most of us would be lost without them. Over the next 30 seconds you may hear any number of the following: a radio or TV, noises from next door, a lawnmower, a tractor, someone shouting, snatches of conversation, doors banging, dogs barking, birds singing, babies crying, cars driving by, footballs being kicked, water rushing through pipes, planes overhead, someone laughing...

The ability to hear gives us constant information about our surroundings, whether we're asleep or awake. A child crying in the garden may signal the fact they've fallen down and hurt themselves. A barking dog may warn us that someone has just arrived at the house. A ringing alarm clock alerts us that it's time to get up. The radio blasts out the latest news, views, opinions, gossip and music. In many developing countries, and even some parts of the UK and USA, where poverty and illiteracy levels are very high, hearing is the only way to communicate complex information. And through the telephone we can hear and speak to people across the other side of the world instantly, as if they were in the next room.

Hearing is a precious sense which, like vision, we so often take for granted. Through listening to sounds at a very early age, we develop speech. Through speaking and listening we learn, we absorb, we discuss and debate ideas, we entertain and are entertained, we form opinions, we develop contact and relationships with others. We learn to associate some sounds with danger and others with pleasure. We learn to recognize the sound of a person's voice so accurately that we can tell it's them almost instantly. And we can learn to interpret complicated, repetitive vocal sounds not just to understand what someone's saying and what language they're speaking, but even to identify by their accent where in the world they grew up.

Vocal language is the most common means of communicating in our churches and communities. But how much do we consider and cater for those people whose hearing is in some way and to some degree impaired – for whom speaking and listening aren't easy methods of communication?

hearing / *n*. 1 the faculty of perceiving sounds. 2 the range within which sounds may be heard; earshot. 3 an opportunity to state one's case. 4 the listening to evidence and pleadings in a law court. ❏ hearing-aid / a small device to amplify sound, worn by a partially deaf person.
Oxford English Dictionary

A Muffled World

About 20 per cent of people in Britain have some loss of hearing. One in eight people under the age of 60 is hard of hearing, with the ratio rising to one in *three* over that age. This world of distorted sounds – or without sounds altogether – can lead to feelings of great exclusion, discrimination and isolation.

By the age of 65, Lil had lost the hearing in her right ear but didn't like to admit it. She also found it increasingly hard to follow what people were saying to her when there were a number of simultaneous conversations in the room. She grew frustrated, and even started accusing her family of talking about her behind her back. Lil's sunny nature gradually gave way to biting remarks, anger and withdrawal. Some people thought she was being rather rude and ignoring them. Like so many people who have become hard of hearing with age, she became ever more prone to bouts of frustration, fear and loss of self-confidence. It's often hard for people with good hearing to understand the extent of this frustration, but we still need to encourage greater tolerance and accommodation in our local churches and communities, helping to create a loving environment that values and supports one another, whatever our disabilities.

Everyone who is hard of hearing has some ability to hear or communicate, unlike those who are profoundly deaf. That ability will partly depend on the clarity, pitch and volume of the sound, as well as the amount of background noise. So splitting into small groups for discussions, for example, can make it difficult for some hard-of-hearing people to follow conversations. Many rely on elementary lip-reading skills to augment the sounds they hear, and when the person speaking changes quickly and constantly – as they tend to in small groups – it can be tricky for hearing-impaired people to keep up. It becomes even more difficult when people unwittingly hide their lips, either behind a hand or because they're looking in the opposite direction as they're speaking. Clear speech, good lighting and a healthy dose of loving consideration can all help bring vocal clarity to a muffled world.

Hearing-aids have obviously led to an improved quality of life for many partially deaf people. Roughly one in ten people who find it difficult to hear now use one. But it's worth remembering that hearing-aids also amplify background sounds. So if there's a lot of noise in the area, or a number of conversations going on around them at the same time, it will be difficult for someone wearing a hearing-aid to understand what's being said. So having coffee and a chat beside a noisy kitchen isn't easy for people with impaired hearing, for example.

An increasing number of churches are installing loop systems. This is a cable loop which runs around a 'listening area', producing a magnetic field. Hearing-aids can be switched to a special 'T' position, so when someone talks into a microphone, their words are amplified with very little distracting noise. At an average cost of less than £500, this is a relatively inexpensive way to make a very big difference in people's lives.

Some churches question the need for this kind of expense. 'We don't need a loop,' they argue. 'We don't have that many deaf people. We'll install a loop when there are enough people who'd use it to make it worth our while.' But this kind of thinking is not merely inconsiderate, it's also short sighted.

Jane was the only member of her family to go to church. Her partially deaf husband, Peter, had started going with her, but had given up when he found the sense of isolation at being unable to follow the service properly or even hear people's conversation over coffee afterwards too much to bear. And because Peter never went, their two children opted to stay at home as well. As a result, what Jane had hoped would be a real family experience – something they could all share and enjoy together – turned out to be a stark reminder to her of her own isolation. She'd always had a stronger faith than Peter, and nothing made that clearer than his refusal to accompany her. So when the church installed a loop system, Peter wasn't the only one to feel less isolated during services: because he and the children started going to church regularly, Jane's feelings of isolation came to an end as well.

> **If there are any of you at the back who do not hear me, please don't raise your hand because I am nearsighted.**
> *Poet W. H. Auden at the start of a lecture in a large hall*

The Goldfish Bowl

For people who are profoundly deaf, the world can seem even more alienating and excluding. So, too, can our local churches. 'We take them to church and what do they see?' asks John Pollendine, a signer for the deaf. 'A goldfish bowl! They're surrounded by people who open and shut their mouths like goldfish.'

Christians were integral in setting up a number of organizations to care for profoundly deaf people. The Church set up deaf communities, or 'Missions', in the early nineteenth century. Church and worship formed a significant part of these centres, where deaf people could socialize, relax, learn and have fun with other deaf people, communicating in a new language they all understood: sign language. But with advances in technology and changes in education, deaf clubs and communities have seen a decline in numbers. Fax machines, text telephones, text subtitling on TV and other technological wonders are enabling deaf people to enjoy greater independence and integration in society. Politician Jack Ashley and world-renowned percussionist Evelyn Glennie have shown that deaf people can – and do – live full, interactive lives.

No longer is the 'deaf community' a homogenous group. Instead, it's changing as deaf people choose to opt in and out according to *their* will. The barriers of a predominantly hearing-based culture are gradually being eroded as deaf people are being allowed access into a larger world. Some deaf people will choose to meet regularly with other deaf people for worship, pastoral care and evangelism. Others will choose to attend their local church, in which case churches need to be ready and welcoming. That means challenging our assumptions about people who can't hear, welcoming them unconditionally.

Trevor is profoundly deaf. He's a member of his local church, where he generally feels welcomed. Occasionally he has the luxury of an interpreter; most of the time he sits next to someone who writes down what's going on. The printed service sheet enables him to follow the service. He sings with gusto, and no one minds that he isn't technically 'in tune' because his singing is every bit as valuable as that of someone with perfect pitch. When the words are printed on an overhead projector screen, his hands are free to sign. After the service, Trevor chats to people using a pen and wodges of paper. One or two members of the church are even beginning to learn very basic sign language, and he was asked to sign an opening prayer at the Christmas service, interpreted by Joanna. Spoken words and sign language together were rich and effective channels of communication.

> **Deaf people ask the same questions as hearing people; questions like: why are there wars and suffering?**
> **The Church among Deaf People, *Church of England Advisory Board of Mission***

'Can You Hear Me at the Back?'

Billions of pounds are spent in the communications industry: in publishing, broadcasting, advertising, telecommunications, marketing, journalism. In the 1980s, magazines were a boom industry, and the 1990s saw the birth of the 'spin doctor', whose job is to put the right 'spin' on a news story to give it the best possible reception both in the papers and with the public. As we turn the century, hundreds of digital TV channels are bursting onto our screens. Advertising, entertainment, information. Communication is big business.

Churches are called to communicate the good news of who Jesus is and what he came to do for us all. But to do that, we need to make sure of a basic communication requirement – quite simply, that our message can actually be heard! Sadly, the story at the beginning of this chapter about a sermon on deafness that fell on deaf ears is absolutely true. A great message failed to get across because someone had forgotten to check the amplification system. As the preacher exclaimed afterwards, 'Why didn't you tell me? Even if there was a fault with the microphone, I could have spoken up – I have a very loud voice!'

Fifty years ago, amplification in churches was not only rare, it was virtually unheard of. Voice projection was a vital part of any preacher's or minister's skill. If you listen to tapes of some of the greatest and most inspirational preachers of the century, you'll notice that, almost without exception, their style betrays their 'stage' origins, when they couldn't rely on speakers and microphones and had to learn instead how to project their voice so as to be heard at the back of a church or auditorium. Today, amplification has made such an impact on vocal and preaching technique that the recorded sermons of Martin Luther King or the early Billy Graham seem to be a bit over dramatic. Yet their lyrical style evolved as much from the need to be heard in the back row as from anything poetic in their natures.

Sometimes the reason we don't always hear as well as we might is just that the speaker or reader isn't speaking slowly and clearly enough into the microphone, or projecting their voice adequately if there are no microphones. Teaching people to read the Bible in public can be a great help not only in ensuring that everyone can hear, but also in assisting them to understand what they're hearing. Nerves and mumbling can obscure the full meaning of a Bible passage under a bland, inaudible monotone.

A number of people were finding it hard to listen to Richard, the assistant minister. He'd always had a tendency to speak quickly, but as he started to get enthusiastic about his subject, both his decibel level and his vocal register seemed to rise uncomfortably high! In the end, Richard decided to contact someone nearby who taught speech and drama. She explained that shouting – instead of projecting the voice – encourages the throat muscles to tense up, which in turn makes the voice rise in pitch. She taught him a few simple voice and breathing exercises to do on a regular basis, and helped him to express his enthusiasm without starting to shout. After several months, he had learnt how to speak more slowly, project his voice without shouting, and develop his lower vocal range so his voice became more relaxed and easier on the ears.

Our services are largely made up of spoken or sung words, whether through words of welcome, hymns, psalms and songs, prayer and liturgy, Bible readings, sermons or notices. Our home groups or weekly meetings are also predominantly speech based. So we need to make sure that in our churches and our communities we can be adequately 'heard' or people will vote with their feet and give us – and quite possibly even the gospel – a wide berth.

The Minister shall read with a loud voice...
The Minister shall ... say ... with an audible voice...
The Book of Common Prayer

'G'fhrr ¿Higggrrrrh###hhah Qa'ark!!!! ... Erm, We Appear To Be Experiencing Some Technical Difficulties'

Whilst an increasing number of churches have the right technology – microphones, radio mikes, loudspeaker systems, amplifiers, video and computer links – we don't always know how to use it effectively! Maybe you've sat in a service and nearly jumped out of your seat when the amplifier suddenly howled. Or, like a British Rail announcement, you've listened to a cacophony of indistinguishable words. Sometimes technology can help us to get our point across, but unless we understand how to use it effectively it's just as likely to get in the way of what we're trying to communicate.

Andrew and Rachel lead a church in the inner city. There's a small core of regulars, but a growing number of locals attend less frequently. Because 'going to church' is new for many of them,

Andrew finds ways of communicating that they find more familiar. Film clips played onto a large screen, computer graphics, illustrations and cartoons all help him illustrate his sermons, for example. Sometimes he even takes a camcorder out to the local market to record 'vox pops' from ordinary passers-by (who are unsually intrigued by the idea of a vicar collecting soundbites from the public, to say the least). There are usually games, dramatized readings, and traditional and contemporary music, all woven into the fabric of an Anglican morning service. They help to communicate the gospel message and biblical teaching in ways that people can hear and understand, especially if they're unused to singing traditional hymns, repeating the same (or very similar) words week after week and sitting through at least 20 minutes of someone talking to them from the front of a building. But in order to work most effectively, these innovations require planning – and a certain degree of technical know-how!

When Andrew first started, there were no end of technical hitches. No one was sure which of the three microphones to use, for example, and Andrew found himself having to leap around, working all the technical equipment as well as leading most of the service. Whilst nobody minded, it was a little distracting! But a small team gradually evolved to take on the technical side of things and ensure a smoother run. Nick now 'produces' the service: he knows who's doing what, makes sure people know which microphone to use and 'cues' any tapes that need to be played. Tim has had basic training on the sound equipment, and is now busy teaching two other people how to use it. William has got to grips with the computer and video equipment. Sound checks are done half an hour before people arrive.

The result is that everyone can now hear clearly, and the earlier technical hitches are minimal, which helps the flow of communication. What's more, Andrew has more time to plan the content of the service each week now that he doesn't have to think about the technical aspects, and the whole team works on devising new ways of getting the message across and making sure that everyone can hear properly.

There's nothing new about the idea of a multi-media presentation in church, of course. Before the Reformation, the majority of church buildings were highly decorated inside with murals and icons – the ancient equivalent of banners and video screens. This wasn't just a way of brightening up an otherwise dull wall – it meant that the words of the service were reinforced by 'artists' impressions' of Bible stories or well-known events in church history. In addition, a lot of what went on during the service was highly visual and far less reliant than services today on words as a means of getting the message across. Candles, colours, costumes and crucifixes all served as visual reminders of deep spiritual themes. Incense – which was partly used as a deodorant – helped people visualize their prayers wafting up to heaven, and bowing and kneeling ('genuflecting') emphasized our worship of God in all his glory, much as raising hands did in the early Church and continues to do in charismatic circles today.

The spoken word only gained its dominance after the Reformation, when many church leaders threw the baby out with the bathwater. Not only did they advocate whitewashing walls, they also chose to reject – rather than reform – a number of practices that had stood the test of time. In a way, this reached a peak with the Nonconformist churches, because although groups like the Baptists actually emphasized the things that were most important to them in a *visual* way (hence the move towards baptism by total immersion), what stood out in most people's minds was the preaching. As pulpits replaced altars at the front of so many church buildings, so the spoken word was allowed to drown out the visual word.

In our multi-media age, there's a need to balance the two, ensuring that words aren't used as the only way of expressing the good news of Jesus and our response to it. But we do need to be careful: a multi-media presentation, though less reliant on the spoken word, needs to be able to deliver its message silently as well as with soundtrack, because it will be that much harder for partially deaf people to catch any of the words used. What's more, most multi-media services require subdued lighting, which will make lip reading virtually impossible.

> *Flustered Vicar*: 'I think there's something wrong with this microphone.'
> *Half-Asleep Congregation*: 'And also with you.'

His Master's Voice

Jesus was undoubtedly the greatest communicator on earth. He talked to government and church leaders as easily as he was able to communicate with lepers, prostitutes and social outcasts. He spoke to thousands without the advantages of audio-enhancing technology or computer-generated graphics. He used words and images that ordinary people understood and related to, and he frequently made his point by telling his audience a story (parable). Yet, in spite of his communication gifts, some people chose to remain deaf, unmoved and unchallenged by his words.

Let's go back to the story of the deaf man in Mark 7. Not only was this man deaf, but he had a speech impediment. The two main forms of communication – speech and hearing – were denied him. Jesus took him away from the crowd, put his fingers into his ears, spat and touched his tongue. It was a form of language – symbolic gestures – the man could understand. As Jesus said the word '*ephphatha*' ('be opened'), the man was able to hear and speak. By doing this, Jesus showed the love, compassion and concern of his Father … and gave the man an end not only to his physical isolation, but his social ostracism as well. We don't have the healing powers of Christ, but we do have the means and the opportunity to show love and compassion to all in our communities – including those who can't hear, or who have speech impediments, or who are blind.

Our churches need to encourage and empower deaf people to appreciate their gifts, allowing them to play a full part in the life and work of our church communities. Deaf and partially deaf people should not be apart from the body. As we've already seen in this book, we're all part of the Body of Christ and we all need to hear.

IDEAS

We're called to go and tell people the good news of Jesus and vocal communication is the most common form of communication that we use in our churches and in our society. We therefore need to check our *communication skills* to make sure that we're being heard and understood. In our technological age, we need to make sure that we make the best use of the *technology* available to us and that we're able to use it effectively. But for many people, speaking and listening aren't easy methods of communication. We need to think creatively and positively about ways in which we can include and cater for people with *hearing difficulties*.

Communication skills to help people hear clearly

- Hold a workshop where everyone who needs to speak or sing publicly in the service (reading, prayers, notices, welcome, kids' spot, music and worship group, etc.) has a chance to practise projecting their voices in the church. You may need to contact someone at a local school who teaches drama or singing to help you run the workshop as they'll have useful techniques to pass on. Make it open to all ages and turn it into a positive, fun event. Encourage people to project their voices to the back row. Help people to familiarize themselves with the acoustics at different points of the church – although they'll vary when a number of people are in the church and absorb some of the sound. Encourage people to check out sight lines and audibility.

- Even if you don't run a workshop, encourage anyone who speaks or sings in church to practise reading or singing aloud. Encourage them by saying some people find it hard to hear and so we need to be more helpful to people with hearing difficulties. Good enunciation, projecting the voice, speaking more slowly than a normal speed of speech, etc., are all good tips.
- If you're a preacher, have a good look at the way *you* communicate and check out the way Jesus communicated. Are you using stories and visual aids to illustrate your talk? Are you communicating in a language that your listeners understand? Do you take time to look at tabloid and broadsheet newspapers and magazines to see what people are reading? Are you watching some of the popular TV series (*Coronation Street*, *Eastenders*, *The Bill*, etc.) to see what people in your church and community are watching? These are often the talking points at home and at work! If you want to encourage feedback and check how you're communicating, see *The Three-Eared Preacher* under the Resources section.

Using technology effectively to help people hear clearly

- Not all churches require microphones, but they're increasingly used. Have you checked to see whether audio equipment would help you communicate more easily? Or if you had equipment installed a while ago, is there anyone locally who might be able to assess whether it needs updating or improving? (Check to see if there's anyone in your congregation who may be able to advise you in the first instance.)
- If you use a radio microphone or fixed microphone (on a stand, fixed to the pulpit or lectern, etc.), make sure you don't keep turning your head from side to side. You'll be 'off mike' and will sound like a Monty Python sketch when people only pick up one word in five!

- If the microphones are fixed and the audio level pre-set, make sure everyone who uses the microphone in the same service stands – or sits – at roughly the *same* distance. That will help keep the sound levels similar.
- Check your sound levels and audio equipment *before* the service starts and before people arrive. It's better to search out the gremlins *before* the service and to set the right levels, rather than trying to address the problems in the actual service. There'll always be the odd gremlin in the system, but it's best to try to minimize the risk!
- If you use several microphones and a reasonable amount of audio equipment, do your operators receive regular training? It's a great idea to make sure you have enough operators who know how to work the equipment, particularly for holiday times and sick cover. It's also a good idea to provide your operator with a 'running order' so they know what's happening in the service, who's taking part and which microphones need to be in place. If extra microphones or audio equipment are needed, make sure the operator or technical team know a few days *before* the service!
- If you have a self-operating PA system at the *front* of the church, think about putting it at the *back* of the church and encouraging a teenager or young person to operate it for you.
- Have you thought of recording your sermon? There are simple recording systems available and, as the recording is taken directly off the microphone, the quality is even better than 'live'. It's a good way of enabling anyone who is hard of hearing to listen to the recording at home. It's also helpful for those who are housebound, ill or unable to get to church.
- Is there any technology which would really help your communication in your services? Have you thought of using any of the following: video clips, audio tapes, audio-visual presentations, pre-filmed video, cartoon clips, computer-generated graphics, overhead projectors, TV monitors, video screen, etc.? Dream dreams, think 'big' and make a 'wish list'.

Then work out what would be really helpful. Then see if there are ways of fundraising, or getting the church council to approve a budget. You may need a two- or three-year plan.

- If there are other churches in your area who use a range of sound and vision equipment, is there a simple way of organizing an occasional 'loan system' – especially if one church has additional equipment which is used infrequently.
- Check out your lighting. Atmospheric lighting and candles are extremely effective. But it can be very difficult for some people to read in such low lighting. It also makes it hard for people with hearing difficulties to lip read.

Helping people with hearing difficulties, and those who are profoundly deaf, to hear clearly

- Encourage people with hearing difficulties to sit at or near the front of the church and make sure there's good lighting. We naturally tend to shy away from the front, but it's harder to hear at the back!
- If you use order-of-service books, don't assume people will know what page you're on! Make sure people know the page numbers so they can at least follow the written word.
- Don't let cost put you off installing a loop system. If you put off installing a loop system, you may be putting people off joining the church! And you may find the loop system attracts other groups into your church as they'd like to make use of the facility (e.g. local history society, talks, lectures, interviews, etc.). Put the loop system on the church agenda. All you need is an ordinary microphone, an amplifier and some wire for a basic system. The Royal National Institute for the Deaf publish a detailed leaflet, *Induction Loops in Public Places*. A phone call to your local authority's offices might produce a grant towards the purchase and installation of the induction loop system, under the Chronically Sick and Disabled Persons Act. Note: make sure any installation conforms to

BS6083 Part 4. Contact RNID for advice regarding the type of installation, etc.

- Encourage Deaf Awareness in your church and community. Your local deaf association may well be able to provide a speaker or help run a workshop, advice and skills course. As many of us will experience hearing difficulties as we get older, Deaf Awareness is a positive way of encouraging us to understand, to be more sensitive, and prepared to cope. You could have a special Deaf or Disability Awareness Sunday service.

- There may be profoundly deaf people in your community who'd love to come to church. Find out from your local deaf association (generally listed under 'Deaf' or 'Social Services' in the phone book) whether there are any signers in your area.

- If you do have a signer, remember that they need to use their hands – they can't hold a hymn book *and* sign! Make sure they have a stand available where they can put their notes, service sheets, etc. Where possible, give them the words to any solos, songs, Bible readings, main sermon points, etc., *before* the service (enlarged words are best). Some words and idioms are more difficult to translate and difficult words and names need to be finger-spelt. An overhead projector or video screen is really helpful as it means words can be projected, enabling people who are deaf to sign *at the same time* as people are singing.

- Advertise the fact you have services and events for people who are hard of hearing or deaf. They're used to being excluded by society, so won't be aware they're welcome unless you let them know!

- Do you – or someone at church – have access to e-mail or a website? Sermons, notices, prayers, etc. could be transcribed onto the web for people who are deaf or hard of hearing. Or they could be printed off and duplicated. E-mail is also a good way of keeping in contact and in communication with the hard of hearing.

- Include hard-of-hearing and deaf people in social events. Be sensitive – remember that sitting in small groups and a lot of background noise isn't easy for hearing-impaired people. Hearing-aids amplify sounds, including background noises. Be patient, tolerant, understanding, and speak clearly. A group of young deaf people attend their local church with their interpreter. They're regular members of the Friday night and Saturday morning social events. They chat and gossip in their own sign language. Although they can't totally integrate with other church members, they're made to feel very welcome, people come up and say hello and a number of the congregation are learning basic signing.
- Befriend people who have hearing difficulties. Talk to *them* and not simply to their interpreters or carers.

RESOURCES

Resources

The Three-Eared Preacher. A practical resource by former advertising executive Mark Greene, if you want to improve your preaching and get honest feedback from the congregation. Available from London Bible College.

Directory of all registered and trained interpreters. Listed in the CACDP (Council for the Advancement of Communication with Deaf People) *Directory 1996/7.*

Addresses of all organizations, services and educational establishments for deaf people. Listed in *RNID Information Directory 1994/5.*

See Hear! Magazine with news, features and advice empowering people with a hearing loss to get the best out of life. Available from the RNID.

Hands Together provides newsletter, conference, Bible Training Day, interpreter workshops, Deaf Awareness, literature, evangelism.

ITV Teletext Religious Pages provides five pages of 'Godlines' on ITV Teletext daily.

BBC Ceefax Religious Word provides religious material for BBC Ceefax.

Check out the interactive CDs, Exploring Bible CDs, text videos, etc. available from leading Christian booksellers.

PA, audio equipment, etc. There are a number of companies which specialize in installing sound systems (see *UK Christian Handbook* for full listings). Check if they offer a free advisory service.

- Keith Monks Sound Systems, Brodrick Hall, Brodrick Road, London SW17 7DY. Tel: 0181 682 3456. Fax: 0181 767 8525. Also install loop systems.
- HW Audio Ltd, 174 St George's Road, Bolton BL1 2NZ. Tel: 01204 385199. Fax: 01204 364057. Also install loop systems.
- B & H Sound Services Ltd, The Old School Studio, Crowland Road, Eye, Peterborough, PE6 7TN. Tel: 01733 223535. Fax: 01733 223545.
- Wigwam Acoustics Ltd, Green Lane, Heywood, OL10 1NB. Tel: 01706 368766. Fax: 01706 365565.

Installers and suppliers of loop systems. See listings on the back of *Is the gospel really heard in your church?* leaflet published by the Church of England Council for the Deaf.

Low-cost overhead projectors. Try Morrison Reprographics, Town Street, Shiptonthorpe, York, YO4 3PE. Tel: 01430 872729. Fax: 01430 871116.

Agencies

British Deaf Association, 1–3 Worship Street, London EC2A 2AB. Tel: 0171 588 3529. Minicom: 0171 588 3527.

Church of England Council for the Deaf, Church House, Great Smith Street, London SW1P 3NZ. Tel: 0171 222 9011.

Committee for Ministry among Deaf People, Advisory Board of Ministry, Church House, Great Smith Street, London SW1P 3NZ. Tel: 0171 222 9011. Fax: 0171 976 7625.

Council for the Advancement of Communication with Deaf
   People (CACDP), Pelaw House, School of Education,
   University of Durham, Durham DH1 1TA. Tel and Minicom:
   0191 374 3607. Fax: 0191 374 3605.
Friends for Young Deaf People, East Court Mansion Council
   Offices, College Lane, East Grinstead, West Sussex RH19 3LT.
   Tel: 01342 232444. Minicom: 01342 312639. Fax: 01342 410232.
Hands Together/Deaf Christian Network, PO Box 212,
   Doncaster DN2 5XA. Tel: 01302 369684. Fax: 01302 739660.
Hearing Concern, 7/11 Armstrong Road, London W3 7JL. Tel:
   0181 743 1110. Minicom: 0181 742 9151. Fax: 0181 742 9043.
Link Centre for Deafened People, 19 Hartfield Road,
   Eastbourne, East Sussex, BN21 2AR. Tel and Minicom: 01323
   638230. Fax: 01323 642968.
London Bible College, Green Lane, Northwood, Middlesex HA6
   2UW. Tel: 01923 826061.
National Deaf Children's Society, 15 Dufferin Street, London
   EC1Y 8PD. Tel and Minicom: 0171 250 0123. Fax: 0171 251
   5020.
Royal Association in Aid of Deaf People, Walshingham Road,
   Colchester, Essex CO2 7BP. Tel: 01206 509509. Minicom:
   01206 577090. Fax: 01206 769755.
The Royal National Institute for Deaf People (RNID), 19–23
   Featherstone Street, London EC1Y 8SL. Tel: 0171 296 8000.
   Text: 0171 296 8001. Fax: 0171 296 8199.

Books

Communication

Richard Bewes, *Speaking in Public – Effectively* (Christian Focus
   Publications, 1998)
G. B. Harrison and J. McCabe, *The Reader's Handbook* (Catholic
   Truth Society, 1986)
Michael Hodgin, *1001 Humorous Illustrations for Public Speaking*
   (Zondervan 1994)

Charles Spurgeon and Harold Shaw, *The Quotable Spurgeon* (Harold Shaw Publishers, 1990)
John Stott, *I Believe in Preaching* (Hodder & Stoughton, 1998)
Graham Twelftree, *Drive the Point Home* (Monarch, 1994)

Practical

The acoustics of rooms for speech and *Loudspeaker systems for speech* – two pamphlets available from Building Research Establishment
Lighting and Wiring of Churches (Church House Publishing, 1988)
Jennifer Zarek, *Sound Amplification in Churches* (Church House Publishing, 1990)

Understanding people who are deaf

Jack Ashley, *Journey into Silence* (The Bodley Head, 1973)
The Church Among Deaf People (Church House Publishing, 1997)
G. Taylor and J. Bishop (eds), *Being Deaf* (Open University Press, 1991)
M. Weir, 'A deaf theological perspective' in *Made Deaf in God's Image* (Visible Communications, 1996)

4 We Will Be Practical and Relevant

Preface by Archbishop George Carey

'By their fruits you shall know them,' said Jesus. Mission and evangelism are inseparable. A church which is only interested in the spiritual lives of people is a 'gnostic' Church. (In the early Church there were gnostic Christians for whom the flesh was unimportant, even disgusting, and of secondary importance.) If people, as whole people, matter to God, then they should matter to us. So I'd encourage Christians to use their facilities to make this point in the local community. Try to identify local needs. Is it an area with lots of elderly people? Then are there gaps in the provision of needs for the elderly? What about young people? The unemployed? Young women with children? And so on. Try not to do everything! I often say to congregations: 'Do fewer things better!' So, be selective.

But it's important to remember that when we care for others, we do so not because we're using it as an excuse to get them into church, but because we genuinely care for people and are meeting a social need. God's care is holistic – so ours should be.

Of particular relevance is a ministry to children and young people. I DON'T BELIEVE OUR CHURCHES ARE DOING ENOUGH! Remember that we're always one generation away from extinction. From experience I've found that if you put resources into children's work, you draw parents in. If you put resources into young people, you'll eventually get young marrieds in your congregation.

We Will Be Practical and Relevant

The previous week had been difficult. As Steve sat in his pew that Sunday morning, he was at his wits' end. But rather than providing the help he so desperately needed, the sermon – which dealt in some depth with the three Hebrew words for 'worship' used in one of the Psalms – only multiplied his frustration and despair.

He left the building after the service, praying with all the sarcasm he could muster, 'Well thanks a lot, God! I'm really struggling with my various roles: sensitive husband, wise father, good boss, loyal friend and responsible member of society. I can't say I've had much help in any of these areas this morning, but at least I now have a much better grasp of some Hebrew words for worship!'

This isn't just a story about one Sunday sermon. It's a parable of how the Church all too often fails to address society's most pressing and important issues with a clear, practical spirituality that ordinary people can understand, relate to and benefit from. The sad truth is that so many sermons on so many Sundays in so many churches are theologically sound, exegetically precise … and utterly irrelevant!

'The only value of religious services,' writes John Stott in *New Issues Facing Christians Today*, 'is that they concentrate into an hour or so of public, vocal, congregational activity the devotion of our whole life. If they do not do this, if instead we say and sing things in church which have no corollary in our everyday life outside church, at home and work, they are worse than worthless; their hypocrisy is positively nauseating to God.'

We need to make sure that our understanding of God is bigger and more extensive than religion on Sundays. All too often, what passes for good, biblical expository teaching, for example, is wholly unworthy of the name. In fact, some of the most irrelevant and unhelpful preaching masquerades under the name of 'exposition', obscuring or ignoring the real issues by using references and concepts that are hard enough for seasoned Christians to grapple with, let alone anyone whose links with the Church are more tenuous. What's more, many of the churches that pride themselves the most on their biblical teaching, and voice the strongest criticisms of others for not using the Bible well in their sermon or teaching programmes, have in fact cut themselves off from reality and the practical necessities of life so much that they are preaching an irrelevant gospel ... which, of course, is no gospel at all.

> **You don't find truth in a theological library. You find it when you take your theological library out into the streets with you and interact. Truth is only found in the tension of the reality of life. The rest is just hogwash.**
> *Australian preacher John Smith*

Boring and Irrelevant?

If you were to walk into your local school and ask the children for the first word that came into their minds when they thought of church, what kind of reply would you get? Having done it, we can tell you – most of them would reply spontaneously and in unison: 'boring'. If pushed, one or two might tell you that church is 'out of date' or 'irrelevant'. Words like 'vibrant', 'dynamic', 'enthusiastic', 'creative', 'passionate', 'life affirming' or 'loving' won't come up: guaranteed.

Most of the children you ask, of course, will never have been to church. One or two may base their perception on a memory of having had to endure a wedding, baptism or funeral service in a freezing, old, musty church building. Most, however, will simply be reflecting the myths and misconceptions about the Church so often portrayed in the media.

There are certainly few positive representations of the Church on TV or radio, and just as few – if not fewer – in the newspapers. More often than not, vicars are portrayed as being wimpy, effeminate and ineffective, as in the classic BBC comedy series *Dad's Army*. Even the ever-popular *Vicar of Dibley* hardly reflects the local church in a positive, dynamic light, in spite of its success in portraying the vicar herself as a real human being. There was a slight ray of hope when, in 1997, a young, hard-working priest walked onto the set of *Eastenders*, full of idealism and gritty determination. But then, with tiresome predictability and without even the hint of a realistic moral dilemma, he embarked on a torrid affair with a married woman.

When it comes to breaking down the stereotype, the Church faces an uphill struggle. Its portrayal as an utter irrelevance is widespread and deep seated. Its leaders must somehow convince both a sceptical media and an unimpressed public that they are neither 'crusty clerics' nor 'bonking bishops', whilst its ordinary punters must square down the charge that they are merely emotional cripples in search of a crutch. In fact, if the general perception of the Church has moved on at all from Peter Sellers' damningly effete liberal vicar in the film *Heavens Above*, it's only towards the happy-clappy, tambourine-swinging brigade whose style often comes across as seeming no less ridiculous or irrelevant.

In recent times, we have probably never experienced an age like ours where there has been such a negative picture of God – and it is extremely important that we recognize this.
Evangelist Laurence Singlehurst

Old Habits...

But blaming ignorance or the media for all this is too easy. The truth is, the Church has been every bit as guilty for projecting the wrong image, and feeding people the wrong caricature, in the first place. Over the years, we've evolved our own distinct subculture and way of doing things. We've developed our own language, style and behaviour patterns without really stopping to think how intelligible or relevant they may seem to outsiders.

Harry grew up going to St Peter's, the local 'high' Anglican church. Though his mum and dad seemed to like the services, Harry found them a bewildering mix of smells, bells, candles, costumes, creeds, crucifixes and chanting: the whole 'Anglo-Catholic' shebang. At 16, bored beyond belief and little wiser as to what it was all about, he left and joined the local charismatic 'house church' instead. At first it was liberating. Where St Peter's relied on a clapped-out organ, Pelham Road had a state-of-the-art worship band. Instead of worn copies of *Hymns: Ancient and Prehistoric*, they used overhead projectors to spray the walls with words of choruses so new the ink was still wet. And the sermons, though two or three times as long, seemed two or three times more interesting.

One day, Harry's mum decided to come with him to Pelham Road, to 'see what all the fuss was about', as she put it. Sitting next to her through the service, he could tell she was uncomfortable. And when he asked her about it afterwards, she confessed that she hadn't really understood a word of what was going on. 'It's all so different,' she said. But when Harry tried to explain what the various components of the service were, he was surprised by her reaction. For everything Pelham Road did, Harry's mum found an equivalent at St Peter's. When he explained that singing in tongues was a way of 'praising God from the heart, using a language you've never learnt so the words can't get in the way', she replied, 'Oh, you mean like those Latin anthems the choir always sings?' And when he told her that the 'words of prophecy' were a chance for church members to express what they 'felt God was putting on their heart for his people' – often a snippet from the Bible – she compared it with the lectionary Bible readings at St Peter's.

'It's not quite the same, mum,' Harry countered, a bit frustrated that she didn't seem to understand or appreciate the huge gap between the 'dull and dying' church he'd left and the 'vibrant' church he'd joined. 'These are spontaneous words – what God's saying for now, for this moment, you know? Your Bible readings are set years in advance.'

'Harry,' she replied, 'are you suggesting that God can't plan ahead?'

It was a sobering moment for them both. Harry's mum had never realized how little he'd understood the Anglo-Catholic traditions he'd grown up with, and Harry had never really thought before how bewildering charismatic worship could be for the uninitiated. As they compared notes, they came to see that the different traditions each church had evolved to express their worship of God had unwittingly served to make the gap between them seem wider than it was. What was beautiful and deeply spiritual to one was strange, baffling and suspicious to the other. And if it was strange and baffling to *them*, they wondered, what on earth would it seem like to someone with no real experience of church whatsoever?

'Why can't there be a Campaign for Real Church like the campaigns for Real Ale and Plain English?' wailed one frustrated churchgoer. 'Every time I go to church, I either get "happy-clappy tambourines" or "smells and bells". I'm not interested in all that stuff. What I want is practical, down-to-earth spirituality –

something I can relate to.' His cries are echoed time and again throughout the country by people who don't understand why *they* should have to learn a new language and adapt themselves to a new Christian culture just in order to hear the good news of Jesus ... especially since it was *he* who did the adapting the first time around!

> **We have reduced Christianity into a religion that brings people to use the right language and to use the right words instead of compassionately identifying with people's needs. We have made Christianity into a lifestyle of middle-class propriety instead of a call to have one's heart broken by the things that break the heart of Jesus.**
> *American sociologist Tony Campolo*

Breaking Open the Time Capsule

A century or two ago, the sermons of Wesley or Spurgeon drew crowds numbering in the thousands. The actions of Shaftesbury, Müller, Wilberforce and Barnardo changed the face of a nation. The spirituality of Newman, Keble and Pusey rejuvenated the Church. These men were the radical rebels of their day – the ecclesiastical 'cutting edge'. Unlike their contemporaries, they found a way to tap into the popular mindset and demonstrate the gospel in fresh, dynamic, exciting and relevant ways, and were rewarded by phenomenal success. Ordinary people related to what they did and said. Yet today it's not only their words that sound dated. Sadly, many of their followers and the institutions they left behind haven't moved an inch since their deaths.

Many churches found their style or sank their roots during a particular time in history. Alive to the 'signs of the times', they found how to respond to people's spiritual hunger with the 'bread of heaven'. Their reputations grew, their numbers swelled and they tasted the fruits of the harvest. And then ... nothing. Having found a form of evangelism or care that worked, they stuck with it. As the saying goes, 'If it ain't broke, don't fix it!' The trouble is, although they stayed the same, the world around them changed.

Tragically, it's not hard to find churches like this. It's as though they've become 'time capsules' – a little bit of yesterday set aside to remind today's world what it was once like. Not just their language, but their whole way of understanding and responding to the world belongs to the past. How many churches still hold evangelistic 'guest services', for example, even when there are no 'guests' present, just because they've always done it that way and don't have either the courage or the common sense to call it a day? How many churches still consider house-to-house visiting an essential ingredient of any authentic evangelistic programme – even if no one in the church has a real 'gift' for it and everyone on the receiving end hates it – simply because it was considered an essential ingredient 30 years ago and no one has ever told them differently?

It's not that there's anything wrong with 'guest services' or house-to-house visiting; in some circumstances and with some churches they're still very effective evangelistic tools. But for most churches, they're tools whose time of usefulness has come to an end. Rather than producing the great results they once did, they're now merely a drain on the church's resources. They simply don't work any more, and haven't for some time. It's the height of folly to keep doing what didn't work yesterday and doesn't work today in the belief that it *will* somehow work tomorrow. A new approach is needed.

All traditions have a sell-by date, even if it's still a long way off. We must learn to ditch ways of doing and saying things that may be personally valuable to us – or just that we're sentimentally attached to – but which no longer adequately communicate the relevance and life-changing nature of the (eternal) gospel to those outside the Church community. We need to find new and more effective traditions: new ways of saying and doing things.

For many, the Church is 'irrelevant' because it is no longer central to their needs or interests.
Archbishop George Carey

Liturgy and Worship

In the Middle Ages, the church building stood in the centre of every town or village, right next to the marketplace and tall enough to be visible for miles around. People came through its doors Sunday by Sunday, even if it meant walking some distance to get there. They understood the symbolism of the building's position: the church stood in the centre of the town just as the gospel stood at the centre of their lives. Over the years, however, the 'marketplace' has moved out of town into purpose-built shopping centres and retail parks, and the church has been dwarfed on the skyline by banks and corporate buildings. At the same time, people have stopped seeing the gospel as central to their lives.

If they go to church once in a while, they're likely to have trouble seeing the connection between the service (including the sermon) and their everyday life. If a local church isn't constantly changing in order to make this link more obvious, then it's effectively obscuring it, hiding the gospel's relevance from the people who need to hear it most. Effectively, the Church is playing catch-up. Language and culture are constantly evolving, and if we're to be true to our task of expressing the gospel in a clear and relevant way, we'll have to ensure that *our* language and culture evolve alongside everyone else's. As the Red Queen tells Alice in Lewis Carroll's *Through the Looking Glass*, 'Now *here*, you see, it takes all the running *you* can do, to keep in the same place.' If we keep doing what we've always done the way we've always done it, the relevance of the gospel and our Sunday morning activities will become less and less apparent to everyone but ourselves.

The Iona Community in Scotland have found a particularly graphic way of relating their worship to their everyday lives.

When they gather each day for morning prayer, their conventional service has an unconventional ending. To be more precise, it has no ending at all. Unlike most worship services, there's no blessing or 'benediction' ... until the end of the evening service. Instead, community members go about their everyday tasks as if they were a continuation of the worship service – which they are. There's no hard distinction between worship and work, liturgy and life. Nor should there be.

The word 'worship' is short for 'wor*th*ship' – meaning any kind of 'worthy' activity, but especially those that show the 'worthiness' of God. Similarly, 'liturgy' comes from a word that literally means 'the people's work': in classical Greek it referred to a person's 'civic duties', but the New Testament uses it to describe a range of activities from the priestly duties of Zechariah (Luke 1:23) to the 'works of service' of the entire Corinthian church (2 Corinthians 9:12). Even our word 'service' clearly points to the whole mission of the Church during the whole of the week, not just to a couple of hours on a Sunday morning!

So if our Sunday morning activities don't clearly relate to our lives during the rest of the week, somewhere along the line we must have forgotten the importance of 'running to stand still' ... and lost touch ourselves with the relevance of the gospel.

> **Worship and the Christian's daily life ... are not separate spheres, but two concentric circles, of which worship is the inner and gives to the outer its content and character.**
> *Jim Wallis, leader of the Sojourners Community in Washington DC*

Back to the Future

The way forward, curiously, is to go back. Back to basics. Back to the lessons of the New Testament. If we look at Paul's letters to the churches, for example, we see a picture of a Church with its own problems, many familiar to us today: in-fighting, infidelity, adultery, idolatry, peer pressure ... Paul's response was to give them *practical, applied* teaching and guidance. Sometimes he was stern and even rude in his approach ('You foolish Galatians!' Galatians 3:1); at other times he was gentle, supportive and encouraging ('I thank my God every time I remember you,' Philippians 1:3); but he was always focused and to the point.

As he wrote to his friend Titus, leader of the church in Crete (Titus 3:14): 'Let people learn to devote themselves to good works in order to meet urgent needs, so that they may not be unproductive.' Having been instrumental in organizing the ship-ment of emergency aid from churches throughout the Roman Empire to famine-stricken Jerusalem, Paul was in no doubt what kind of things could be included under the heading 'urgent needs'. It wasn't just 'spiritual' needs he was referring to.

In fact, to Paul the whole division between 'spiritual' and 'material' needs would have smacked of the kind of disastrous compartmentalizing of life that some pagan philosophers seemed to like, but the Hebrew Bible tended to steer well clear of. The Old Testament prophets had had nothing but condem-nation, for example, for those kings of Israel and Judah who had lined their own pockets at the expense of the people they were meant to be protecting (e.g. 1 Kings 21; Jeremiah 22:13–17). This 'material' gain was condemned by God as a 'spiritual' crime. For Paul, as for the Old Testament writers, 'soul' and 'body' weren't two different things; they were two different ways of looking at the *same* thing.

Perhaps that's why the early Jerusalem church is depicted as a community not only of *spiritual* unity, but of *material* unity as well. They 'were of one heart and soul', Luke tells us, and 'every-thing they owned was held in common' (Acts 4:32). They were a body in which everyone had a purpose, a talent, a skill, a gift, a 'ministry' (e.g. 1 Corinthians 12). Each member of the church community was seen as valuable and *inter*dependent. And the church didn't merely concern itself with people's spiritual needs. It concerned itself with *all* their needs.

We, too, must provide clear, Bible-based teaching in our churches that will help people not only to grow in their relationship with God, but also to deal with the pressures and relationships of day-to-day life. The Bible is brim full of practical, relevant truth that's as challenging today as it was two thousand or more years ago. It's past time this practicality was let loose on a hungry world.

> **A spirituality is a concrete manner, inspired by the Spirit, of living the gospel.**
> *Peruvian theologian Gustavo Gutierrez*

Care in the Community

If we're to be relevant and practical in the care we offer people, we need to listen to and understand the culture we live in, and constantly work hard to relate our faith to our local community. We need to speak its language fluidly and idiomatically, but at the same time maintain our unique challenge to its mores. We need to become totally immersed 'in', but never be 'of', the world around us.

Society has changed. For example, there are more older people, more single parents, more divorce and separation, and more people living alone than ever before. Loneliness and isolation are now commonplace. Many people are looking for a supportive community, where they are accepted and their needs are met, but don't know where to turn. Like a house of cards, the old structures that held things together are fragmenting, plunging society into further confusion and uncertainty. 'Without marriage and the family,' wrote Patricia Morgan in the *Daily Express*, 'we lose our links to the rest of the community, our sources of support in adversity and care in old age. These amount to the loss of the framework of society itself.'

It's up to the Church to offer the same kind of help and practical support to people now that it offered in its youth in Jerusalem. It's our job to be salt and light, offering practical guidance and help, and relating to people where they're at rather than trying to get them to accommodate themselves to our standards and language *first*. That means responding to people's *perceived needs*, showing them (with as little religious language as possible) what light the gospel can shed on their present situation, as opposed to insisting that they join some 'fast track' to conversion. Our task is to present the good news about Jesus in a way that people can understand and apply to their lives – not just in Sunday services, but in all we do – because the gospel affects and transforms every area of our existence.

So, for example, the local church can offer help to parents. For many people both inside and outside the church, the question of how to be a good parent is the most pressing one on their agenda. They struggle with finding the time to be with their kids, or maintaining discipline when they're naughty or unruly. They worry about protecting them from harm. Above all, they harbour strong doubts about how they're doing as a mum or dad. There's hardly a parent in the country who wouldn't welcome practical advice, support, help and encouragement in improving their parenting skills. Sunday after Sunday, Christians call God 'Our Father': so what lessons have we learnt – and what can we pass on – about being a *good* father or mother?

One church in the Midlands set up a parenting workshop, advertising it in their local paper and throughout the local community. It was held on a Saturday in their church hall, and they provided a crèche and children's activities. They were staggered to find that 60 parents wanted to start the course, and even more surprised to discover that over half the parents had no real Christian background (many were Hindus) and wouldn't normally have come near a church building!

The course was a huge success on three levels. First, it gave local parents much-needed practical advice, encouragement and ongoing support. Second, it communicated values that form the bedrock of the Christian faith – unconditional love, forgiveness, responsibility for others, and the fact that it's never too late to begin again – within the context of parenting, making it significantly easier to understand the faith itself at a later time. Third, it was a brilliant piece of public relations: people now see the church in a positive light, as a friend, where before it never struck them as anything more than an irritating irrelevance.

Some churches have found setting up a baby-sitting service really helpful and effective. A monthly support group offering time for relaxing, socializing and discussing is often a lifeline for harassed parents. What's more, an accountant, solicitor or marriage counsellor in the church may be willing to offer support services, helping families who are encountering problems to see a way forward – a light at the end of the tunnel.

Do you have a happy family? Or are the kids still at home?
Anonymous

All Work and No Play...

Let's take the workplace as another example – an environment full of all kinds of people, with all kinds of problems, pressures and fears: ambition, greed, illness, fear of redundancy or unemployment, relationships, grief, confusion, adultery, ethical dilemmas, money, dirty tricks, purposelessness, retirement, criminal negligence ... If it happens in life, you can pretty much guarantee it happens at work.

It's calculated that we spend around 65 per cent of our time in the workplace. For 20, 30, 40, 50 hours a week, we have an opportunity to develop relationships, build bridges, make peace, and show the difference Christ can make in a life – in short, to show love in action. So we need to be concerned for our colleagues. We need to pray for opportunities to share our practical, relevant faith in the workplace, served up in such a way that its relevance is immediately obvious to those around us. We need to read and think carefully about important issues and thorny ethical dilemmas, so that our 'Christian' point of view is both informed and enlightening. We need to be salt and light.

Mark Greene, now Vice Principal of London Bible College, spent 10 years working for an advertising agency in London and New York. In his book *Thank God It's Monday*, he tells the story of how he was able to offer a Christian perspective to a former work colleague. As he was leaving the office one evening, he bumped into a woman he'd once worked with. As they got chatting and catching up on each other's news, she told Mark that she was trying to decide whether or not to marry a man who'd proposed to her.

'By coincidence, perhaps,' he recalls, 'I happened to have with me a copy of Jack and Carole Mayhall's *Marriage Takes More than Love*. I gave it to her. I saw her again on Monday. She had read the whole thing, had accepted its perspective on marriage, though not on the gospel, and it had helped her to see why this particular man wasn't right for her.' As far as Mark knows, she hasn't become a Christian, but he holds out hope, 'that the seed planted will bear fruit, that one day she will remember that when she needed wisdom for her life, she got it from a book based on the Bible. I couldn't have given her a Bible at that point, but I could give her something relevant to her life situation.'

But it's not just those in work we need to help. It's those out of work as well. Mary had been unemployed for three years. A committed Christian, she'd nevertheless lost most of her self-confidence and self-esteem, and felt constantly despondent. A businesswoman in her church, Clare, aware of her situation, helped her apply for clerical jobs in town. She talked Mary through the application forms, helping her to see her strengths and past experience. She even conducted a mock interview, offering advice and encouragement and revealing the kinds of things she looked for when she was interviewing candidates for jobs in her firm. As a result of the work they'd both done on Mary's application forms, she was invited for two interviews. And thanks to Clare's practical help, advice and friendship, she had the self-confidence to do well in them. Three years of unemployment and depression ended when she accepted a clerical job at the council offices.

> **The Christian community has a specific task ...**
> **to regain the lost sense of work as a divine calling.**
> *Emil Brunner*

'To Boldly Go...'

Being 'full of compassion' *sounds* alright in theory. It's safe and comfortable. But actually *engaging* in practical compassion is a different matter. The idea of it makes most of us feel daunted, inadequate and guilty. Often our response is to 'leave it to the experts', so we do nothing. But as John Stott says, 'witness' and 'service' are 'inseparable twins'. Faith, love, service is the striking sequence. 'True faith issues in love, and true love issues in service.'

As Christians, our task is to communicate God's love, acceptance and forgiveness. We're challenged to live out a practical and relevant gospel in our specific culture. After all, that's the spirit of incarnation. That means we have to take a good, hard look at ourselves as churches, working out what strengths and weaknesses we have, and what we can do to make God's love obvious to all and sundry. We have to *engage* with our community at the bus stop, at the school gates, in the workplace, among the homeless, in the pub, or on the rugby pitch. We're called to be salt and light to those around us, offering a clear, practical, down-to-earth spirituality that people can understand, relate to and benefit from.

It is easier for people to feel that they belong to the church community if they sense a caring atmosphere and realize that here are others that they can trust and turn to if the going gets tough.
Philip Richter and Leslie J. Francis, **Gone But Not Forgotten**

IDEAS

We don't have to attend the Faith and Love in Action Training College in order to show practical and relevant service! There are times when, yes, we'll need to bring in the experts and those who've received specific training. But there are a whole range of ways in which we can get involved and show practical concern in our *community* and in our *place of work*, ways in which we can engage in *social action*. We shouldn't feel daunted or inadequate. We just need to find relevant ways in which we can offer practical, down-to-earth spirituality seven days a week.

Practical and relevant ... in the community

- Every parent longs for advice on how to do the job better! Run a parenting course, such as *Parentalk*, *The Parent Assertiveness Programme*, or *Help! I'm a Parent* (see Resources section in this Chapter and in Chapter 2).
- Build up a monthly parents' group offering relevant speakers, social activities, information network and support/advice. Choose relevant subjects such as a health visitor talking about child care; 'meet the schools' to find out more about the local schools in your area; an update or swap-shop on family-friendly leisure activities in the area; a drugs awareness workshop. Make sure there's plenty of time for socializing, questions, relaxing, discussion and offering one another support. Plan the subjects with the parents.

- Run a kids' holiday club or play scheme (with other churches?) in your area. Encourage parents or child carers to stay on for a cup of coffee when they come to pick up the kids. Build in a Family Fun night, barbeque, Family Breakfast, It's a Knockout, etc. Relationship-building with the children and parents is important and will make it easier to invite them to a family service.

- Run an over-sixties club. Offer a range of activities: table tennis, snooker, keep fit, flower arranging, book swap, topical talks ('Security in the Home', 'Lifeline', 'Legal Matters', 'Health Matters', 'Sex and the Over-sixties', etc.). A church in Eastbourne found it a great way of offering practical support, especially during August when many older people are on their own.

- It's a good idea to have a Resource Board in the entrance of the church, with key numbers: GP, hospital, police, church leader, Citizen's Advice Bureau, Relate, local social services, dentist, etc.

- Set up a Skills Shop. People from the church can advertise their skills and services on a noticeboard (e.g. gardening, baking, sewing, accounting, car lifts, hospital visiting, baby-sitting, maths coaching, hairdressing, carpentry, music lessons, plumbing, etc.). They could choose to offer their skills on a voluntary basis, make a charge, or do a 'skills swap'. One church not only found this a great way of raising money for their major rebuilding project, but also discovered the range of people's gifts!

- Debt is an issue which a lot of people are struggling with. Debt clinics or a debt counselling service, offering practical advice, counselling and awareness, have proved very helpful. Some churches have worked together to set up a service in their area. Churches could also join to offer some form of local credit union, providing a savings and loan service. Specialist groups such as Credit Action can help with advice, materials, speakers and experience.

- A baby-sitting service is a good way of supporting people within the church family and those in the community. Obviously some baby-sitters want payment. Others operate a 'tokens system', whereby everyone who wants a baby-sitting service forms part of the baby-sitting rota and receives a number of tokens. When they use a baby-sitter, they pay them a token. When they baby-sit themselves for someone else on the rota, they receive a token.

- Set up a day centre in your church building or church hall. As well as providing food, think of other services you could offer: occupational therapy, chiropody, health-care advice, crèche, mobile library (check with the council), laundry facilities, sports, general advice on local services. If you have access to transport services, you may also be able to offer day trips and outings. Chessington Evangelical Church, for example, has built a multi-purpose Community, Recreational and Church complex in partnership with the local council. The King's Centre offers a range of leisure, recreational, educational and Christian activities through the week in a relaxed and caring environment. The Centre started out a number of years earlier as one man's dream!

- Host practical workshops on issues relevant to your community, e.g. Dealing with Stress, Drug Awareness, Racial Injustice, Coping with Ageing Relatives, Preparing for Retirement, etc.

- Make sure you include practical issues in your preaching and fellowship groups or home group material. You may want to focus on a specific topic. Check, too, to see if your groups are non-judgemental places where members can share their fears, concerns, anxieties, hurts and success. Are they places where the pastoral skills are matched with relevant biblical teaching?

- If you have a number of international visitors, or newcomers to Britain in your community, make sure they feel welcome. Help them get to know the area, provide them with useful phone numbers, introduce them to people. Some may need help with language skills. If there are a number in your community for whom English is not their first language, could you offer weekly language classes?

- Put on an International Night, where people from other countries can take part. They could dress in traditional costume, cook traditional dishes, show videos or slides, play their music, teach a song or greeting, show local art or craft, explain traditional customs, etc.

- Could you set up a young people's drop-in centre? It could include sports activities, employment opportunities, workshops on coping with stress, drugs awareness, safe sex, etc., getting involved in social action (homeless project, overseas project, etc.), information kiosk.

- Get involved in local government – parish, district or regional councils. It's a good way of engaging in the community, highlighting issues, affecting change, making a difference.

Practical and relevant ... getting involved in social action

'I was hungry and you gave me food, I was thirsty and you gave me something to drink, I was a stranger and you welcomed me, I was naked and you gave me clothing, I was sick and you took care of me, I was in prison and you visited me' (Matthew 25:35–6).

- Set up a soup kitchen, a breakfast or night run for the homeless. Church halls and kitchens can be opened up late at night or first thing in the morning, offering tea, coffee and breakfast. Donated clothes, sleeping bags and blankets can be collected and distributed among the homeless.

- Run a furniture project. The idea is to collect furniture from people who no longer need it and give it to those who do. *Love in Action*, produced by The Shaftesbury Society, have further information on how to set this up. You can try other recycling services (crockery, children's clothes, books, etc.). A group in

Bristol have set up a sofa project which re-upholsters sofas before selling them on. The project also offers training in upholstery, providing skills training and employment opportunities for local people.

- Offer support services. If you have an accountant, solicitor, marriage guidance counsellor, etc., in your church, they may be willing to help people in the church and community who are encountering problems.

- Read about some of the issues that affect people in your community. Support the work of charities and organizations involved with the homeless, the unemployed, prison visiting, the sick, etc. Could you organize some fundraising events or invite speakers to increase your awareness and response?

Practical and relevant ... at work

- Get alongside people at work. Look for practical ways of showing love in action. They don't have to be massive – it could be getting the teas or coffees, buying ice creams, being a listening ear, encouraging and praising someone who's done a good job.

- If you have colleagues with similar interests to some of your Christian friends (golf, squash, kids, theatre, cinema, football, etc.), meet up after work. Gently build up the relationships.

- Stress management. A lot of people are under stress at work. *The WorkNet Partnership* runs courses on stress management as well as a number of other work-based issues.

- Be an activist! Without getting under your employer's skin, identify if there are any obvious improvements which could be introduced at work (e.g. crèche, staff room, low-interest loans, company subscription to sports club or gym, social trips, etc.). You'll need to suggest ideas sensitively to your employer or line manager!

RESONDCES
RESOURCES

Resources

Love in Action. A resource pack with suggestions and practical
advice to help churches move into caring action in the
community. Produced by The Shaftesbury Society.

Hope UK offers training, advice and support about drugs, alcohol
and substance abuse. The Christian-based charity offers a
range of resources (for 5+s), plus training, speakers, seminars
and workshops.

Parentalk. An eight-session course for up to 10 people. The pack
includes a video, expert advice from Rob Parsons and Steve
Chalke, course guide, suggestions for practical activities,
course material, OHP masters.

The Parent Assertiveness Programme, *The Noughts to Sixes Parenting
Programme*. Just two of a number of programmes to provide
support at all stages of the family life cycle. Easy-to-run,
flexible, self-help courses for groups of 8–12 participants.
Developed by Family Caring. (The basic parenting
programme is also available in Welsh.)

Help! I'm a Parent. A multi-format resource for use in church
and home groups. Produced by CPAS.

Wake up to Work. Thought-provoking material on workplace
issues available in CD or cassette format. Produced by Geoff
Shattock, National Director of The WorkNet Partnership,
which also runs courses for churches and church groups,
training courses and workshops on stress management.

Making Sunday Best … and every other day of the week. A free
practical resource to help you evaluate your church and its
role in the community. Available from Fanfare for a New
Generation.

The Racial Justice Sunday Pack. Youth and adult resource packs for
churches to work through issues of racial justice. Available
from Evangelical Christians for Racial Justice.
A Debt Cutter's Handbook. Resource material, games and fun
material about Jubilee in the Old Testament. A history of
the debt crisis, case studies of the impact of debt and practical
ideas to raise awareness about debt. Linked with Jubilee
2000.
Justice and Jubilee. A booklet and study guide to get to grips with
the gospel's call to deal fairly with those around us. Available
from Churches' Millennium Office.
New Start at Home: practical steps towards a fairer Britain.
Discussion booklet with five sessions for home group or
personal use. (Available from Church House Bookshop, Great
Smith Street, London SW1P 3NZ. Tel: 0171 340 0276.)

Agencies

Age Concern, Astral House, 1268 London Road, London SW16
4ER. Tel: 0181 679 8000. Many books, leaflets, resources for
older people.
Age Concern Northern Ireland, 3 Lower Crescent, Belfast BT7
1NR. Tel: 01232 245729.
Age Concern Cymru, 4th Floor, 1 Cathedral Road, Cardiff CF1
9SD. Tel: 01222 371566.
Age Concern Scotland, 113 Rose Street, Edinburgh EH2 3DT.
Tel: 0131 220 3345.
Association of British Credit Unions Ltd, Unit 307, Westminster
Business Square, 339 Kennington Lane, London SE11 5QY.
Tel: 0171 582 2626.
Care for the Family, Garth House, Leon Avenue, Cardiff CF4
7RG. Tel: 01222 811733. Offers advice, plus runs special
low-cost, Outward-Bound-type holidays for single-parent
families.

Christian Action Networks. Operating in many larger cities, they network projects, churches and organizations. Contact them via the Evangelical Alliance.

Church Action on Poverty, Central Buildings, Oldham Street, Manchester, M1 1JT. Tel: 0161 236 9321.

Church Army, Independents Road, Blackheath, London SE3 9LG. Tel: 0181 318 1226.

Churches' Millennium Office, Church House, Great Smith Street, London SW1P 3NZ. Tel: 0171 340 0250.

Churches National Housing Coalition (CHNC), Central Buildings, Oldham Street, Manchester M1 1JT. Tel: 0161 236 9321.

Church Pastoral Aid Society (CPAS), Athena Drive, Tachbrook Park, Warwick CV34 6NG. Tel. 01926 334242.

Community Action Network, PO Box 14785, Bromley by Bow, London E3 3SJ. Tel: 0181 983 3816.

Credit Action, Jubilee Centre, 3 Hooper Street, Cambridge CB1 2NZ. Tel: 01223 324034.

Cruse Bereavement Care, Cruse House, 126 Sheen Road, Richmond, Surrey TW9 1UR. Tel: 0181 940 4818. Counselling service for people who've been bereaved.

The Evangelical Alliance, Whitefield House, 186 Kennington Park Road, London SE11 4BT. Tel: 0171 582 0228. The EA will put you in touch with many organizations involved in most areas of community work.

Evangelical Christians for Racial Justice, 107 Homiton High Street, London E9 6DL. Tel: 0181 985 2764.

Evangelical Coalition on Drugs (c/o Evangelical Alliance). A coalition of representatives of Christian organizations involved in drug and alcohol abuse.

Family Caring Trust, 44 Rathfriland Road, Newry, Co. Down, BT34 1LD. Tel: 01693 64174. Fax: 01693 69077.

Fanfare for a New Generation, 115 Southwark Bridge Road, London SE1 0AX. Tel: 0171 450 9070/1. E-mail: fanfare@btconnect.com

Help the Aged, St James's Walk, Clerkenwell Green, London
 EC1R 0BE. Tel: 0171 253 0253. Fax: 0171 250 4474.
Hope UK, 25f Copperfield Street, London SE1 0EN. Tel: 0171
 928 0848. Fax 0171 401 3477.
Jubilee 2000, PO Box 100, London SE1 7RT. Tel: 0171 401 9999.
Oasis Trust, 115 Southwark Bridge Road, London SE1 0AX. Tel:
 0171 450 9000. Involved with local churches in communicating
 faith through social care, training and evangelism.
Parentalk, PO Box 23142, London SE1 0ZT. Tel: 0171 450
 9072/3. Fax: 0171 450 9060.
The Shaftesbury Society, 16 Kingston Road, London SW19 1JZ.
 Tel: 0181 239 5555.
Tearfund, 100 Church Road, Teddington, Middlesex, TW11
 8QE. Tel: 0181 977 9144. Promoting social concern in the
 third world.
The WorkNet Partnership, 56 Baldry Gardens, London SW16
 3DJ. Tel: 0181 764 8080. E-mail:
 training@worknetpartnership.org.uk

Books

Fran Beckett, *Called to Action* (Fount, 1989)
Steve Chalke, *I Believe in Taking Action* (Hodder & Stoughton,
 1996)
Steve Chalke and Paul Hansford, *The Truth about Suffering*
 (Kingsway, 1996)
Graham Cray, *The Gospel and Tomorrow's Culture* (CPAS, 1994)
Peter Curran, *Handling Redundancy* (Grove booklet, 1995)
David Evans and Mike Fearon, *From Strangers to Neighbours. How
 you can make the difference in your community* (Hodder &
 Stoughton, 1998)
Paul Goodliff, *Care in a Confused Climate: Pastoral Care and
 Postmodern Culture* (DLT, 1998)
Mark Greene, *Thank God it's Monday* (Scripture Union, 1997)

Jack and Carole Mayhall, *Marriage Takes More Than Love* (Navpress, USA)

Philip Mohabir, *Building Bridges* (Hodder & Stoughton, 1992)

Laurence Singlehurst, *Sowing, Reaping, Keeping People* (Crossway Books, 1995)

John Stott, *New Issues Facing Christians Today* (Marshall Pickering, 1999)

Keith Tondeur, *Escape from Debt* and *Helping People in Debt* (available from Credit Action)

5 We Will Help You Explore Answers to Your Deepest Questions

Preface by Archbishop George Carey

Remember that 'belonging' usually comes before 'believing'. It may surprise us to find that very few come to faith through intellectual argument. They are more likely – far more likely – to come through friendship, fellowship and inspiring worship. Preaching, though, should be intelligent, drawing upon human experience and well illustrated – and not too long!

The same goes for worship. I remember the late Bishop Mervyn Stockwood once saying fiercely: 'I don't mind if people call me "high church", "low church" or "middle church", but they can't call me "long church"'! I have a theory that more people would come to church if they knew that the service wouldn't go on more than one hour, preferably less...

But to go back to life's questions. When I was in Durham, I started an 'Agnostics Anonymous' group at the vicarage. I invited anyone to come with their questions and promised them a cup of tea, and that I was willing to listen. I couldn't promise them that I had the answers! It proved to be a most enjoyable group which was at times uncomfortable for me, and at times deeply significant spiritually for some of those seeking faith. Courses like Alpha, Emmaus and others such as Cursillo are tremendous resources.

We Will Help You Explore Answers to Your Deepest Questions

Four years ago, Val was diagnosed as having breast cancer. Since the tumour had begun to spread, she opted to have a mastectomy – the most drastic form of surgical cure. Soon afterwards, she went back to her job as a teacher at a local secondary school. She attended regular check-ups, and life quickly returned to normal for her and husband Mike.

But then, a few months ago, a routine x-ray revealed a shadow on one of Val's lungs. She'd noticed she was getting short of breath; in addition, she'd started to develop an infuriating cough and felt increasingly lethargic. Further tests revealed the presence of secondary, 'mestatic' cancers in other organs throughout her body. The prognosis was very bleak: the doctors confirmed that she had just a few months left to live.

'How do you deal with a moment like this?' asked Mike.

People are searching for answers.

Roger was a successful businessman, working for a large, multinational corporation. A committed Christian, he was happily married to Carol, with a seven-year-old daughter, Emily. The family lived in a beautiful house in a desirable commuter-belt village, where they were very involved in both the village community and the local church.

Then, one day, Roger was called into a hastily convened meeting at work. The company had relied heavily on trade with the Asian 'tiger' economies, and had been severely hit by their collapse in early 1998. As a result, it was going to have to 'downsize' its operation. His entire section, including Roger as section head, would have to be 'let go'. At 41, Roger knew that it would be tough to find another comparable job. He couldn't help feeling that he was letting his family down, and wondered what he'd done to deserve such a fate.

'I'm so sorry,' he cried on his wife's shoulder.

People are looking for meaning.

Man cannot live without seeking to describe and explain the universe.
British philosopher and historian, Sir Isaiah Berlin

Brave New World?

As we turn the corner into the twenty-first century, people are still trying to make sense of life. 'Twenty-eight murdered in Omagh bomb blast,' reveal the headlines. 'Nine hundred more jobs to go as Tyneside factory closes.' 'Thousands die as flood waters cover two-thirds of Bangladesh.' 'Over-population threatens more endangered species.' 'Gang-rape victim's nightmare ordeal.'

Magazines and newspapers are littered with features on sexuality, violence, genetics, war, suffering, lifestyle issues and medical ethics. The staggering advance of technology witnessed by the twentieth century presents us all with a moral maze infinitely more perplexing than the one that greeted our great-grandparents one hundred years ago. Our ability to do things, manipulating the world around us, has rapidly overtaken our capacity for deciding what's right and wrong. In effect, the scientific revolution has now reached such a pace that we're 'shooting' first and asking questions later.

In February 1997, Ian Wilmut and colleagues at Edinburgh's Roslin Institute announced that they had successfully cloned a sheep – Dolly – from an adult udder cell. A year later, Dolly gave birth (naturally) to Bonnie, proving that she's a normal sheep in spite of her abnormal origins. Meanwhile, other geneticists around the world succeeded in cloning two rhesus monkeys, two cows and more than 50 mice, some of which are clones of clones.

In 1998, Dr Robert J. White, an eminent American brain surgeon, spoke of the imminent possibility of carrying out 'a total body transplant' – removing the head from one patient and transplanting it to the body of another. With the increasing success rate of multiple organ swaps and major developments in the areas of medical research, genetic engineering and biotechnology, the fantasy creations of *Robocop* and the *Six Million Dollar Man* – not to mention the dinosaurs of *Jurassic Park* – are beginning to look less and less like science fiction and more and more as if they belong to the realms of eventual science fact.

Medical technology already allows many of us to fulfil some of our deepest desires, especially when it comes to those who find themselves unable to have children. *In vitro* fertilization offers would-be mothers a miracle opportunity to conceive and give birth that would have been beyond even their wildest dreams just 30 years ago. The Human Fertilization and Embryology Authority reports that, in a 15-month period between 1996 and 1997, there were as many as 37,000 attempts at IVF treatment in 22,000 mothers. The result was 5,500 live births, costing a staggering £75 million!

And in the not-too-distant future, it may be possible to test and even engineer embryos to determine aspects of their intelligence, physical strength, size and susceptibility to disease. Princeton biologist Lee Silver warns that, in the long term, genetic engineering could lead to an even greater widening of the gap between rich and poor, as rich parents become able to build genetic advantages into their children's DNA which poorer parents will never be able to afford.

Professor John Wyatt, of University College London Hospital, urged his audience at the 1997 London Lectures in Contemporary Christianity to consider the possibility that soon, 'For the first time in history, couples will be able genuinely to select the child of their choice. Perhaps before too long, selecting the best embryo will be seen as an essential part of responsible parenthood. The god of consumerism will have finally extended its stranglehold to parenthood.'

Brave New World indeed.

Ironically, the muting of traditional voices of moral authority by modern science has taken place at precisely the same time modern science is forcing us to face a growing number of difficult ethical issues – many of them unprecedented in human history.
Canadian geneticist David Suzuki

The Fountain of Eternal Youth

As ethics debates continue to rage, more and more people look for 'quick-fix' ways to stay young and find happiness and fulfilment. Convinced it will provide the answer to at least some of their problems, vast numbers of women have surgical nips, tucks, implants and enlargements to stay young and beautiful and achieve the body of their dreams.

According to one American doctor, few baby boomers are happy about turning 50. Dr Jody Robinson told the US press that her surgery is packed with women (and a few men) searching for a miracle cure for their bulges, sags, aching joints and encroaching wrinkles. Vitamins and hormone replacements are being consumed by the shovelful, and the craving to look young is producing an orgy of plastic surgery. Doctors may be able to unclog arteries and replace worn-out parts, she said, but there's still a natural course of events in the flow of life. The sooner people come to terms with their inevitable demise, the happier they'll be.

In March 1998, thousands of American men welcomed the introduction of the new anti-impotence drug Viagra. Designed for those with 'erectile dysfunction', its potential for use as the latest and most efficient in a long line of aphrodisiacs became immediately apparent. 'It's wonderful, amazing. It's the greatest recreational drug ever,' exclaimed Hugh Hefner, the 72-year-old publishing tycoon whose *Playboy* empire once stretched around the world. But what worked wonders for Hefner's libido clearly couldn't do the same for his nine-year marriage, which came to an awkward and embarrassing end at about the same time.

What's more, it soon became clear that the so-called 'wonder drug', which has raked in millions for its New York-based manufacturer, Pfizer, couldn't live up to its astonishing hype. There were doubts about the effectiveness of the drug to remedy erectile dysfunction. Ophthalmologists were concerned about possible side effects that could turn patients permanently blind. And if that wasn't bad enough, a small number of US users – many advanced in age and with poor blood circulation – found the increased blood flow around the body, combined with the other drugs they were taking, just too much to cope with … and died.

The search for eternal youth, it would seem, is as fruitless in our modern, technological age as it has ever been, even though the desire for it is far stronger. As one newspaper put it, 'The only sin left in the UK is being old … and getting found out!'

Old or young, we're all on our last cruise.
Robert Louis Stevenson

The Undiscover'd Country

A hundred years ago it was sex. Thirty years ago it was cancer. Today it's death. Death is the great taboo – a subject to be avoided at all costs. When the 1998 BBC TV series *The Human Body* broke this taboo by broadcasting the final moments in the life of cancer victim Herbie Mowes, the public outcry made our awkwardness with death very obvious.

Some commentators, ignoring the fact that Mowes had invited the cameras to film his last months and his dying breath, accused the BBC of invading his most private moment. Others complained that screening a genuine death was a massive breach of good taste. But one thing became perfectly clear from all the hype surrounding the programme: people's fear of death is real and runs deep.

Most of the time we can successfully ignore death: change the conversation, flick over the page, switch over the TV or radio channel. Perhaps one of the reasons why the tragic and sudden death of Diana, Princess of Wales, in August 1997 provoked such a display of national grief and a genuine outpouring of public emotion was that it was such a stark and compelling reminder that we're all mortal. The life of a beautiful, famous, vivacious 36-year-old woman being so unexpectedly and prematurely snuffed out exposed our own fear, pain and vulnerability.

Roy Castle, the popular entertainer, gave a press conference a short while before he died. The lung cancer that eventually claimed his life was already well advanced, and it was clear to everyone concerned that he wasn't going to make a miraculous recovery. 'How does it feel to know that you only have a few months to live?' asked a reporter from a national newspaper. 'If I knew I had a few months to live,' replied Roy, 'I'd be unique. *You* don't even know whether you'll still be alive this time tomorrow.'

A few weeks later, as his wife Fiona was sitting at his bedside, she noticed a smile cross Roy's lips. After 24 hours of almost constant vomiting and enormous pain, she was surprised and asked him what had prompted the smile. His whispered reply was barely audible: 'It's beautiful,' she recalls him saying in her book, *No Flowers … Just Lots of Joy*. 'The most wonderful gardens. What a gardener! I thought I was a gardener, but this gardener's something else ... It's so lovely – don't hang about, darling! I don't know that I'm going to die yet, but I've got to be patient.'

In traditional forms of Christian spirituality, death has usually been seen as a friend. Like Roy Castle, the old Negro spiritual 'Swing low, sweet chariot', for example, welcomed death as the great liberator 'comin' for to carry me home'. It offered the gateway to a new life beyond the grave. Believers – who made up a majority of the population – died, in the words of the funeral service, 'in sure and certain hope of the resurrection to eternal life'. Death, with what Paul called its 'sting' removed, offered a new and exciting chapter in the book of life. People could even take comfort from the inevitability of it all. As the author of Ecclesiastes put it, 'For everything there is a season, and a time for every matter under heaven: a time to be born, and a time to die' (Ecclesiastes 3:2).

But for many people today, having abandoned all but the last vestiges of an authentic and life-affirming Christian spirituality, death is anything but a positive prospect. Rather than being seen as a friend, death is perceived as the ultimate enemy, to be avoided by any means necessary – from cryogenic suspension to crystals and from wrinkle cream to a belief in reincarnation. Like Shakespeare's Hamlet, they cling to youth in a desperate attempt to stave off 'the dread of something after death, the undiscover'd country from whose bourn no traveller returns'. But whilst Hamlet feared that this 'country' would turn out to be the flames of hell, the most common dread now is that it's ... nothing – permanent extinction.

It's hardly surprising that this idea fills people with horror, pushing them to search for some kind of ultimate meaning to their existence. After all, if everything you've done has been with the aim of increasing your own sense of pleasure and self-importance, you'll do almost anything you can to avoid the realization that it's all been for nothing. If you're proud of the sleek, black 'sweet chariot' marked BMW sitting on your driveway, and what it says about you as a success in life, the last thing you want is for another 'sweet chariot' to arrive labelled RIP! Like the man in Jesus' parable who tore down his barns and built bigger ones to store all his grain, rather than sharing his success with others, the thing you'll dread the most is finding out that your time's up, and that you've been a terrible fool.

> It's not that I'm afraid to die, I just don't want to be there when it happens.
> *Woody Allen*

The Search for Spirituality

England football manager Glenn Hoddle believes that if he'd taken his spiritualist faith healer with him to France, his team might have won the 1998 World Cup. The former governor of Hong Kong, Chris Patten, a Roman Catholic, is said to have used the Chinese technique of Feng Shui to ensure that his official residence was ordered so as to maximize the amount of energy flowing through it. The Duchess of York, not to be outdone, tried to search for meaning sitting in a pyramid. Spirituality is big business.

Eastern mysticism, horoscopes, meditation, tarot cards, healing techniques, scientology. Since the drug-hazed, Beatles-soundtracked, counter-culture explosion of the late 1960s, there's been an increasing interest in spiritual things. A trip to almost any rock music festival, a visit to the annual Mind, Body, Spirit exhibitions in London, or even a browse through the bookshelves of your local WHSmith will confirm that atheism is out and 'alternative' religion is in. Faith-healing techniques, witches, druids and pagans now have more credibility, in many areas, than traditional organized religions such as Christianity. There's Buddhism for business executives, yoga for young people, horoscopes for housewives, meditation for mums, crystals for caterers, alien abduction for accountants, spiritism for students, and Hare Krishna for the genuinely helpless.

'Rapidly increasing numbers are finding it possible to believe in reincarnation, spirit guides and extra-terrestrials, and all sorts of other esoteric ideas,' says John Drane in his book *What Is the New Age Saying to the Church?* 'To traditional Christians, this might be unfamiliar territory. But it certainly means that these people are spiritually open as no other generation within living memory has been.'

We may not be too keen on some of the ideas people latch onto, or their prejudiced dismissal of traditional, time-tested Christianity in favour of the weird and frequently not so wonderful. But the truth is that it represents an undeniable spiritual 'renaissance'. The solutions science promised us to life's problems have failed to materialize. In fact, the twentieth century has raised far more questions than it has answered. As a result, there's a real spiritual hunger throughout the nation and across the Western world. Millions of people are now exploring their spiritual options.

> **I still haven't found what I'm looking for.**
> **Bono, of the band U2**

A Voyage of Discovery

The great Age of Exploration began in earnest with Marco Polo in the fourteenth century. It ended when Neil Armstrong first set foot on the moon in 1969. His 'one small step for a man, a giant leap for mankind' was, in many ways, a giant leap over the finishing line. Satellites have mapped every square inch of the earth, and the Voyager probe has relayed pictures of almost the whole solar system. The era of outward-looking exploration is essentially over. Instead, the voyage of discovery has turned inwards.

More and more people are searching for meaning. The challenge they face is not on the high seas, but in the largely uncharted waters of their own souls.

> **explore** / *v.tr.* **1** travel extensively through (a country etc.) in order to learn or discover about it. **2** inquire into; investigate thoroughly. **3** *Surgery* examine (a part of the body) in detail. ❏ **explorative.**
> *Oxford English Dictionary*

Like a rebellious adolescent, our society is in the process of rejecting many of its Christian parents' core values, even before it properly understands them. Having nurtured Western culture for 2,000 years, Christianity is now being indiscriminately and sometimes angrily tossed aside in favour of almost *anything* different. It's a frantic search for identity and independence.

How should the Church respond to this? Should it clamp down hard, exerting what little authority it has left in an attempt to impose its own brand of 'traditional values' and force its prodigal son's compliance? Or, like a wise parent, should it make itself available and easily accessible in the hope that, by removing obstacles and keeping the communication channels open, its child will feel able to ask for help in exploring life's deepest questions as and when they need it?

> **Our society is asking profound questions about what it means to be human. The church should seize the opportunity to help today's men and women discover God's answers to the questions that many are already asking.**
> *Archbishop of Canterbury's Evangelism Officer,*
> *Robert Warren*

Hold the Front Page!

When a news journalist receives a phone call giving them a lead on a story, their job is to find out the facts – to answer the who, what, where, when, how and why. If they're any good, they'll verify the story using a number of different sources, provide substantiating evidence, and then write a balanced and 'objective' report based on their investigations. No responsible journalist would write an article based exclusively and unquestioningly on just one source of information. Instead, they'd try to corroborate or criticize the story using other, independent sources.

If people come to our churches and our communities exploring the big questions in life, we must enable and allow them to investigate, scrutinize and examine our beliefs and our actions in just the same way that a journalist would. We must be welcoming towards those who don't yet fully believe, but come to church anyway in search of meaning. Rather than insisting that they agree with us and toe the party line, we need to create space for them to be able to explore the truth of the gospel for themselves.

In the past, even some of the best-intentioned churches have unwittingly come across as being suspicious of, or even downright hostile to, those 'seekers after truth' who've dared to ask awkward questions or voice opinions they don't quite agree with. When Sheila's church ran its first Alpha course, it attracted both established church members, who wanted a quick 'refresher course', and those more on the fringes of involvement with the church, who wanted a 'just-looking course'. Alpha (which we discuss in a bit more detail in Chapter 7) seemed to cater perfectly for both, and the church advertised it as being a no-holds-barred chance to explore the basics of the Christian faith.

However, it wasn't long before problems arose. Not used to having their faith carefully scrutinized and questioned, a few of the established Christians on the course began to give some of the 'just-lookers' a hard time. 'Believe this or get out!' was the impression many of the fringe members carried away with them, and it took all of their persuasive powers for Sheila and the other group leaders to get them to come back again the following week. Of course, none of the Christian 'hard-liners' wanted to give this impression. It's just that they'd become so used to their church being filled with *believers*, rather than *explorers*, that they gave off the vibe, without meaning to, that unless someone believed all the right doctrines (orthodoxy), they wouldn't be fully accepted.

It's ironic, really. After all, the biblical pattern is for full acceptance (what Paul called 'justification by grace through faith', in which God fully accepts us before we fully accept him) to come *before* the kind of root-and-branch transformation that leads to a renewed understanding and 'orthodox' belief. (Paul calls this transformation a 'metamorphosis' in Romans 12:2. The Reformers, following both Paul and a long-standing Church tradition, referred to it as 'sanctification', meaning 'becoming holy', and viewed it as the necessary second step *after* 'justification'.)

Similarly, for all their commitment and dedication, Jesus' first disciples were very short on understanding. Think back to the time when Peter stumbled onto Jesus' 'true identity' (Matthew 16:16/Mark 8:29/Luke 9:20). 'You are the Messiah,' he blurted out, 'the Son of the living God.' Never has a truer word been spoken, but only moments later Peter was being harshly reprimanded by Jesus: 'Get behind me, Satan! You are a stumbling block to me.' The reason for this sudden attack? Although Peter was right on the ball to spot that Jesus was the Messiah, he had his own – and, as it turned out, completely wrong – ideas about what that meant. For Jesus it meant certain death; for Peter this was unthinkable. In fact, Peter didn't really understand what it was all about until *after* the resurrection – and as his run-in with Paul (described in Galatians 2) shows, perhaps not even then.

To return to the analogy of the rebellious adolescent for a moment. Just as a wise parent tries to avoid bluntly telling their teenager, 'You're wrong' – opting instead if possible to help them discover their mistake for themselves – so we must learn to make our churches more tolerant of the kind of mistakes that most of us, if we're honest, have made at one time or another. We need to work hard to make them 'places' where people feel confident about exploring opinions and beliefs, especially Christian ones, safe in the knowledge that they won't get shot down for saying the 'wrong' thing.

We need to take Peter's subsequent advice to heart (1 Peter 3:15–16): 'Always be ready to make your defense to anyone who demands from you an accounting for the hope that is in you; yet do it with gentleness and reverence.'

> **Jesus does not want me for a cabbage. Church is not the ecclesiastical equivalent of the Red Army or Hitler Youth, where lots of unthinking clones do what they're told and, when asked to jump, ask only 'How high?' We need to bring all our critical faculties to bear on our belonging. It is this that has the potential to make church such a rewarding experience.**
> *Simon Jones*

'Jesus Is the Answer ... What's the Question?'

Theresa had no real experience of church. She didn't know any of its teachings, having not been sent off to Sunday school as a child. She certainly hadn't read the Bible. As a result, she found the services a bit bewildering. She only went because her daughter had joined the choir with a friend. When the friend's mother started confirmation classes, Theresa went along to keep her company.

At first, she didn't know what to expect. It was a little intimidating. But Sarah, the woman leading the classes, soon made her feel at home. She didn't expect Theresa or the others to know very much about the Christian faith. Instead she asked them what they did know, and used that as her starting point for exploring what it was all about. Feeling she was in a 'safe environment', Theresa began to open up. As the classes progressed, all the really big questions – God, death, sex, guilt, poverty, religion, evil, suffering, happiness, parenting and work, not to mention the meaning of life – seemed to crop up naturally.

Sarah never pushed answers at them, but steered them in the direction of the Bible. She gave Theresa an easy-to-read version, which Theresa was surprised to find herself hungrily devouring. She asked lots of questions about Jesus, and wanted answers. By the time the course was over, Theresa had not only become a Christian, she'd also become one of the group's most enthusiastic members. Sarah couldn't believe the transformation: the shy and suspicious woman who'd always sat in the corner had blossomed into someone whose obvious excitement at what she was discovering was infectious.

Helping people explore life's deepest questions, of course, means letting them set the agenda. Christians are often so enthusiastic to introduce people to Jesus as 'The Answer' that we forget actually to listen to the questions they're asking. As a result, we often come across like politicians, determined to say what's on our mind whether it's relevant to the question or not.

Steve had had a number of affairs. His marriage was decidedly on the rocks. At 27, he had a steady job as a technician and two young daughters, but he was dissatisfied with his lot in life. Carol worked in the same building as a secretary, and they'd met a few times. One night there was a works social at the local ten-pin bowling club. Steve started talking to Carol at the bar, at first trying to chat her up. She left him in no doubt that she wasn't interested, but rather than wandering off, he stayed at the bar. Gradually they got to talking, and he told her about his marriage and his boredom at work.

'You always seem pretty happy and content,' he told her. 'What's your secret?'

'You may find this strange, Steve, but if you really want to know – I'm a Christian.'

Steve silently groaned. He'd encountered Christians before. But she gently explained how she'd found faith at a difficult time in her life, when her father had been dying. She'd been unsure at first, but it had really helped her cope with the impact of her dad's death. In fact, it had turned her life around.

Carol didn't want to push it, so she left it at that. She got the impression that he was interested in what she was saying, but that any more would have been too much. Over the next couple of years, however, she and Steve had several further heart-to-hearts – always in public places so as not to generate any office gossip. He came to admire her faith, and found that she was someone he could trust and talk openly to. He still hasn't become a Christian, but he's asking a lot of questions about God, religion, morality, commitment and the point of it all.

Like Carol and Sarah, we'll have to learn to meet people where they are if we're going to be able to help them in their quest for meaning and understanding. When Philip met an Ethiopian official on the road from Jerusalem to Gaza (Acts 8), he didn't launch headlong into a fully illustrated, NICAM digital stereo explanation of the gospel. Instead, he asked a simple question: 'Do you understand what you are reading?' When the official asked for help, *that's* when Philip moved in – at the official's invitation. And rather than taking him back to some theoretical starting point, he used the same passage of Isaiah that the Ethiopian had been reading to explain the gospel message. In other words, he used the Ethiopian's own deep questions and exploration as a starting point, and steered him from there *naturally* to a real understanding of Jesus.

We, too, need to allow people to explore at their own pace. We're a part of a process, moving people on in their journey with God. We're called to be salt and light, reflecting the 'good news' of Jesus in who we are, and in what we do and say. But like the parable of the sower (Matthew 13/Mark 4/Luke 8), we won't always know where the seeds will end up, or be there to harvest them.

IDEAS

As people are looking for answers to some of the big questions in today's society, we're going to need to know the concerns and understand the culture in which we live. So we'll need to be *ready to explore the questions* with people. In our churches and in our communities we can provide an opportunity for people to *explore the answers*. We won't necessarily provide the answers, but we need to allow people the freedom to explore and develop at their own pace.

For being ready to explore the questions

- Take time to read about the issues that matter to people. Make sure you read a cross section of newspapers and magazines. The *Sun* and the *Mirror*, for example, are the most widely read papers. Like Paul, we need to understand and speak the language of the people – tabloid or broadsheet – and be ready to explore the questions.
- If you have house groups or fellowship groups, try this exercise. Buy a cross section of newspapers and magazines. Get people to cut out stories which raise the Big Issues. Discuss the main points and angles in each story. Discuss the biblical teachings relating to the main issues. (You can do the same exercise by choosing a popular TV programme like *Eastenders*, *Coronation Street*, *Brookside*, etc.)
- In your home groups, sermons, school Christian Unions, etc., spend a few sessions looking at issues like image, spiritual awareness, death, medical ethics. There may be someone in your church who could tackle one of these subjects.
- Learn to listen! It's very easy to let ourselves jump in with what we think and believe on certain subjects. But we need to let people talk and we often need to learn how to listen. This simple exercise works well in twos: Person A spends three

minutes telling Person B something about themselves and any issue they feel strongly about. Person B does the same to Person A. Then tell each other what you remember. It's a good test of concentration!

For exploring the answers

- If you're a member of a group in your community (e.g. Mums and Toddlers, youth group, parenting group, lunch club for the elderly, etc.), set up a 'Big Issue' debate. Invite a local Christian who's a good communicator to set up the 'hot topic' – e.g. relationships, euthanasia, image, bereavement, facing the future, etc.
- Is there someone who does a follow-up visit after a funeral, baptism, operation, illness, etc.? A visit not only lets them know you care for people in the community, it also allows them an opportunity to talk privately *if* they want to. We need to find ways of enabling people to ask the questions. Not everyone will want the answers just yet!
- If you're a member of a sports club (golf, rugby, football, cricket, etc.), host a match, followed by a dinner with a speaker and/or entertainment. A number of churches have found this a really good way of getting people who wouldn't easily come into church to think about 'the meaning of life'. Christians in Sport can help and provide resources in local church sports ministry.
- Business Breakfasts or Lunches are another good forum for inviting good speakers. They can be held in a local hotel with an 'after-breakfast' speaker, for example.
- Pub Nights have been a very successful way of getting people to think about life issues. Pubs make a great venue for hosting pub quizzes, fun nights, film nights, etc. A relaxed, fun way of getting people together. You may want to include a short, punchy thought/talk or interview touching on one of the Big Issues.

- Set up an 'Agnostics Anonymous' group. A relaxed, 'no-limits' forum where people can come and ask questions and say what they like about life, the universe, and Christianity! The aim is to get people talking, discussing and raising the issues that matter to them. It has proved a successful way of getting people to open up, discuss and think about what's important to them. It's also a good group for people who aren't quite ready for a Christian basics or enquiry group.

- Build up relationships in your community. Do something practical as a church, such as building or gardening, to give you an opportunity of drawing your contacts into the Christian circle naturally.

- You may want to run something like *The Jesus Video Project*, either showing the film of the Gospel of Luke in a hall, hotel, etc., or distributing it round your area. If anyone has burning questions or is obviously really looking for some answers, try to follow them up afterwards. They may want to talk further in a small group or one-to-one setting.

- Run a 'just-looking' course such as *Open to Question*, *Alpha*, etc. The *Alpha Course*, for example, offers 'an opportunity to explore the meaning of life'. It tackles questions such as 'What is the point of life?', 'What happens when we die?', 'How do we deal with guilt?' It's aimed at those who want to investigate Christianity, newcomers and those who want to brush up on the basics. There are a number of other Christian Basics courses available, including: *Emmaus*, *Christianity Explained* (see Resource section, Chapter 7).

- Run a holiday or half-term Holiday Club for young people, giving them an opportunity to explore some of the questions: friendships, relationships, being loved and valued, image, etc.

- Prayer! Have prayer clusters, prayer cells, prayer chains, prayer triplets for any events or groups you put on. Pray for the courses and the people. Pray with expectancy!

RESOURCES

Resources

Time ... to Make a Difference. Sir Cliff Richard, Fiona Castle, Jonathan Edwards talk to Steve Chalke about what their faith means to them in terms of success, ambition, suffering and bereavement. A low-cost audio cassette to help people think about the issues. Produced by ICC with Fanfare for a New Generation. Available from Fanfare.

Time ... to Make a Difference training pack. Designed to help people build up relationships in the community, in the workplace, among friends and family, and developing natural openings for sharing your faith. Features Nicky Gumbel, Steve Chalke, J John and others. Produced by ICC with Fanfare. Available from Fanfare.

Open to Question. An eight-week enquirers' course for sceptics and those who are looking. Available from CPAS.

The Jesus Video. Film dramatization of Luke's Gospel. Available from Agape.

How to Organise a Men's Evangelistic Event by John Arkell. User-friendly workbook on how to put on an event, choose the right venue, follow-up, etc. Available from CPAS.

Men: The Challenge of Change. Innovative workbook focusing on understanding men and developing relevant evangelistic strategies. Available from CPAS.

Church Leadership Pack. Folder of ready-to-use ideas and information for those in church leadership. Available from CPAS.

How to Lead Group Discussions with those who are not yet Christians. Practical guide on how to lead a discussion, how to handle difficult questions, etc. Produced by Agape, available from CPAS.

Mind the Gap. Studies on creation, the fall, redemption and future hope, showing the importance of work. Useful for small groups and business groups. Available from CPAS.

Out on the Cutting Edge. Video and resource pack, answering the top six questions posed by young people. Good for discussion groups or road shows. Part of the *Discovery Flatpack* designed for work in schools. Produced by Discovery and available from CPAS.

Children's Holiday Club material available from: Scripture Union, CPAS, the Bible Society, Scripture Press and others.

Agencies

Agape, Fairgate House, King's Road, Tyseley, Birmingham B11 2AA. Tel: 0121 765 4404.

Alpha, Holy Trinity Brompton, Brompton Road, London SW7 1JA. Tel: 0171 581 8255. Hotline: 0345 581278.

Bible Society, Stonehill Green, Westlea, Swindon SN5 7DG. Tel: 01793 418100.

Christians in Sport, Bryan Mason, 29 Glamis Close, Garforth, Leeds LS25 2NQ. Tel: 0113 287 0411.

Christian Viewpoint for Men, PO Box 26, Sevenoaks TN15 0ZP. Tel: 01732 834297.

Christian Viewpoint for Women, 14 Parkfield Road, Stourbridge, DY8 1HD. Tel: 01384 370775.

Church Pastoral Aid Society (CPAS), Athena Drive, Tachbrook Park, Warwick, CV34 6NG. Tel: 01926 334242.

Fanfare for a New Generation, 115 Southwark Bridge Road, London SE1 0AX. Tel: 0171 450 9070/1. E-mail:fanfare@btconnect.com

Food for Thought, 27 Radstock Lane, Earley, Reading RG6 5RX. Tel: 0118 986 1545. How to use meals for outreach.

Scripture Press (SP Valley Trust Ltd), Triangle Business Park, Stoke Mandeville, Aylesbury HP2 5BL. Tel: 01296 614430.

Scripture Union, Queensway House, 207–9 Queensway, Bletchley, Milton Keynes, Bucks MK2 2EB. Tel: 01908 856000.

Women Reaching Women, 49 West End Avenue, Pinner HA5 1BN. Tel: 0181 866 8013.

Books

There are a vast number of books for people enquiring about the Christian faith. The following is just a sample selection:

Fiona Castle, *No Flowers ... Just Lots of Joy* (Kingsway, 1996)

Steve Chalke, *More than Meets the Eye* (Hodder & Stoughton, 1995)

Steve Chalke and Paul Hansford, *The Truth About Suffering* (Kingsway, 1996)

John Drane, *What is the New Age Saying to the Church?* (Lakeland Paperbacks, 1991)

R. T. France, *The Evidence for Jesus* (Hodder & Stoughton, 1986)

Stephen Gaukroger, *It Makes Sense* (Scripture Union, 1987)

Sheena Gillies, Steve Chilcraft, Rory Keegan, *Single Issues* (CPAS, 1997)

Michael Green, *Why Bother with Jesus?/You Must Be Joking!/New Life, New Lifestyle: Omnibus edition* (Hodder & Stoughton, 1997)

Nicky Gumbel, *Questions of Life* (Kingsway, 1993)

Jennifer Rees Larcombe, *Turning Point: Is there hope for broken lives?* (Hodder & Stoughton, 1994)

C. S. Lewis, *Mere Christianity* (Fontana, 1955)

Josh McDowell, *More than a Carpenter* (Kingsway, 1979)

Josh McDowell, *His Image, My Image* (Alpha, 1985)

Stepping Stones (Agape, 1995)

Norman Warren, *Is God There?* (Kingsway, 1990 ed.)

6   We Will Offer You Time to Stop and Think in a Busy Life

Preface by Joel Edwards

People are living under great pressure. Many need time to stop and think – to simply find some space to 'be'.

In a high-speed, high-tech noisy world, what we do with those two to four hours each Sunday becomes very important. Exuberant praise and worship is important; but do we simply fill our time with activities and decibels? Or should we not offer busy people opportunities to reflect on God and what it means to belong to one another?

We all agree that the Sabbath remains an important biblical principle. But I suspect that the average Sunday agenda, with its heavy demands, may be something alien to what the Old Testament had in mind: a day of rest. So often our busy programmes and creative innovations can turn up the pressure on busy people and over-stretched parents, and build up our own egos and statistics rather than building up people, our society and the Kingdom.

So here is a challenge for the contemporary Church: if we give way to the demands of a secular calendar, which forces our members to hit the ground running on Monday morning, we may see a serious reduction in church-based activities. If we keep the pressure up, we may be a part of the problem of an over-heated society. We could, on the other hand, courageously offer an alternative to the rush-hour culture by building fellowship and belonging, vibrant witness and strong families. In fact, we could end up with a kind of Church which looks like the family model in the book of Acts.

We Will Offer You Time to Stop and Think in a Busy Life

Tom and Sarah sat on top of the mountain, looking out onto a vast expanse of valleys, forests, mountain peaks and rivers. It was a far cry from their usual round of business breakfasts, traffic jams, meetings, deadlines, briefing sessions and business trips. Then at weekends there were friends to meet, football training for Tom, squash matches for Sarah, regular household chores, parents to visit, DIY and gardening. As they sat in the sunshine, breathing in the fresh air, Tom turned to Sarah: 'There's got to be more than the rat race.'

Di was aching with tiredness as she sat down at the kitchen table. She'd just managed to get her 15-month-old son to settle down for his mid-morning sleep. Earlier on there'd been the usual battle against the clock to get her three-year-old daughter Clare to nursery and five-year-old son Josh to school. There was a pile of ironing waiting to be done, two loads of washing, the kids' rooms were in a mess and her mum – who somehow always made her feel like a failure as a housekeeper and mother – was due to pop in for a cup of coffee. On top of that, the car sounded as if it was in need of urgent attention and her ex-husband was getting married again at the weekend. 'I can't go on like this,' she cried as she slumped over the kitchen table.

Progress is man's ability to complicate simplicity.
Norwegian anthropologist Thor Heyerdahl

No Time to Stand and Stare

From the moment life begins, we're launched headlong into a race against time. We climb aboard a rollercoaster that may speed us through school, work, marriage, children, retirement, old age and finally death. The track may change course, but the rollercoaster keeps going. Each morning, millions of alarm clocks buzz or ring to signal the start of another day. From that moment, we're under the relentless power of the ticking clock. Ours is a culture dominated by time.

In his book *Spirituality and Time*, Michael Botting describes modern life as, 'People commuting up and down the motorways or across the Atlantic, washing down a sharp deal with a few drinks – not even time for the extended business lunches these days!' The rat race sucks people in and squeezes them dry, fuelled by a need to keep going at all costs. 'Between times there may be some rushing into co-habitation, occasionally marriage, and unhappily out again. There may be the anxiety about children's exam results, because they must get their offspring launched as fast as possible into the same rat race. And if they do manage some time off, the pattern can be much the same. The weekend can be filled with DIY home improvement. Or they could be flying off somewhere or other for an exhausting round of pleasures, night and day with no time to stop and stare.'

We live in a society of 'instants'. We want instant access, instant communication, instant results, instant answers, instant gratification. In the last 50 years, technological advances have revolutionized our society. We can fly at twice the speed of sound. We can measure time in nanoseconds (one thousand-millionth of a second). We can send and receive mail instantly across the globe via e-mail. We can pay bills and even shop on the Internet.

Mobile phones enable us to have an instant 'one to one' with friends. There's 24-hour banking and 24-hour news.

When US Special Prosecutor Kenneth Starr published his report into the Clinton/Lewinsky affair in September 1998, it was quickly posted on the Internet. Within minutes, the most private and intimate details of *the* political scandal of the decade was making its way around the world on the information super-highway, available for downloading to anyone with a modem-linked computer and an ordinary phone line.

We can travel to the other side of the world within 24 hours – a journey that would have taken three months a century ago. Satellites enable us to watch live-action broadcasts and news reports from around the globe. Video conferencing lets us have meetings without delegates having to be physically present with us in the same room. Our world has become a smaller, more accessible place. But the results are bittersweet. Our rollercoaster 'instant culture' means we're often pressured and fighting against the clock. Like the White Rabbit in *Alice in Wonderland*, we're often rushing around muttering, 'Oh dear! Oh dear! I shall be too late!'

Rob Parsons, Executive Director of Care for the Family and a practising lawyer, often asks the jam-packed crowds who attend his acclaimed stress-busting seminars for a show of hands as to how many labour-saving devices they have at home. An electric iron? Every hand goes up. A hoover? A washing machine? Every hand goes up. A dishwasher? A food processor? Almost every hand goes up.

'Now let me ask you something,' he addresses his audience. 'Did your grandparents have any of these time- and labour-saving devices?' Five hundred people shake their heads. 'So you have a lot more time on your hands than they did, right?' Five hundred people laugh, shaking their heads again. Wrong.

Technology designed to help us find the time to relax has actually quickened the pace of our lives, adding to the pressures and strains on us. Rather than giving us the extra leisure time its manufacturers promise, new technology seems, if anything, to make us busier than ever. Labour-saving devices at home are joined by computers, fax machines, answerphones, mobile phones, ISDN and e-mail in the office. And although they make life easier, they don't make us any less busy.

In fact, you could be forgiven for thinking that the amount of leisure time people have is inversely proportional to the number of labour-saving devices they use. Instead of giving us more time, technology has multiplied the options available to us, hugely increasing the number of choices and decisions we're faced with. Our lives are becoming steadily busier and more complex. We seem to be locked in a battle against time – a battle many of us appear to be losing.

We've become too busy for our friends and families, and we wonder why relationships suffer as a consequence. One of the reasons couples split up is a breakdown of communications. We spend more time at work than we do with our families, striving for promotion or simply to keep our jobs. In September 1998, a Lifestyle Revolution Report revealed that men would prefer to work from home so they could spend more time with their families. Even within church circles, we tend to be so busy and involved with groups and church activities that we often fail to engage actively in the community.

> **What is this life if, full of care,**
> **We have no time to stand and stare?**
> **Poet W. H. Davies**

Sabbath Rest?

The great American evangelist Billy Graham, when asked what advice he'd give to someone on how to make the most of their life, paused to think for a long time before answering. Then, at last, he offered a deceptively simple piece of advice. 'Life goes a lot quicker than you expect it to,' he said, 'so use each day wisely.'

We're not made in the image of machines. We're made in the image of God. And on the seventh day, Genesis (2:2) tells us, God took a breather. Arguments over whether or not the first chapter of Genesis should be taken literally to mean that the earth was created in seven days, and whether evolution is therefore a modern-day myth or even a threat to a belief in God, have generally over-shadowed one of the most important questions the book has to pose to us: why would God, an omnipotent being with absolute power over time, choose to take a break? After all, couldn't he put the universe on 'pause' for a bit if he needed to, and then 'fast for-ward' to the next crucial moment? The inescapable conclusion is that, having emphasized that we're made in God's image, Genesis tells us God rested in order to lend the fullest possible weight to the command of Leviticus 23:3: 'The seventh day is a sabbath of complete rest, a holy convocation; you shall do no work.'

There has been a lot of confusion about the meaning of this verse. By the time of Jesus, and still today, strict Jews interpreted it to mean that anything that could be construed as work, from plucking grains of corn to turning on a light switch, couldn't be done from sundown on Friday to sundown on Saturday – the time known as the 'Sabbath'. In the last century, and in our own, the Church has often used it to quash trading on the Christian 'Sab-bath' and keep Sunday 'special'. But although these ways of both understanding and applying Leviticus 23:3 (not to mention the fourth Commandment of Exodus 20:8–11; Deuteronomy 5:12–15) have undoubtedly been fuelled by the best intentions, they have not always produced the best results.

At the beginning of the nineteenth century, Sunday was a day very much like any other. Although services were held at church – usually in the mid-morning, to allow dairy farmers the chance to tend to their cattle beforehand – business could carry on as usual. Only with the start of the ultra-religious Victorian era did 'Sun-day Observance' laws force shops and businesses to close and push all but the poorest people into the pews, dressed up in their 'Sunday best'. Partly aimed at 'honouring' God, partly aimed at ensuring that people had at least one day of rest in the week, this Victorian equivalent of the Keep Sunday Special Campaign (the 'Lord's Day Observance Society') was successful in reshaping the nature of people's weeks, ultimately leading to the setting aside of both Saturday and Sunday as rest days. But all was not roses.

Whilst some campaigners were content to establish Sunday as a day of rest, available for worship for those who wanted, others insisted on *imposing* their concept of 'Sabbath rest' on everyone else. After all, they argued, wasn't it a divine command? When rail company bosses first proposed running trains on a Sunday, for example, the reaction amongst most 'Sabbatarians' was extreme. And Michael Faraday, the famous physicist, was expelled from his church just for accepting a dinner invitation from Queen Victoria on a Sunday!

Like the Pharisees before them, many Victorian-era Sunday Observance campaigners unwittingly turned a day of rest and relaxation into a day of ritual, religious observance. In the mid-nineteenth century, it was common for people to spend almost all day at church, attending three separate services. The irony is, not only did Sunday therefore become the busiest working day of the week for those same pastors and preachers who argued most passionately for it to become a legally protected 'Sabbath' (literally, a day of 'rest' or 'full stop'), but it also became synonymous with 'going to church', rather than 'resting'.

As a result, when people think of the word 'Sabbath', they're more likely to conjure up images in their minds of dull church services and petty regulations than of life-affirming rest and *re*creation. This is precisely the image of the 'Sabbath' Jesus attacked when he lashed out at the Pharisees after they'd accused him of letting his disciples break the Sabbath Commandment (Mark 2:27–8): 'The sabbath was made for humankind, and not humankind for the sabbath; so the Son of Man is lord even of the sabbath.'

**I heard the voice of Jesus say,
'Come unto me and rest;
Lay down, thou weary one, lay down
Thy head upon My breast.'**
Hymn writer Horatius Bonar

Shopping for a God?

Yet how often do we stop, rest, reflect, and spend time with our families and God? The busier we are, the harder it gets to filter out the hustle and bustle of everyday life. Sundays are no longer regarded as rest days. Social attitudes and habits have changed over the last century, with people tending to treat it as another Saturday, a day for doing the DIY, the gardening, catching up with work, household chores ... and shopping.

Nearly half of Britain's stores now open on Sundays. 'Has shopping become the new religion, the opium of the masses?' asked a journalist in an article in the *Daily Mail* after the opening of Manchester's Trafford Centre in September 1998. With its portals, dome features and vast murals, 'the most sensational, the most breathtaking shopping centre in the country' was more like a magnficent cathedral, argued journalist James Bartholomew. 'It is only a pity that when we are brought together in this way, our minds remain unstimulated, our souls unelevated, and we are not made to consider the worthiness of our behaviour,' he continued. 'Shopping imitates the form of religion but, in truth, it cannot replace its substance.'

Whilst shopping can be a leisure activity – a family outing, helping cement relationships between mums and dads and kids – it can also be a source of pressure. We can't, and shouldn't try to, turn the clock back and repeal the Sunday trading laws, which were enacted to stop people being forced to work seven days a week, being fined and sometimes even arrested for faking a day off to relax or worship with their family. But we *can* and *should* work hard to ensure that the freedom to worship on a Sunday continues to be enshrined in law.

Eric Liddell, the runner whose achievements at the 1924 Olympic Games were celebrated in the film *Chariots of Fire*, famously refused to run on a Sunday because, for him, it was a day of complete rest, set aside for God. Even though he considered his running to be both a gift from God and a form of worship, he wouldn't compromise his principles and treat Sunday like any other day. He didn't impose his beliefs on anyone else, campaigning for the 100-yard heats to be held on the following day, for instance. He simply refused to compete himself. As a result, until his historic gold medal in the 400 yards, he was subjected to huge pressure to conform and treated as a traitor and Public Enemy Number One.

In many ways, this is the same stand the Church must make today. We don't want to impose Sunday on other people as a special 'day of rest', but we also don't want to lose the *right* not to work on a Sunday if that's what we choose. This will mean opposing any laws that allow employers to discriminate against people who refuse to work on a Sunday. Shopping may be a much-needed form of 'rest' for some, but it's a form of work for others.

At the same time, we need to make people realize that they were created not only to work, but also to rest. The problem with Sunday shopping – especially if we buy into it as a consumerist version of churchgoing – is that it doesn't guarantee rest. So if we are to be faithful to the idea of a biblical Sabbath, we will have to broaden our concern beyond Sunday trading laws towards a wholescale campaign promoting the vital importance of rest. In fact, rest is an essential part of life. Without it, we're not only physically and emotionally drained, we're *inefficient*. We start to lose our enthusiasm and our ability to concentrate.

When Henry arrived in Stuttgart to start his new job, he was a bit intimidated by the famous 'efficiency' of the German workforce. He found to his dismay that his colleagues arrived at work at 8.30 a.m. and didn't leave until about 8.30 p.m., often taking extra work home with them. The office environment was such that anyone doing less than about a 12-hour day was considered lazy and inefficient. Only Henry seemed to leave work at 6.00, in time to tuck his two young children into bed and read them a story before spending the rest of the evening with his wife. But the strange thing is, he wasn't lagging behind his colleagues in terms of his workload. Though he did an average of 10 hours a week less work than they did, he was, if anything, working more efficiently. The reason? He was better motivated and more able to concentrate because he was getting more rest.

I haven't got time to be tired.
Wilhelm I, King of Prussia

Time Out

People may not always *choose* to take time out on a Sunday, but they *need* to take time out. They need the space to recuperate, but they also need to spend time with their friends and families, enjoying their company and building up their relationships. As John Donne put it at the turn of the seventeenth century, 'No man is an Island, entire of itself; every man is a piece of the Continent, a part of the main.'

A research team from Duke University, North Carolina, studied the lifestyles of four thousand 65-year-olds over a period of six years. Their results, published in mid-1998 and reported in *The Times*, revealed that those who attended church at least once a week had 40 per cent lower blood pressure than those who didn't, which significantly lowered the chances of them having a stroke or developing heart disease. Dr Harold Koenig, the head of the research team, had talked to thousands of older people who'd lived through wars and the Great Depression. 'What gets you through the bad times?' he asked. 'My faith,' they replied. People who prayed and had the support of a church community coped better with stress, he concluded, adding, 'I'm a sceptic, but I've been affected by the findings.'

Commenting on the report, Dr Geoff Scobie, senior psychologist at the University of Glasgow, pointed to the importance of being amongst friends and family in terms of going to church. Not only did it give people time out, it helped them to refocus their lives and appreciate their dependence on, and support of, others. 'Our lives are more stressful,' he suggested, 'and the only group-cohesiveness seems to be through the church. Small-group systems operate within a church, with support that focuses on individual concerns. If you are under stress, this will be reduced.'

All of us need time with those we care about in order to hear ourselves think clearly, reorganize our priorities and regroup for whatever lies ahead. It may be a cliché, but it's true nonetheless: no one ever said on their deathbed that they wished they'd spent more time at the office. There's nothing like a brush with death to remind us of what really matters in life.

Alfred Nobel, the nineteenth-century genius who invented nitroglycerine, detonators, dynamite and gelignite, got the shock of his life one day in 1888 when he found himself reading his own obituary in the newspaper. A careless journalist had unwittingly got him mixed up with his recently deceased brother, so Nobel had the rare chance to see how the rest of the world really viewed him: a multi-millionaire merchant of death who'd made his money from the manufacture of weapons. Having devised his explosives for use in mining and road-building, Nobel had always been troubled by their lucrative military application. The premature obituary gave him just the impetus he needed to ensure that he'd be remembered differently when his obituary was written for real, and he set about changing his will so that, when he died, the bulk of his vast fortune would fund the prizes that bear his name in physics, chemistry, medicine, literature and, most importantly of all, peace.

Most of us will never read our own obituary. In fact, most of us will never be famous enough to warrant having our obituary written in a newspaper. Instead, it will be written in the hearts and lives of those we know and love. Sometimes it takes a dramatic shock, or even something physical like a stroke or a heart attack, to make us sit up and take notice of the direction our lives are headed. We can so easily become distracted by other things that we end up as spectators rather than players in our children's lives, for example; we don't even spend enough time with them to find out that we're not spending enough time with them!

Churches are in a unique position to offer people both a *place* to go in order to find time to stop and think (provided they own their own buildings) and a *powerful message* to think about. The gospel has an uncanny way of cutting people to the bone, helping them sort out what's important and what's not. On top of that, churches themselves are groups of people who are constantly reassessing their lives in the light of the gospel, allowing God to transform them slowly into better, more focused, more creative, more loving and more supportive human beings.

Europeans have clocks, we have time.
African proverb

The Still Small Voice

In his book *The Church in the Market Place*, Archbishop George Carey tells of a period in his life when he'd become so self-centred and so busy at work that he'd managed to push God out of the picture. You might be tempted to think, being a bishop, that God would have been centre stage not only in Carey's life, but also in his work. Ask any professional Christian worker, however, and they'll tell you that things don't work like that. It's very easy when God – or, at least, the Church – is your employer, to forget that he's also your friend ... not to mention your redeemer! Carey eventually found himself on his knees, praying, 'I can't live a hypocritical life any more. Unless you fill me again with your Spirit, I cannot go on!' In the calm of that Sunday evening, God spoke to the busy clergyman – there was nothing dramatic, but an amazing quality of peace.

This story is remarkably similar to one that happened over 2,800 years ago, almost halfway round the world in a land and culture very different from our own. After a three-year standoff with an increasingly unstable King Ahab, and a duel of truly epic proportions on Mount Carmel, Israel's greatest prophet was ready just to lie down and die. On the run from Ahab's wife, Jezebel, Elijah had reached the end of his tether. He went to the desert, sat down under a tree and prayed for a swift death. Then, worn out, he fell asleep. When he woke, he found that God had provided lunch; nothing fancy, just freshly baked bread and water. After lunch, Elijah fell asleep again. Once more he was woken, and told to eat and drink before beginning the long journey to Mount Horeb. When he finally arrived there, he found a cave in which to spend the night. In the morning, God told him to stand at the mouth of the cave and wait.

'Now there was a great wind, so strong that it was splitting mountains and breaking rocks in pieces before the Lord, but the Lord was not in the wind; and after the wind an earthquake, but the Lord was not in the earthquake; and after the earthquake a fire, but the Lord was not in the fire; and after the fire a sound of sheer silence. When Elijah heard it, he wrapped his face in his mantle and went out and stood at the entrance of the cave. Then there came a voice to him' (1 Kings 19:11–13).

For Elijah, the 'sound of silence' – and the reassurance of God's presence in the stillness – was what gave him the strength to continue. The battle with Ahab and Jezebel was far from over. Ahab was to die as Elijah predicted, with the dogs licking his blood as they'd licked the blood of his victim Naboth. But for Elijah, the 'time to stop and think' was vital. It allowed him to get things straight in his own mind, focusing his priorities in preparation for the time ahead. It also prepared him to hear God speaking.

Over 800 years later, God spoke in a similar way to a very similar man. John the Baptist had modelled himself on Elijah … right down to the dress code. At a time of great political instability, and before a dramatic showdown with Herod Antipas that would seal both their fates and lead to John's death, he wandered into the desert like his predecessor and waited for instructions.

Luke (3:1–2) adds drama to the occasion and sets the scene by telling readers about the political leaders of the day: Pilate, Herod and Caiaphas, the real 'movers and shakers' of their generation. We can only speculate as to what they might have been doing. Pilate, ensconced in his office in the heart of the city, could have been in meetings, the nation's fate balanced precariously in his hands. Across town, Herod may have been entertaining another round of foreign dignitaries at a state banquet in an attempt to stabilize relations with neighbouring countries. Caiaphas, the high priest, taking time out from the relentless (and rather bloody) onslaught of official business, was perhaps snatching a few treasured moments of private prayer. And suddenly, out of the blue, God spoke … to a scruffily dressed vagrant in the desert.

In contrast to the busy lives and self-importance of Pilate, Herod and Caiaphas, which would have served to drown out God's prophetic voice, John the Baptist specifically went to the desert in order to hear God call. There's nothing unusual about this. When Jesus heard the news of John's death, he went by boat to a quiet place (Matthew 14:13). After the feeding of the five thousand, he went up the mountainside to pray alone for several hours (Matthew 14:23). And when he knew he was about to be betrayed, arrested and executed, he withdrew to Gethsemane to be with his Father (Matthew 26).

Through contemplation, we realize that our own power proves inadequate, and we learn to trust a power that is beyond ourselves. We are shaken from our natural talents to accept our spiritual gifts. Our slow movement is from achievement to self-giving, from filling up to emptying out, from being the centre to becoming a channel. Only then will we finally relax and act out of gratitude more than obligation, grace instead of law, hope rather than expectation.
Jim Wallis, leader of the Sojourners Community, Washington DC

Pilgrim's Progress

We all need time to stop and think in our lives, and to listen and pray to God. Churches need to offer the time and space for quiet reflection not only on Sundays but throughout the week. In spite of the threat of vandalism and theft, there are ways to ensure that your church building is open every day to those who want to use it to stop and think.

Of course, reflection and time out don't have to take place in a church building, though many people find churches a helpful oasis. Some prefer to go for walks in the country, or climb a hill. Some even find opportunities for quiet contemplation in grave-yards, among the 'souls of the faithful departed'. We need to encourage people to take stock, to spend time reflecting, in whatever ways they find helpful.

You don't need to be alone to find the time to stop and think. More and more churches organize 'retreats' or 'weekends away' once or twice a year, where church members have the chance to spend a day or two enjoying each other's company and listening to God's voice together in the quiet of the countryside, or in the grounds of a monastery, retreat centre or conference centre.

What's more, pilgrimages, once considered the loyal duty of all able-bodied Christians, are back in fashion. People are travelling hundreds or thousands of miles to experience a more tangible,

first-hand connection with the site of a genuine spiritual phenom-
enon or renaissance: from the Celtic monasteries of Lindisfarne,
Jarrow or Iona – the first monastery in Britain, established by the
missionaries of St Columba, who arrived from Ireland in 563 (30
years before the arrival of St Augustine in the south of England) –
to the ecumenical monastic community in Taizé; from the shrines
of the Virgin Mary at Walsingham and Lourdes to the charismatic pilgrimage centre at the Airport Vineyard Church in
Toronto (home of the famous 'Blessing'); or following in the steps
of the Master in the Holy Land. Standing in the footsteps of 'spiritual giants' can provide just the impetus people need to let the
Holy Spirit further transform them, or else act as a powerful cata-
lyst in focusing their thoughts and reordering their priorities.

As people return to seeing their lives as spiritual journeys, the
idea of a retreat or pilgrimage will be a helpful one. All too often,
however, it begins by creating a peaceful space somewhere in our
buildings and services where members of the church and people
from the local community can come and find time to stop, think
and re-evaluate where they are in their lives, as well as where God
fits into the picture.

IDEAS

Compared with the hectic pace of life, the tranquillity of entering
a church during the day seems like an oasis. Whether sitting in
the sanctuary, wandering round ancient tombs and crypts, sitting
in silence, or listening to music, people want time to reflect, to
take stock. Our churches offer a great opportunity for enabling
people to do just that. But we can also take the lead in encouraging and helping people to relax – to find ways of taking time out
of their pressurized lives.

Helping people in our church and community to take the time...

- Take time out on your own, in your own family unit, or with a larger group. Go for a walk or a picnic. Swimming can be relaxing. Find something that you enjoy doing, that relaxes you, and make the time to do it, say, once a month.
- Could you offer creche facilities and baby-sitting services to allow mums and dads some time out? Encourage them to go shopping without the kids, and to take an extra half an hour to chat over a cup of coffee!
- Make sure people in your church aren't taking on too much. Generally it's the same few people doing a myriad of tasks. But we can be so busily caught up in church work and church meetings that we're not spending enough time with our friends and family.
- If you have a car, take someone who doesn't have one on a day trip into the country. Many elderly people who no longer drive really appreciate even a short trip in the area. (Try to include a tea stop, too!)
- Book in a 'family day'. Decide what you want to do as a family and enjoy it! The process of doing it may make you stop and reprioritize what's important in your life.
- If you have children, try a 'one to one' with them. Take one of them out on a date – e.g. Breakfast at McDonalds, cinema trip, football match, etc. Spend some quality time together.
- Have a TLC Night. Once a fortnight, try to have a night in. If you're a family, have a Pizza and Video Evening. If you're single, invite some friends round for something to eat, or simply relax with a book or video and a bottle of beer or wine. Anything that relaxes you. Pamper yourself. REST! Give yourself a little 'tender loving care' – if *you* don't, nobody else will!
- Sundays can be very pressurized days. Don't feel guilty if, once in a while, you don't go to church (although that may be a problem for the church leader – in which case make sure *they*

take a day off sometime, too!). Go for a bike ride, read a book, go for a long walk, go to the park, take a day trip. Make it a special day.

- Many churches find weekends away or church family holidays a good way of helping people to relax and take time to think. A lot of boarding schools and youth hostels offer very competitive weekend or weekly rates. Some churches do 'swaps' with a church in another part of the county or country and use their facilities. Build in plenty of time for 'chilling out', getting to know people, relaxing, having free time.

- Plan a retreat – on your own, with friends, as a family or as a church. There are a number of organizations who specialize in this, including: Lee Abbey, Iona Community, Ashburnham Prayer Centre, Ellel Ministries. Or you might think about going further away – to the Taizé Community and Lourdes in France, or to the Holy Land.

- Run a course on effective time management. Administry have resources to help with this. Or use *Managing Your Time* (see Books section below) and develop it into a seminar. Or perhaps there's someone in your community who could run a workshop for you. The workshop/seminar could be opened up to include the wider community.

Using our church buildings to help people take the time...

- If your church is in a town or city, are you able to put on a lunchtime service? A number of churches have found it a really helpful way of enabling people to find the space and time to think during a busy day. The services generally last around half an hour, with soup and sandwiches afterwards. Many elderly people enjoy worshipping together during the week and you may have the facilities to be able to offer lunch afterwards. Check, too, whether a creche facility would be useful.

- Are there ways of opening up your church during the week? Unfortunately the rise in crime, theft and vandalism has forced

many churches to remain locked during the day. Are there imaginative ways in which you could open up the building?
- Could the church be manned for, say, two hours over the lunchtime period?
- Is there a separate room accessible between the main building and the street? There may be a way of keeping the outside door open, whilst closing entry into the church. Perhaps you could establish it as a prayer room.
- Perhaps you could remove any valuables and then leave the building open!
- The Open Churches Trust is committed to finding ways of unlocking the doors so that people can use churches for peace, quiet and prayer.

RESOURCES

Agencies

Administry, PO Box 57, St Albans, AL1 3DT. Tel: 01727 856370.
The Open Churches Trust, c/o The Really Useful Group Ltd, 22 Tower Street, London WC2H 9NS. Tel: 0171 240 0880.

Retreat Centres

Ashburnham Prayer Centre, Ashburnham Place, Battle, East Sussex TN33 9NF. Tel: 01424 892244.
Ellel Ministries, Ellel Grange, Ellel, Lancaster LA2 OHN. Tel: 01524 751651.
Iona Abbey, Isle of Iona, Argyll, Scotland PA76. Tel: 01681 700404.
L'Eau Vive Provence, 13122 Ventabren, France. Tel: 00-33-4-42-28-77-53.
Lee Abbey, Lynton, North Devon EX35 6JJ. Tel: 01598 752621.

Quiet Garden Retreat, a chance to rest, pray and simply 'be':
Stoke Park Farm, Park Road, Stoke Poges, Bucks SL2 4PG.
Taizé Community, 71250 Taizé, France. Tel: 0033-385503002.
Fax: 0033-385503016. Web site: http://www.taize.fr

Books

Michael Botting, *Spirituality and Time* (Grove Spirituality Series, 1997)

George Carey, *The Church in the Market Place* (Kingsway, 1995 ed.)

Steve Chalke, *How to Succeed as a Parent* (Hodder & Stoughton, 1997)

Steve Chalke with Penny Relph, *Managing Your Time* (Kingsway, 1998)

Gordon MacDonald, *Ordering Your Private World* (Highland Books, 1998 ed.)

Rob Parsons, *The Sixty Minute Father* (Hodder & Stoughton, 1995)

Rob Parsons, *The Sixty Minute Marriage* (Hodder & Stoughton, 1997)

Rob Parsons, *What They Didn't Teach Me in Sunday School* (Hodder & Stoughton, 1997)

Prayer and meditation

Nick Aitken, *Complete Prayers for Teenagers* (Marshall Pickering, 1989/93)

Michael Botting (ed.), *Prayers for all the Family* (Kingsway, 1993)

Ronald Dunn, *Don't Just Stand There, Pray Something* (Scripture Press, 1992)

Joni Eareckson Tada, *A Quiet Place in a Crazy World* (JAF Ministries, 1998)

Richard Foster, *Seeking the Kingdom: 20 Minutes with God* (Hodder & Stoughton, 1995)

Joyce Huggett, *Finding God in the Fast Lane* (Eagle, 1993)

Joyce Huggett, *Listening to God* (Hodder & Stoughton, 1986)

Bill Hybels, *Too Busy Not to Pray* (IVP, 1998)

C. S. Lewis, *Readings for Meditation and Reflection* (HarperCollins, 1996)

Henri Nouwen, *Bread for the Journey* (DLT, 1996)

Henri Nouwen, *The Return of the Prodigal Son* (DLT, 1994)

Brendan O'Malley, *Celtic Blessings* (Canterbury Press, 1998)

Ian Reid, *Meditations from the Iona Community* (Wild Goose, 1998)

Thank You God: The Prayers of Children (Hunt & Thorpe, 1997)

David Torkington, *Inner Life* (DLT, 1997)

John White, *People in Prayer* (IVP, 1977)

See also the Resources section in Chapter 7.

7 We Will Help You Make Sense of the Bible and Who Jesus Is

Preface by Faith Forster

Faith Forster, together with her husband Roger, set up the Ichthus Christian Fellowship in 1974. A well-known speaker and writer, Faith is also involved in evangelism and training church leaders.

I firmly believe the Bible has enormous power. As the written Word of God, inspired by the Holy Spirit, the Scriptures have power in our lives. As we read the Bible and pray, God speaks through his written Word.

That's why it's so important to have our daily intake of the Bible and to help people in their understanding of it. It's rather like eating food. You don't always remember what you've eaten, but you know you've had it and that it's still working in you, sustaining and nourishing you. Similarly, we may not always remember what we've read in the Bible, but it has gone into our minds and hearts and is working away. In fact we may not be aware of its effects for months to come!

It can be difficult to make time to read regularly in our busy, pressurized lives. I went through a stage when I didn't read the Bible very much.

I had three small children, my husband Roger was away a lot and life was just too busy. I was even too busy to eat! For days I'd pick at food, skip meals or eat junk food. When you have young children, are suffering from stress and sleep deprivation, feeding yourself is the last thing on your mind! I suddenly realized how easy it would be for my irregular eating patterns to turn into a habit, which could lead to an eating disorder and all sorts of health problems. I also realized I'd done the same thing with the Word of God.

What I had to do was develop an appetite for the Bible, and to feed on it regularly. I didn't need to be convinced that God's Word was good for me. But I did need to enlarge my appetite. I started with a short, but regular, daily input using Bible-reading notes. Gradually my appetite grew. I found I craved more and more and I was back in the swing of regular Bible reading.

Like food, we need variety in our approach to Bible reading. Contemporary translations such as the *Living Bible* are easier to read. Meditating on a verse or two, reading a verse off a calendar each day, discussing passages in a regular Bible study group – these are all ways of helping us to read, understand and listen to God's voice.

The Bible is a very powerful tool. We need to find ways of encouraging appetites to grow – not only ours, but those of others, too. Perhaps we need to review our lives every few weeks, to see if we've taken in something from the Bible – whether it's a little crumb or a great big chunk! That way we'll keep our spirit and appetite alive.

We Will Help You Make Sense of the Bible and Who Jesus Is

Karl Barth ranks as one of the greatest Church leaders of the twentieth century. In the early 1930s, he was sacked from his job as a professor in a German university and sent packing back to his native Switzerland after spearheading church opposition to Hitler. And though few churchgoers have even heard of him, his multi-volume epic *Church Dogmatics* has had more impact on the European church than any other book since the Reformation, leading to a renewed academic interest in the Bible as a work of divine revelation. He's largely credited with having put 'Christ' back at the heart of *Christ*ian theology.

On one occasion a student asked him, 'Dr Barth, what's the greatest single thought that ever crossed your mind?' The great theologian slowly bowed his head and puffed on his pipe, thinking for a moment. His students all waited in eager anticipation for some great, earth-shattering spiritual answer. But lifting his head, Karl Barth replied, in the words of the children's hymn, 'Jesus loves me: this I know, for the Bible tells me so.'

> **You cannot criticize the New Testament. It criticizes you.**
> **John Jay Chapman**

Bestseller

The Bible, one of the first books ever to be printed after the invention of 'moveable type' printing presses at the start of the sixteenth century, remains the annual bestselling book worldwide by a very long way. Around 44 million copies are sold every year, with the UK seeing annual sales of nearly 1.25 million. It has been translated into more languages than any other book ever written. There are numerous translations in English alone, ranging from the almost Shakespearean tones of the *King James* (*'Authorized'*) *Version* to the more tabloid style of easy-to-read contemporary versions like the *Good News* or *New Light* Bibles.

In 1998, publishing company Canongate's decision to repackage 12 of its books into £1 mini-editions, with introductions written by top contemporary writers and personalities, caused a certain amount of controversy. Singer Nick Cave, whose passionate introduction to the Gospel of Mark made him few friends within the Church, had mixed feelings about the project. 'I like the fact that the Bible is difficult and requires quite an effort,' he said, 'but this does make it more accessible. I would like people to read the Bible. I would hope that through my introduction, some people who might not otherwise, will read it.'

Sadly, many people don't read the Bible and don't know what it tells them because they haven't actually taken their copy off the shelf in years. It's a strange bestseller, remaining largely unopened, gathering dust, its vast treasure trove of knowledge undiscovered. They suspect it of being dull, difficult, dogmatic and depressing.

Believe it or not, reading books isn't popular culture. Although literacy levels have risen sharply this century, and most people can now read, whatever their social standing, nearly a quarter of the UK population have apparently never read a book and don't regularly read a newspaper. Radio and TV have altered the way in which people absorb information, and magazines – which have adapted to the new style more successfully than any other written medium – are now the primary reading matter of the majority of people in the UK. Rather than subjecting readers to long, complicated and involved arguments, they offer short, colour-illustrated, human-interest stories and statistics that can be read and applied quickly and with the minimum of fuss.

We may find this kind of approach shallow and short sighted. We may feel that it lends weight to the cynical view expressed by French dramatist Jean Anouilh in one of his plays: 'An Englishman should never think. It's bad for his health.' We may nostalgically long for the supposed 'Golden Age' of a Wesley or Spurgeon, when preachers and Church leaders could explore deep, complicated spiritual themes at length before a sympathetic audience drawn from all walks of life. But even if such a 'Golden Age' existed – and all the evidence suggests that it *didn't* – it's now long gone. We have, on the whole, entered the post-literate era: people *can* read, but they tend not to if they think it will involve effort.

As everyone knows, there are two ways to get an unwilling donkey to move: beat it with a stick, or entice it with a carrot. Nine times out of ten, the carrot is more effective, and reading the Bible is no exception to this rule. People *will* read – articles or books – if they feel motivated enough to do it.

There are two main reasons why people leave their Bibles on their shelves to collect dust, instead of devouring them ravenously. Firstly, the contents are uncharted waters to them. Rather than being an 'open book', it remains very much a closed book because its language, culture, contents and concerns seem strange and forbidding. Like Pandora's Box, it's better not to open it because you never know what might come out. It's so much easier to approve of the Bible if you've never read enough of it to have been disturbed by it. Secondly, they just don't see what relevance it has to their everyday lives. What could a long, complex, ancient and translated book, full of 'thee's and 'thou's, possibly have to say to people's intimate problems today?

So if we want newcomers and even regular churchgoers to make sense of the Bible and read it regularly, we need to make sure we're communicating its message effectively and creatively. We need to give them a flavour of its dynamic, gritty, relevant, life-changing contents – enough to make them want to read it for themselves.

> *A Classic*: A book everyone wants to have read and no one
> wants to read!
> *Mark Twain*

Extra! Extra! Read All About It!

Steve was at a conference for Church leaders on 'Effective Communication'. At lunchtime, the manager of the conference centre asked all the delegates which newspapers they'd like to order for the following morning's breakfast, in roughly what numbers. He asked for a show of hands as he ran through a list of available options, starting with *The Times*. In the days before Rupert Murdoch bought the paper, *The Times* prided itself on the selectiveness of its readership, and gently mocking tones of 'Ooooohh!' came out as some delegates raised their hands and opened themselves up to the allegation of being 'snooty'. Then the other broadsheets followed: the *Telegraph*, the *Independent* and the *Guardian*. Most of the delegates requested one of these. Only those who were trying to earn 'street credibility' opted for the *Daily Mail*, the 'respectable' face of the tabloids and the last paper on the list, earning themselves a few 'tuts' of mock disapproval. Almost without exception these were college-educated men.

Steve, who'd scraped through theological college by the skin of his teeth, was amazed to find that there was no possibility of ordering any other tabloid. Neither the manager nor any of the other delegates even appeared to notice that the *Sun* and the *Mirror* had been left off the list, for example. It never occurred to them that a Christian leader would want to read a 'red-cap' tabloid. Yet with daily sales of over 4 million copies and a daily readership of 12 million, the *Sun* is by far and away the market leader. Between them the *Sun* and the *Mirror* account for nearly half the total daily newspaper sales.

The Bible itself tells us that 'the Word became flesh and lived among us' (John 1:14). In other words, God revealed himself to humanity by becoming human. Living in a particular community, speaking a particular language, God communicated through his Son, making eternal truth brutally relevant to a specific culture. As Marshall McCluhan might have said, and Stephen Gaukroger and David Cohen *do* say in their book *How to Close Your Church in a Decade*, Jesus was the *message*, the content of the good news, as well as the supreme *means* of communication by which God revealed himself.

But looking at Jesus, seeing the world's greatest-ever communicator in action, we notice something intriguing. Whether he was teaching the theologians, talking to the outcasts or addressing large crowds, he invariably spoke *their* language. He used stories, symbols and other visual aids to illustrate his message. He told quirky stories about women losing coins through their floorboards, indiscriminate fishing, crooked businessmen, nagging widows, teenage tearaways and fancy slap-up dinners. He got alongside people, understood them, recognized their fears, their anxieties, their failings, and spoke to them in such a way that they could understand really profound things in really simple ways. And he was always challenging, always demanding a response.

Our preaching and teaching, if it's to be faithfully *Christ*ian, must be more than simply 'rooted' in the Bible: it must also be fully accessible and intelligible to those listening in the pews and front rooms of house groups. Otherwise, as John Smith suggests, it'll be nothing but 'hogwash'. So we too need to get alongside people in our churches and communities to find out what's important in their lives, what they know and understand, and how they take in information. As John Stott puts it in his book *The Contemporary Christian* (taking his cue from the idea of 'doublethink' in George Orwell's *Nineteen Eighty-Four*) we need to learn how to 'double-listen' – which he defines as 'the faculty of listening to two voices at the same time, the voice of God through Scripture and the voices of men and women around us'.

Though more than three-quarters of all daily newspapers sold are tabloids, for example, we often tend to preach and teach in a style that's unashamedly broadsheet. The famous Baptist preacher Charles Spurgeon once said, 'The Christian preacher is one who carries the Bible in one hand, the newspaper in the other … and reads both.' Perhaps we need to rephrase his words:

'The Christian preacher is one who carries the Bible in one hand, a broadsheet and a tabloid in the other ... and reads all three.'

For many the Gospel is news because they have never heard a coherent account of it before.
John Martin, Gospel People

The Good Book Guide

Getting to grips with the language and concepts of the world around us isn't easy, of course. But it's child's play compared to the task of getting to grips with the language and concepts of the Bible. In many ways it's an enormously bewildering book. It spans two thousand years of history at the crossroads of three continents. It was composed over a period of about one thousand years by a multitude of different authors from very different backgrounds. It was written in poetry, prose and song, combining fiction with non-fiction, in three different languages. It addresses the whole gamut of human experience against the backdrop of several distinct and unique political and social situations.

Some Christians act as though not a day has passed since the ink dried on the parchment of Revelation (the last book of the Bible to be written, and coincidentally the last in terms of its running order). They pay little attention to what a passage means in the context of a book or the Bible as a whole, and seem uninterested in the history behind it. Instead, they treat it as if the meaning of its words were self-evident and easy to understand. But as the one-time Bishop of Liverpool, J. C. Ryle, once said, 'The Bible would not be the book of God if it had not deep places here and there which man has no line to fathom.'

The truth is, some of the Bible is very hard to understand. That's why we have sermons, for example, and why preachers are usually expected to have studied the Bible at college for a couple of years before being let loose on a congregation. It's not so much that they need to take in a lot of information – after all, there are plenty of biblical reference books available in any Christian bookshop for that. It's more that they need to develop a feel for the various cultures that inhabit the Bible – so different from our own – and for how it fits together as a whole. These are essential qualities for helping both Christians and people from outside the Church to steer their way through the Bible's wafer-thin pages.

After all, you'd hardly take medical advice from someone who'd never trained as a doctor. Nor would you allow someone who'd never trained as a lawyer to handle your legal affairs. It wouldn't matter how many medical or law books they had access to – they still wouldn't have the background knowledge to make proper use of them. And without this background knowledge, we miss so much of the treasure to be found in the Bible.

Take the humour, for example. As Australian theologian Michael Frost says in his book *Jesus the Fool*, 'In the mists of time, we have lost the insight to see the great humour and comedy of the life of Jesus. Things that would have been quite hilarious, or even mildly amusing, to Jesus' contemporaries are taken all so very gravely today … We miss the humour because of our cultural distance from first-century Palestine. We need to work a little harder and dig a little deeper to find the original intent or the original setting.'

In fact, there's humour throughout the Bible. Paul, for example, indulged in a little sick humour in Galatians 5:12 when he wished that those 'agitators' who insisted on Galatian Christians being circumcised would go all the way and castrate themselves! The image – 'snip a little further down' – is funny by itself, but it gains a little extra depth (and acidity) when you realize as Paul did that, though no man could be fully accepted into the Jewish religion or worship unless they were circumcised, they could *never* be fully accepted if they were castrated (Deuteronomy 23:1). As with so much humour, of course, there's a rich vein of truth as well: by insisting on circumcision as a condition of genuine faith, the 'agitators' were essentially denying the *unconditional love* of God that formed the core of Paul's gospel message to the Galatians.

Frost himself points to the humour involved in Jesus' first recorded miracle, when he turned water into wine at a wedding feast in Cana. Wedding feasts were often week-long events in those days, and the host – whose obligation it was to entertain everyone – would have felt terribly ashamed at running out of wine before the end. In response, Jesus told the servants to *act* as if the huge stone vats of water used for ceremonial washing really contained wine. When you think about it, it's funny: grown men pretending that water is wine … and then finding out that it *is*! Who has the 'last laugh'?

There would have been added mischievous humour in the fact that it was ritual cleansing water – usually a symbol of austerity – that was turned into wine, and then used to fuel the 'good time' being had by all at a party that would have been anything but austere. What's more, the presence of his mother suggests that Jesus had been invited because of a family connection, and had brought his disciples along almost as gate-crashers. The host would have welcomed them, of course, but been only too aware that they were about to set off empty handed on a preaching tour, and so would share the limited stock of wine without bringing anything to contribute to the feast (as was sometimes the custom). Yet suddenly these gate-crashers turned out to have 'brought' not only *more* wine than anyone else, but *better* wine than anyone else!

It's the job of a preacher or house group leader to help people step into the pages of the Bible by 'fleshing out' the 'Word of God' in the Bible – presenting the human-interest or even the humorous side not only of what the Bible means to us today, but what it meant to people when it was first written. This has to be done in a lively, relevant way, of course, if it's to avoid making the Bible seem even more dull and antiquated than it already does to a great many people. But only with this kind of humanizing work can we help people to appreciate the eternal relevance of the Bible's message. As the saying goes, 'God is in the details.'

Kenyan theologian John Mbiti suggests, 'We can add nothing to the Gospel, for this is an eternal gift of God. But Christianity is always a beggar seeking food and drink, cover and shelter from the cultures and times it encounters in its never-ending journeys and wanderings.' It's our job as churches to supply that shelter, so that people can understand what the Bible has to say to them, and learn to appreciate Jesus in all the vivid colour that the New Testament uses to paint him.

If God intended us to pickle our brains and put them aside, if he hadn't wanted us to struggle with the great issues of human history and culture, then he would not have sent us a Middle-Eastern book spanning many centuries and cultures – he would have sent us a small tract.
Australian biker minister John Smith

Food for Life

But it's not only visitors who rarely touch their Bibles. Regular churchgoers, it seems, aren't exactly voracious readers of the Bible either. A survey carried out by the Bible Society in 1997 revealed that, outside church services, nearly two-thirds of churchgoers don't read the Bible regularly, and 18 per cent had never read anything from it at all at *any* time in their lives.

It was always the intention for ordinary people to be able to read and understand the Bible. That's why it was originally written in everyday Hebrew and Aramaic and common Greek. It's also why it was translated into Latin at a time when Latin had replaced Greek as the dominant language in the Western part of the Roman Empire, and why it has been translated into English so many times. Sermons can and should add flavour to people's understanding of the Bible and Jesus (whose story is told in its pages), but they shouldn't be the be-all and end-all of that understanding.

As Christians, we believe the Bible is God inspired, authoritative and life changing. It's 'living and active, sharper than any two-edged sword, piercing until it divides soul from spirit, joints from marrow; it is able to judge the thoughts and intentions of the heart' (Hebrews 3:12). With such a vital resource at our fingertips, our task is to encourage regular churchgoers and visitors alike to discover or rediscover that the Bible is as relevant for our lives today as it was when it was first written.

How we do this will partly depend on the way the Bible is taught in our churches. A complex argument and cerebral expository preaching may win theological points, but half the congregation will be asleep or wondering whether they've remembered to turn on the oven or the video recorder. Rather than nodding in agreement with you, they're likely to be nodding off! They want to learn and to be taught, but they don't want to be bored in the process. And they want answers to the questions and issues they face in their everyday lives.

Millions of people all over the world can testify that the Bible has changed and guided their lives. Actor David Suchet, like many other Christians, found faith by reading the Bible. Lying in a bath in a hotel room, he had a sudden, inexplicable need to read the New Testament again. 'I suddenly discovered the way that life should be followed,' he said. But for many, a motivation for reading the Bible will come as they grow in their understanding of who Jesus was, and is, and in their journey with God. So as churches we need to find interesting and fun ways to help people get to know Jesus better, slowly maturing in their faith in him.

The evangelists shaped and developed the traditions in order to make them relevant to their reader. They felt free to do this because their primary concern was to proclaim the significance of Jesus Christ; they did not intend to summarize what Jesus said and did in the manner of a

modern secretary taking minutes as records of important board meetings.
Graham Stanton, Lady Margaret's Professor of Divinity, Cambridge

Stoking Up

We shouldn't simply rely on Sunday services for our weekly dish of spiritual nourishment. Our bodies require regular doses of vitamins, proteins, carbohydrates, iron, fibre, etc., for us to sustain healthy, productive lives. So we try to eat and drink sensibly. Similarly, we need regular nourishment to feed our spiritual appetites each day.

Of course, we all have different tastes. Brian enjoys egg, sausage, chips and baked beans for supper, washed down by a good beer. Caroline is a gourmet girl, who enjoys liberal amounts of fresh garlic in her Mediterranean dishes, accompanied by a full-bodied claret. They have different tastes and spend varying amounts of time preparing their meals. But, at the end of the day, both are fed, watered and satisfied. In the same way, dfferent people need to find different ways of studying the Bible that works for *them*. For some, it'll be a weekly in-depth study. For others it may mean meditating on just a few verses daily. Yet more rely on the 'quick but reasonably regular gulp' before the baby wakes up demanding to be fed, or before they need to leave the house for work.

Grace and Ian were regular church members. Ian was a church warden. Although he read the lesson in church and was actively involved, he'd found doing any sort of daily Bible readings or study rather dry. He'd used Bible reading notes in the past, but quite frankly had found them a bit of a chore. So he relied on Sunday services for his regular biblical input. When he and Grace heard about a series of audio tapes which went through the New Testament over 40 days, they decided to give it a go. Grace listened in the car after she'd dropped the kids off at school. Ian played the tapes in his Walkman as he commuted to and from work. Neither found it a chore. Rather, they both discovered fresh insights into the New Testament as they *heard* the words of strength and encouragement spoken to them.

Small groups are also part of the exploratory journey. Corporately and individually, guided by God's spirit, we get new insights into biblical passages and move deeper in our relationship with God. As we encounter Jesus and discover more about the Bible, we're motivated to read on, and it's this motivation that keeps us going even when the going gets tough and we feel like giving up.

Many churches run beginners' groups or house groups in their communities for nurturing both new Christians and those who have a long-standing faith. They meet in small groups in someone's home to eat, study the Bible and pray for one another. Through this friendly support system, they learn to care for one another both practically and spiritually. These groups are a vital way of encouraging, teaching and supporting enquirers, new Christians and established Christians throughout the year.

Running a Christian basics course – such as *Emmaus*, *Christianity Explained* or *Alpha* – is another good way of encouraging churchgoers and others to find out more about Jesus in a non-pressured environment. The 10-week Alpha course, pioneered by London's Holy Trinity Church, Brompton 20 years ago, has helped almost a million people explore the Christian faith over the past five years. Members of a church in Manchester decided to run their course in the local pub, as they thought people would find it a more comfortable and familiar environment than a church.

> **God enters the human heart by its own ways: he enters the wise through wisdom; he enters the simple through simplicity.**
> *Assassinated Salvadorian Archbishop Oscar Romero*

Variety...

But what happens when we do give up? Many people feel guilty or that they've failed if they stop their regular Bible study and prayer time, or drop out of the small group system. Others feel suddenly liberated.

It can be good to ring the changes, and a 'sabbatical' from reading the Bible can even be healthy! But as David Cohen warns, if we abandon regular times of Bible study altogether, we are 'throwing the baby out with the bathwater'. The Bible becomes peripheral, with prayer and meditation becoming unfamiliar in our busy, frenetic lives. 'This can only result in a superficial spirituality based on what *I* feel or what *I* think, rather than what *God* wants of me.'

Sometimes we need time to reflect, reappraise what we're doing and change our way of doing things. Jogging round the same circuit at the same time every day, seven days a week, 52 weeks a year, gets very dull and tedious. (Let's be honest, even jogging every day sounds very tedious to many people!) But finding different routes, or different forms of exercise to work out, maintains our enthusiasm and motivation, while keeping us fit and healthy.

Similarly, we may need to be more creative in the way we explore the Bible, the way we pray and listen. Individually, we may want to use different Bible reading notes or tapes, or join up with a friend for a weekly study and prayer time. As a church, we may choose to alternate something like Alpha with a course of our own making, deliberately tailored to the needs of our specific community.

IDEAS

The Bible is our manual for life. We need to help people of all ages and abilities to understand it through effective, creative *communication and preaching*. We can encourage people to explore its relevance to our daily lives through *small groups* and *courses*. And we can encourage and motivate people to spend a regular time *reading*, *praying*, and *listening to God* in creative ways.

Making sense ... through our communication and preaching

- Think of creative ways of communicating the message. Use humour, stories, contemporary illustrations from magazines/ newspapers/TV. Drama, poetry and dance can be really helpful *if* they're well done. Or you may have someone artistic who can paint or bring in a painting, craft, etc. A potter once used a beautiful bowl she'd made to explain the passage about the potter and the clay (Isaiah 64:8).
- If you have the technology, use recorded video clips, vox pops, etc., to reinforce your teaching points. The small, all-age congregation in one church regularly take part in acting out the Bible reading in a contemporary way, which is recorded on a simple camcorder and played back after the service. People of all ages can learn through participation. There's a growing range of video material available from main Christian bookshops, the Bible Society, Scripture Union and other Christian organizations.
- Try something different once in a while! Why not have a short sermon, then get into small groups to carry on with the discussion and teaching (over a cup of coffee).
- Run a 'tour of the Bible' to help people understand how the different books fit into the whole picture and to enable them to get an overview. Most Christians haven't read the whole

Bible. Walk Thru the Bible Ministries run regular seminars. It's best to get someone who can lead the tour effectively!

- Look at creative ways of retelling the Bible. *The Open Book*, produced by the Bible Society, is developing new multi-media resource material.

- Do you have Bibles available in your church for people to follow the readings and sermons? Or encourage people to bring their own Bibles so that, together, you can open up the Scriptures. (It's obviously best for everyone to have the same translation.)

- Encourage those who work with children and young people. They're constantly looking for new ways to make the Bible relevant to the young people's lives and culture.

- Many churches find it helpful to do the Stations of the Cross at Easter. People walk around the church to look at pictures, carvings, etc., that point to the incidents in Jesus' last week of life. There are readings, hymns, prayers and meditations at each station.

- Crib services can be really creative and helpful ways of telling the Christmas story.

- Some churches have found it beneficial to act out the Passion Play in the town marketplace, town square, etc., at Easter. But it *does* need to be done well. If it's done badly, it can send out the wrong message!

Making sense ... through small groups and courses

- Christian basics courses are helpful ways of encouraging people to explore the Bible and discover more about Jesus and the Christian faith. *Alpha* has proved incredibly popular, relaxing over a meal and then exploring in small groups. Holy Trinity Brompton has produced a wide range of books, videos, manuals and other resources for running Alpha groups. *Emmaus* and *Christianity Explained* are among a number of other Christians basics courses used by churches throughout the UK.

- Home groups, beginners' and enquirers' groups are ideal ways of enabling people to study, relax, share and pray in small groups. They're often places of great encouragement as members see prayers answered, feel supported and nurtured. Although some older people don't like going out at night, many of them don't mind hosting a group in their home!

- Make sure you have a small group meeting during the day for people with small children, elderly people, shift workers, etc. Provide a creche for young children, and transport for elderly people, if possible. Have time afterwards to relax over lunch or tea!

- Try varying your communication methods in your small groups. Audio tapes, videos, art, photography, etc., can all be used creatively to help make sense of the Bible and who Jesus is. If you live in the country, why not go for a walk to look at God's creation – as well as relaxing together.

- You could use a resource such as *The Jesus Video*, the dramatization of Luke's Gospel. You could show it in one sitting, or use it as a basis for discussion group or house group material.

- You may like to go on a group retreat, weekend away or holiday. There are a number of organizations who specialize in this, including: Lee Abbey, Iona Community, Ashburnham Prayer Centre, Oak Hall at Otford Manor, Ellel Ministries.

- Children's holiday clubs and youth nights are helpful ways of encouraging young people to explore who Jesus is and to ask questions relevant to their worlds.

Making sense ... through reading, praying and listening to God

- People shouldn't be forced into the daily 'quiet time', so that they start feeling guilty if they miss a day, or get stuck in a rut. But, as we've seen, a regular time of reading, praying and listening to God is vital if we're to be really effective. Many people find Bible reading aids very helpful. There are a wide range of materials for all ages available from Christian bookshops and organizations. Some of the most popular are produced by: Bible Reading Fellowship (*New Daylight*), Scripture Union (*Daily Bread*), CWR (*Everyday with Jesus*), and CPAS.

- There are also a wide variety of resources available for people who want to do more in-depth study. A trip to a Christian bookshop will help you find which material suits you best.

- Audio cassettes are a helpful way of learning, meditating, listening to the Bible, etc. The Bible Society has produced *Faith Comes By Hearing*, which enables you to listen to the New Testament over 40 days, at an average of 28 minutes a day! Cassettes are also useful for people with reading difficulties or visual impairments. A number of Christian organizations are involved in producing readings, meditations, interactive material, etc., on tape. Again, it's worth a visit to your Christian bookshop or a phone call to ask for some catalogues.

- There are a number of distance-learning courses available for people who want to undertake more in-depth study. London Bible College, Moore College and Emmaus Bible School have correspondence course material available.

- If you're stuck in a rut with your readings or prayers, try something different. Go for a walk, use candles and music, write your own psalm, use art and craft if you're creative, go sailing, take time out on your own wherever you feel comfortable – even if it's on your bike or soaking in a bubble bath!

- Take time out by going on a retreat (see above for names of organizations).

RESOURCES

Resources

There are plenty of videos, CD-Roms, audio cassettes, videos and books around to help you make sense of the Bible and who Jesus is. The best way to find out is to pay a visit to your local Christian bookshop. Or phone up Christian organizations for a resource catalogue: e.g. Scripture Union, Bible Society, CPAS, Lion, Agape, Grove Books, Bible Reading Fellowship, Kingsway, International Christian Communications, Word, etc.

You can also look up books, tapes and resources on the *Internet* at: http://www.christianbookshop.com

Taizé also produce a website, featuring daily Bible text, pictures and music, plus requests for prayers: http://www.taizé.fr

Basics resource material

The Open Book. A range of resource material, video clips, service ideas, drama sketches, for helping to open the Bible in creative ways. Available from the Bible Society.

Entertaining Angels. Sixteen fast-paced sketches taking a witty but thought-triggering look at the Bible's importance in finding meaning for everyday living, both for Christians and those outside the Church. Produced by the Bible Society.

Alpha Course resource material available from Holy Trinity Brompton, London.

PACT (Post Alpha Catholic Teaching) for Catholic enquirers. Available from the Catholic Alpha Office.

Christianity Explained and new Christians basics course material available from All Souls Church, London.

Emmaus course material published by Church House Publishing and the Bible Society.

Reel Issues. Ian Maher shows how popular films can be used to help young people understand the Bible. Produced by the Bible Society.

Y2000 Course. An eight-session evangelistic course looking at
Jesus. Produced by Y2000.

Youth Alpha Leaders Manual. To fully equip leaders to run Youth
Alpha in a variety of settings (church groups, schools, etc.).

Distance learning

Emmaus Bible School UK offer 90 different correspondence
courses.

God at Work: A Vision for Workplace Ministry. A biblical
introduction to work by Mark Greene. House group material
and video looking at the workplace. From London Bible College.

London Bible College offer a wide range of biblically based
distance learning courses, with an emphasis on practical
application.

Maryvale Institute, Birmingham. Catholic religious education
centre offering courses and degrees, plus distance learning and
adult studies on Catechism.

Moore College Correspondence Course, Crossways Christian
Education Trust.

Audio cassettes/videos

All Souls Tape Library has a catalogue of sermons on audio
cassettes featuring John Stott, Richard Bewes, Michael
Baughen and other past and present members of the team.

Faith Comes By Hearing. Cassettes of the New Testament available
through the Bible Society, Swindon and the National Bible
Society of Scotland.

The Jesus Video, a dramatization of Luke's Gospel. Available from
Agape.

Retreat centres

Ashburnham Prayer Centre, Ashburnham Place, Battle, East
Sussex TN33 9NF. Tel: 01424 892244.

Ellel Ministries, Ellel Grange, Ellel, Lancaster LA2 OHN.
Tel: 01524 751651.

Iona Abbey, Isle of Iona, Argyll, Scotland PA76. Tel: 01681 700404.

L'Eau Vive Provence, 13122 Ventabren, France. Tel: 00-33-4-42-28-77-53.

Lee Abbey, Lynton, North Devon EX35 6JJ. Tel: 01598 752621.

Oak Hall, Otford Manor, Shorehill Lane, Otford, Kent TN15 6XF. Tel: 01732 763131. Also run weekend breaks on 'exploring the Bible' for individuals and groups.

Quiet Garden Retreat, a chance to rest, pray and simply 'be': Stoke Park Farm, Park Road, Stoke Poges, Bucks SL2 4PG.

Taizé Community, 71250 Taizé, France. Tel: 0033-385503002. Fax: 0033-385503016. Web site: http://www.taize.fr

Agencies

Agape, Fairgate House, King's Road, Tyseley, Birmingham, B11 2AA. Tel: 0121 765 4404.

All Souls Church, 2 All Souls Place, London W1N 3DB. Tel: 0171 580 3522.

Alpha, Holy Trinity Brompton, Brompton Road, London SW7 1JA. Tel: 0171 581 8255. Alpha Hotline: 0345 581278.

Bible Reading Fellowship, Peter's Way, Sandy Lane West, Oxford OX4 5HG. Tel: 01865 748227.

Bible Society, Stonehill Green, Westlea, Swindon SN5 7DG. Tel: 01793 418100.

Catholic Alpha Office, PO Box 333, St Albans, Herts AL2 1EL. Tel: 01727 822837.

Catholic Biblical Association, 6 St Helier House, Melville Road, Edgbaston, Birmingham B16 9NG. Tel: 0121 454 3168.

Church Pastoral Aid Society (CPAS), Athena Drive, Tachbrook Park, Warwick CV34 6NG. Tel: 01926 334242.

CWR, Waverley Abbey House, Waverley Lane, Farnham GU9 8EP. Tel: 01252 783761.

Emmaus Bible School, Carlett Boulevard, Eastham, Wirral, Merseyside L62 8BZ. Tel: 0151 327 1172.

London Bible College, Green Lane, Northwood, Middlesex, HA6 2UW. Tel: 01923 826061.

Maryvale Institute, Maryvale House, Old Oscott Hill, Kingstanding, Birmingham B44 9AG. Tel: 0121 3608118.

Moore College, c/o Crossways Christian Education Trust, 11 Preston Road, London SW20 0SS. Tel: 0181 947 4146.

The National Bible Society of Scotland, 7 Hampton Terrace, Edinburgh EH12 5XU. Tel: 0131 337 9701.

Oak Hall, Otford Manor, Shorehill Lane, Otford, Kent TN15 6XF. Tel: 01732 763131.

Scripture Union, Queensway House, 207–9 Queensway, Bletchley, Milton Keynes, Bucks MK2 2EB. Tel: 01908 856000.

Walk Thru the Bible Ministries, Thorpe Green, Thorpe-le-Soken, Essex CO16 0AA. Tel: 01255 861868.

Y2000, PO Box 94, Chessington, Surrey KT9 2YJ. Tel: 0181 287 3147.

Books

Christian basics

P. Butler and G. Piper, *Following Jesus* (Scripture Union, 1993)

Steve Chalke, *More than Meets the Eye* (Hodder & Stoughton, 1995)

David Cohen and Stephen Gaukroger, *How to Close your Church in a Decade* (Scripture Union, 1992)

Terence Copley and others (ed), *Splashes of God-Light* (Bible Society, 1998)

R. and C. Deverell, *Bible Handbook for Young Readers* (Hunt & Thorpe, 1995)

Michael Frost, *Jesus the Fool* (Lion, 1994)

Stephen Gaukroger, *Being Baptized* (Marshall Pickering, 1993)

Michael Green, *After Alpha* (Kingsway, 1998)

Nicky Gumbel, *A Life Worth Living* (Kingsway, 1994)

Nicky Gumbel, *Questions of Life* (Kingsway, 1993)

C. S. Lewis, *Mere Christianity* (Fontana, 1955)

J. I. Packer, *Knowing God* (Hodder & Stoughton, 1993)

Rob Parsons, *What They Didn't Teach Me in Sunday School* (Hodder & Stoughton, 1997)

Rowena Pasco, *Answers to 101 Questions on the Catechism* (Geoffrey Chapman, 1995)

Mike Pilavachi, *Live the Life* (Hodder & Stoughton, 1998)

Father John Redford, *Faith Alive* (Hodder & Stoughton, 1988)

John Stott, *Basic Christianity* (IVP, 1997)

John Stott, *Understanding the Bible* (Scripture Union, 1998 ed.)

I. C. Wojtyla, *The Way to Christ, Spiritual Exercises from Pope John Paul II* (Harper & Row 1984)

Tom Wright, *The Original Jesus* (Lion, 1996)

Prayer and meditation

Josephine Bax, *Help on the Way: A Guide to Personal Prayer* (Lynx, 1997)

Joni Eareckson Tada, *Diamonds in the Dust: 366 Meditations* (Marshall Pickering, 1993)

Rob Frost, *When I Can't Pray* (Kingsway, 1995)

Joyce Huggett, *Open to God* (Eagle, 1997)

Andrew Knowles, *Discovering Prayer* (Lion, 1993)

Peter Miller, *An Iona Prayer Book* (Canterbury Press, 1998)

Henri Nouwen, *Bread for the Journey* (DLT, 1996)

Brendan O'Malley, *Celtic Blessings* (Canterbury Press, 1998)

Michel Quoist, *Prayers of Life* (Gill & Macmillan, 1963)

Rachel Stowe, *Children at Prayer* (Marshall Pickering, 1996)

Mother Teresa, *The Joy of Loving: Daily Wisdom with Mother Teresa* (Hodder & Stoughton, 1997)

Thank You God: The Prayers of Children (Hunt & Thorpe, 1997)

See also the Resources section in Chapter 6.

Bibles

There is a wide range of Bibles, including:

Classic Devotional Bible (NIV, 1996)
Couples' Devotional Bible (NIV, 1994)
The Lion First Bible (Lion, 1997)
New Light Bible (NIRV, 1998)
New Light Bible Stories (6 years+, Hodder & Stoughton, April 1999)
The Parenting Bible (Zondervan, 1994)
The Tabloid Bible, Nick Page (HarperCollins, 1998)
Thompson Chain Reference Study Bible (NIV, 1990)
Youth Bible (New Century Version, 1993)

8 We Will Make Sure Your Visit Will Be Helpful and Challenging

Preface by Faith Forster

The reasons why we go to church are to gather with other Christians for mutual encouragement and building up, to meet with God himself, and to take hold of spiritual food.

Sometimes it can be hard. Perhaps you don't feel you're doing very well spiritually. Perhaps the church you go to is made up of people who attend regularly, but there's no real bonding together as 'the body of Christ'.

I remember sitting in a service where the preacher's sermon consisted of a nice little story, his own personal thoughts on the subject and a few trips down memory lane. Spiritual input had been largely abandoned. It was hard to find God's presence in that particular church. So I picked up the Bible in front of me and read from the Scriptures while quietly listening to the sermon. Then I opened a prayer book and read a prayer from St Francis of Assisi. God fed me and spoke to me more through those words he had inspired, than in the rest of the service. But obviously this isn't the way it's meant to be!

As a church leader, I'm constantly challenging myself to seek God. How can I expect people in my church to seek him if I am not? It's essential that I continually rest in God and lean on him. If I don't, how can I help others and pray for them – especially when I'm struggling with today's pressures and stresses? I need to be constantly feeding on God.

It's important that we meet with God, at whatever stage we are in our journey of faith. And it's important that we seek to meet with God as a church family. We need to allow God to touch us, to help and challenge us in our daily lives.

We Will Make Sure Your Visit Will Be Helpful and Challenging

Danny felt annoyed and frustrated as he sang the final hymn. In the great scheme of life, the problem wasn't anything major. The garage had just given him a pay rise and things were fine with his girlfriend. The youth group was running really well at the moment and he'd been given the job of organizing a big youth event for the area. His main problem was the church service itself. He'd had a great week away at a Christian festival earlier in the year and, ever since, he'd found church frustrating. He felt the prayers lacked real depth, the music didn't allow for any spontaneity, and as for being a caring church *family* – well, that was a joke! He closed the music book, and sat down with his head in his hands for the final prayer.

Danny's story isn't unique. There are people at churches all over the country who echo his sentiments every week. But in fact, Danny's real problem isn't so much to do with his church as with his attitude. We live in a pick-'n'-mix, consumer society. We may buy Kwik-Save's cakes, for example, but shop at Safeway for sausages. Waitrose may sell the best waffles, but for tasty bread it's off to Tesco's! We're used to choosing the things we like, and that work best for us, like dishes from an *à la carte* menu. It's the key element of our 'postmodern' culture. Rather than choosing the best overall package from the limited number of options available and learning to accept and live with its weak spots, we want a custom-made package tailored to our own unique specifications.

And we often do the same with our churches. We may hold a 'loyalty card' with one, but it won't stop us from nipping off to another every now and again for a quick 'topping up the batteries' session. We may enjoy the biblical teaching in one church, but still want to balance it with the meditative prayer ministry of another, the spiritual gifts of a third, and the social events programme of a fourth.

> **One of the great things about church is that it isn't self-selecting. We don't choose who comes to our church. Everyone is welcome.**
> *Former editor of* Christianity, *Simon Jones*

A Well-balanced Diet

In many ways, there's nothing wrong with this. It's a good, healthy thing to do. We're all growing in our individual relationships with God, and need food and sustenance along the way. We need a well-balanced diet if we're to mature into well-balanced Christians. What's more, it's good for us to experience something of the rich variety of styles and specialisms that the broad Church has to offer – the 'Body of Christ' in all its diversity.

Whether it's a one-off event like a Luis Palau mission, a trip to Israel or a pilgrimage to the site of Bede's old monastery at Jarrow; an annual event like Spring Harvest, Keswick, Greenbelt, Soul Survivor or Prom Praise; or regular attendance at another church for their prayer group, praise meeting or evening service, variety can be the spice of life, pepping us up or pushing us on … and giving us fuel for the journey.

James and Philippa met when they were both spending time with a religious community. Each of them had come to a point in their lives when they weren't sure what to do next or what the future held in store for them, and they had each independently made the decision to spend a month or two with the community in order to 'clear away the clutter and tune in to God's voice', as they put it. They were looking for inspiration ... but they found each other. 'It was amazing,' Philippa said later. 'It was as if God told us to stop what we were doing, clear our diaries and spend a few months in the middle of nowhere just so we could meet each other.' And though they came from different backgrounds – James was brought up Anglo-Catholic, whilst Philippa had been part of a charismatic Free Church tradition – they immediately sensed they were 'made for each other', and were quickly married.

After the wedding, they moved to the small village where James had spent his youth and where his parents still lived. It was a bit of a culture shock for Philippa, who'd grown up in the city. And the village church – there was only one – was even more of a shock to her: Anglo-Catholic to the hilt, complete with smells, bells, canticles and rosaries. At first, they seriously considered attending the lively Methodist church in the next village instead, but felt this would, in some ways, be desertion: James had grown up in the village church, and it felt like home to him. Eventually they hit on what seemed like the perfect arrangement – they joined the village church, getting involved in the Sunday school and the small house group, but balanced this out by going to the evening service in a large charismatic church in the nearby town for the more modern, informal worship they'd come to appreciate.

Tonight's sermon: 'What Is Hell?'
Come early and listen to our choir practice.
Note in a church service sheet

On the Side

But there *is* a downside to all this as well. For one thing, it can make us rather 'spoilt for choice' when it comes to how we like our spiritual nourishment. Rather than settling for what's put down in front of us, as we once *had* to do, we now have the opportunity to pick-'n'-mix our way to the perfect 'designer' service or set of activities. We become more and more 'high maintenance', as Billy Crystal describes Meg Ryan in the film *When Harry Met Sally*. Not only does Sally insist on ordering food from the *à la carte* menu, but she's very fussy about how she wants it, with a lot of things being served 'on the side'.

'"On the side" is a big thing for you,' he says.

'I just want it the way I want it,' she replies.

'I know,' he says. 'High maintenance.'

But the more we become used to having things the way we want them, the less tolerant we become when they're not like that. In addition, we become more demanding of those whose responsibility it is to arrange the services for us. There's a distinct danger of 'spoilt for choice' slipping smoothly and silently into plain, old-fashioned 'spoilt'.

The second downside is that, like Danny, the chances are that we'll eventually become frustrated that we can't have the kind of worship, teaching, prayer meetings, small group work or family atmosphere in our local church that we're getting elsewhere. The problem with this, of course, is that everyone's idea of 'perfect' is subtly – and often not-so-subtly – different. The difference between designing a church service and choosing items from an *à la carte* menu is that, when it comes to the church service, we're forced to impose our choices on everyone else or not have them at all. In other words, if we're to be at all responsible in the way we arrange services, we'll have to take account of what's best for others rather than insisting on the type of thing we personally would opt for if given a free choice.

At heart, as any leader will tell you, church is a massive exercise in compromise.

But there's a third reason, as well, why our pick-'n'-mix approach to church is potentially problematic. Danny's attitude, for example, illustrates it perfectly. Without meaning to, he'd become very self-centred in his approach to church. His frustration and dissatisfaction stemmed largely from his feeling that he wasn't really *getting enough out of* his church. He never fully stopped to think about whether or not he was *putting enough into* the worship and service. His main approach to church was *consumerist*: 'What's in it for me?' And this is the wrong question.

The 1994 Finding Faith survey suggests that he's far from alone. Seventy-five per cent of people questioned said they went to church because they enjoyed the worship. The next most popular reason given for going to church was 'a sense of belonging' and fitting in. Other reasons included: the support churches give in living out one's faith; the friendliness of the people in the church; the sense of being drawn closer to God; the personal ministry of the vicar or pastor; and the chance to thank God and pray for one's needs. All good reasons, you'd think. But interestingly, six of these reasons are consumerist in their approach. The last (and least popular) one is *half*-centred on the consumer.

> **The problem with the church is that for years, it has either been pulpit-centred or altar-centred, according to our different traditions. In both situations the dominant role has been played by the minister or priest.**
> *Alpha course 'guru' Nicky Gumbel*

Christmas Presence

Jane and Jamie love Christmas. They particularly enjoy the moment on Christmas morning when it's time to unwrap the presents under the tree, but they enjoy it for very different reasons. At just four years of age, Jamie can hardly contain his excitement as he rips open the paper and hurls it enthusiastically into the air. The pure joy on his face as he discovers a tractor or a game is plain for all to see. For him, the enjoyment of 'pressie time' consists of receiving presents and seeing what's inside them. They're not only something new and exciting to play with, they're also a tangible reminder of how much his mum loves him.

Jane, on the other hand, doesn't get so excited at the prospect of opening her presents. At 34, she can usually guess their contents without needing to touch the wrapping paper: the annual store of notelets, the bottle of wine, the latest P. D. James book. Her family are generous, but predictable. What's more, with the passing of each year she's learnt to appreciate more and more the truth of Jesus' words, 'It is more blessed to give than to receive' (Acts 20:35). In fact, she's every bit as excited as her son Jamie when he discovers the gifts she's chosen for him. She loves to see his little hands gripping the present, tearing off the wrapping and opening up what she jokingly calls 'Pandora's Box'. His sparkling, big brown eyes, his squeals of delight and his grin from ear to ear say it all! Jamie loves *receiving* presents, Jane loves *giving* them.

To a large extent, this is a feature of maturity. As Jamie gets older, he'll gradually find it easier to wait for the present-opening time on Christmas Day rather than pestering Jane every 20 minutes with questions like, 'Can I open a pressie now, *please*?' He'll find that it's not so essential to rip the paper open in record time; in fact, he may even learn to savour the experience, deliberately taking his time so as to make it last longer. And he'll slowly discover that *giving* presents can be even more enjoyable than *getting* them.

In the same way, when they first become Christians, people are far more aware of their own needs and desires than they are of the needs and desires of other people. There's an understandable period of 'intensive nutrition', like a baby suckling, during which they need to be fed and to grow. There's nothing wrong with this whatsoever. In fact, it's essential. Peter used just this imagery when he encouraged new Christians, 'like newborn infants', to 'long for the pure, spiritual milk, so that by it you may grow into salvation' (1 Peter 2:2).

The problem comes when we're allowed or encouraged to continue this intensive 'feed me' approach to our faith past an appropriate 'age'. Our 'spiritual hunger', when added to the hugely consumerist approach to life ('give me') taken by most of society, conspires to keep us like children: often kind and generous, but still more preoccupied with receiving than with giving. Both Paul (1 Corinthians 3:1–3) and the anonymous writer of Hebrews (5:11–13) chastized some of those church members they were writing to for remaining as 'infants' in need of 'milk', rather than graduating to 'solid food'. Paul, for one, made it clear that the proof of this infancy was 'jealousy and quarrelling' – in other words, a 'me'-centred approach to their faith.

The Church's job is to help people move on in their journey with God, at whatever stage they are. Through prayers, liturgy, readings, music, silence, fellowship, whatever forms we use in our services, we're called to help people develop and grow in their relationship with God. But relationships are a two-way process, and they can't develop if one person is unable to move beyond the point where all they can do is receive. If we're constantly looking for what we can get out of a relationship – love, support, care, friendship, etc. – but aren't prepared to give anything back, it'll soon become a lop-sided relationship and our character will fail to develop as it should. If we concentrate on what we can get out of our relationship with God and the Church, our lives will become poorer and more frustrated.

It's essential, therefore, that the visitors to our churches and the people around us who show an interest in spiritual things aren't allowed simply to become passive recipients. A quick glance at most of the 'alternative spiritualities' being peddled and promoted through New Age outlets and in the media is enough to reveal a universal trend: almost without exception, they emphasize and appeal to personal, individual satisfaction. They don't offer people a chance to become active players in society and the world. And that's just where the gospel packs its biggest challenge.

> **An individual has not started living until he can rise above the narrow confines of his individualistic concerns to the broader concerns of all humanity.**
> *Martin Luther King*

The View from the Terraces

The dynamics of most churches are similar to one another. Regardless of their size, style, status, wealth, location or denomination, a relatively small proportion of the congregation is left to do most of the work. Some observers have likened church to a football match: 22 players in need of a rest being watched and cheered on by 22,000 fans in need of exercise!

Nineteenth-century Italian economist Vilfredo Pareto is credited with having discovered that 80 per cent of Italy's wealth was owned by just 20 per cent of its people. Known as Pareto's 80:20 Law, this 'rule' has since been found in a number of other areas of life, including churches. So the odds are, around 80 per cent of the work in your church is being done by just 20 per cent of the members.

There are, of course, many reasons for this, but the main one is undoubtedly that we've been encouraged – by both society and the way in which the Church historically organized its leadership

– to see religion as a spectator sport, with ourselves as individual spectators. We don't see ourselves as part of the team, nor do we have all that much to do with any of the other 'fans' during the rest of the week. We may cheer loudly beside them on the terraces, sing the same anthems when our team is winning and share a word or two of commiseration when things aren't going well, but we don't really *know* any of them. We rarely, if ever, socialize with them on non-match days or go for a drink with them outside the confines of the stadium.

This feeling of being spectators rather than players is reinforced by the architecture in so many of our churches. Many older buildings are usually arranged a bit like a plane or a No. 57 bus, with everyone facing the front and trusting the priest as the 'driver' to get them to where they're meant to be going. Some even have what's called a 'rood screen' separating the clergy and the altar off from the rest of the congregation, a bit like a driver's cockpit. In fact, historically, this arrangement *was* meant to represent a journey (though not a motorized one!), or pilgrimage, with the whole congregation headed in the same direction and arranged like fellow travellers.

By contrast, many nineteenth-century Nonconformist churches – built to emphasize the importance of sound biblical preaching – are arranged more like music halls, complete with a spectators' gallery, but with a raised pulpit where the stage (or altar) would have been. Since the mid-twentieth century, most Nonconformist church buildings have tended to resemble schools more than anything else, often with a raised platform at the front. In each case, church members have been arranged in a face-the-front type of way, with their gaze directed at goings-on ahead of them rather than at their fellow 'spectators'.

The result of this 'spectator' attitude has been that, rather than being the *highlight* of our life together as a church, Sunday services are for many of us the be-all and end-all of our life together. When we *do* meet during the week – at a house group, prayer meeting, etc. – we often do so unconsciously seeing ourselves as fellow spectators. There is a deep-seated notion in all of us that we're really just rank amateurs at heart, and that at best we play a supporting role to our priests and pastors – the professionals who form the 'team'. So, though many churches work hard to encourage members to play a full role in house groups, for instance, house group leaders (rarely ministers, but usually part of the overworked 20 per cent) up and down the country will tell you that it can often feel like pulling teeth to get people to chip in.

As the third millennium has approached, however, there are real signs that the tide is at last beginning to turn. The charismatic movement, choruses, team ministries, the explosion of plain English-language Bibles, and courses such as Alpha have all helped to shift the emphasis away from the minister back towards the congregation.

Social changes have also helped. The trend towards part-time work (as well as the dearth of ministers) has given rise to the part-time priest or pastor, helping to break down the old them-and-us division between 'clergy' and 'laity'. The slow decline of the class system and the onset of postmodernism have eroded our sense of our 'proper place in society' and our respect for 'institutions' as such, with the result that we no longer feel compelled to 'sit there and take it'. And the technological revolution has altered the way we see education and entertainment, giving us a much more interactive, 'hands-on' approach.

The danger for the Church in the third millennium is not therefore that its members will see themselves as spectators. Instead, thanks to the rise of postmodernism's pick-'n'-mix mentality, we're faced with the probability that church members will increasingly come to see themselves as consumers – with all the rights and expectations that entails.

Heckler: 'What's it like being a professional Christian?'
Donald Soper: 'Very much the same as being an amateur, except I don't make so much money.'

Being There

When Richard and Helena moved into a new area, literally oppo-site the local Methodist church, they felt they couldn't have asked for a clearer sign from God about which church to join. They'd both wanted to join a *local* church, and figured they couldn't get more local than across the road. Helena's mum – brought up to treasure the Bible and taught by her Baptist origins to see good sermons as a vital ingredient in any healthy church – was more cautious. 'I don't care where you go,' she told them, loving con-cern written all over her face, 'just as long as you're well "fed".' Richard, brought up in a Catholic environment to see commu-nion as every bit as vital as preaching, resisted the temptation to suggest that the bread and the wine were likely to prove a better source of nutrition than the sermon. He did, however, snap back, 'It's a church, not a restaurant.'

For Richard, being 'fed' wasn't the most important reason for going to church. Nor was the worship, the support, the friend-ship, the sense of belonging, or the sense of being close to God – all given as reasons for going to church in the 1994 Finding Faith survey. Both he and Helena found it just as easy – or sometimes easier – to be fed, worshipful, supported, befriended, 'belonged' and close to God in other ways. They tended to get more targeted teaching through reading the Bible or other books than they did from church, and found that the strongest support to their faith actually came from a close circle of friends, drawn up over many years, who lived in other parts of the city and the country. As for worship, like many of their friends they generally found it easier to praise their creator in wide-open green spaces than in the con-fines of a small, inner-city building!

What mattered to Richard and Helena wasn't being *fed*, but being *there*. 'Church isn't about what you can get *out* of it,' Richard remarked. 'It's about what you can put *into* it. It's about being part of the body, part of a family. When you're a kid, you need stuff from your mum or dad, and other members of your family. But as you get older, you learn to get those things from other people or to cope yourself. So the relationship changes. I think it's the same with church. It's good to get stuff out of it, and I often do. But I go because it's my "family". It's more like a family gathering than a restaurant. There's food there, but you have to bring some of it yourself!'

Most of the people who will cross the threshold of our churches in the new millennium will see both this world and the next in a very consumerist way, in terms of what they can personally get out of it. They won't hesitate to pick what they like from the gospel, reject what they don't, and mix the remainder together with borrowed snippets from other old creeds and traditions in order to construct a form of 'postmodern' gospel tailor-made to their own requirements.

The *authentic* gospel, however, is always a challenge. Paul called it 'a stumbling block to Jews and foolishness to Gentiles', but warned that it was a stumbling block that would shame the strong and a foolishness that would shame the wise (1 Corinthians 1:23–9). So part of our task at the dawn of the new millennium is to challenge people's self-centred, consumerist approaches both to church and to the rest of life, modelling instead a way of living and being there for each other that demonstrates the truth of Jesus' claim, 'It is better to give than to receive.'

In his book *Struggling to Believe*, Simon Jones remembers the first time he encountered this way of being church, intriguingly (in view of the earlier section on church buildings) in an architecturally in-the-round building.

I remember standing in the modern amphitheatre of the university church of Brunswick in Manchester, aware of the other people worshipping with me, and able to see their faces rather than just the backs of their necks. I found myself laughing out loud. It wasn't funny. The preacher wasn't cracking jokes; the worship leader's trousers hadn't fallen down ... I was laughing for joy because I realized in my heart what I had been wrestling with in my mind: God has given me all these people to help me live my life in the world. I am not alone. I do not have to make my way to the pearly gates as a solitary traveller, a sort of spiritual Ranulph Fiennes, pulling my sled solo through the wilderness, frost-bitten, existing on survival rations, with only an unreliable satellite link to an unseen mission control for company.

IDEAS

As we've seen, the task of our churches is to help people in our communities move on in their journey with God: through exploring who God is; through prayers, music, fellowship, liturgy, readings, teaching; through practical and caring action, etc. We've already discussed ways of encouraging these areas in earlier chapters. As we help people grow in their relationship with God – wherever they're at – we need to recognize, too, that a relationship demands a response and the gospel is challenging. Rather than expecting to get things *from* the church and our communities, we need to seek ways of *giving – of our time, of our talents and gifts*, and *of ourselves*.

Giving of our time

- Try to do a 'time survey' of a typical week in your life. At the end of each day, analyse how much time you've spent: giving out to others (practical action, plus listening to the kids, etc.), receiving from others, and time with God. Work out the totals at the end of the week and see if there are any areas that need balancing out! (If a week seems too onerous, try a day. But you'll get a better overall view if you manage to do it for a week.)
- Are there any voluntary groups that are looking for help (e.g. lunch club for the elderly, youth club, Brownies, Scouts, etc.,

among disabled and elderly people, with the homeless, a local charity, the unemployed, etc.)

- If you're a parent with school-age children, are you involved in the Parent Teacher Association? Would you consider becoming a school governor?
- Find out if your school needs a classroom assistant. There may be opportunities for helping children with reading skills, story-telling, etc.
- Is there a neighbour or someone you know who would benefit from: a listening ear, transport, shopping, baby-sitting, help with gardening, freezer meals, a visit, etc?
- Full-time carers are often in need of an hour or two when they can go shopping, or spend 'time out'. If you know someone who's a carer, offer to 'baby-sit' so they can have a break.
- If you need help in your church, make sure people know! Have a 'We Need You!' section on your notice sheet and on your noticeboard, advertising where you need help: looking after the church grounds, Sunday school, coffee rota, PA system, welcome team, magazine distribution, prayer team, admin. skills, etc.).
- Get involved in the church! Find out if there are any areas that need your help – don't wait to be asked.
- Make sure people at church feel they *belong*. Chat over coffee after the service, have social events. Encourage them to feel a part of the family.

Giving of our talents and gifts

- If you have musical skills, would you consider offering to help out at recorder clubs, etc.? Many schools are being forced to drop 'extracurricular activities' such as sports, music, drama, etc., because of funding pressures.
- Help out at a local charity shop. Most high streets have at least one charity shop and they're usually looking for help.

- Do you have technical skills? See if there are any ways in which you might be able to help in your church (advice, practical help, etc.) and/or in your community (school production, music society, youth club, hostel for the homeless, town pageant, etc.).
- If you have business skills, could you help someone who's wanting to set up a small business, someone who's running a charity, a voluntary group, etc.?
- 'Mentoring' in all areas is a great way of passing on valuable skills and encouraging others.
- Get involved in social action in your community. See Chapter 4 for more ideas and suggestions.
- Your church needs you! You've been given God-given gifts. Are there any ways you can use them in your church?
- If you're part of the church leadership team, encourage people to *explore* and *use* their gifts and allow them opportunities for using them! Give them an opportunity to use their talent – don't let the church abuse it!
- Encourage people to get involved in the church. Belonging and taking part in services and the life of the church/community, will help their faith to grow, wherever they're at in their relationship with God.
- Give of your money and give as much as you can! There are a range of ways of doing this: from little and often, to regular standing orders, Gift Aid, legacies, etc.

Giving of ourselves

- Spend time with people. Be available for members of your family, your friends, your neighbours. Try to build in some time each week when you can 'be there' for them.
- Spend time with God. As we've seen, relationships are two-way and we need to make sure we're giving of ourselves to God. Chapter 6 has a range of ideas and suggestions to help you.

- Support your local church! It's easier to criticize than to praise what the church is doing. Remember, we're called to be *engaged* in our churches and communities. Don't concentrate on 'what can I get out of church', rather find ways in which you can *put in* to the church.
- Support charities or causes you feel passionate about or have a personal connection with. Charities and voluntary groups need long-term commitment.

RESOURCES

Resources

Love in Action. A comprehensive resource pack with loads of practical advice to help churches engage in social action. Plus plenty of suggestions to get you going. Available from The Shaftesbury Society.

Generation to Generation. A resource pack encouraging you to support your local school in a whole variety of ways. Suggestions and practical advice for churches. Available from Fanfare for a New Generation.

The Voluntary Agencies Directory. The charities' equivalent of the Yellow Pages, produced by the National Council for Voluntary Organisations.

Running a Local Fundraising Campaign. A 'how-to' guide for small voluntary organizations, by Janet Hilderley. Available from the Charities Aid Foundation.

See also Resources sections in other chapters.

Agencies

Charities Aid Foundation, Kings Hill, West Malling, ME19 4TE.
   Tel: 01732 520000.
Contact the Elderly, 15 Henrietta Street, Covent Garden,
   London WC2E 8QH. Tel: 0171 240 0630.
Fanfare for a New Generation, 115 Southwark Bridge Road,
   London SE1 0AX. Tel: 0171 450 9070/1. E-mail:
   fanfare@btconnect.com
Inland Revenue: Gift Aid Helpline: 0151 472 6038. Covenants
   Helpline: 0151 472 6037.
National Council for Voluntary Organisations, Regent's Wharf,
   8 All Saints Street, London N1 9RL. Tel: 0171 713 6161.
The Shaftesbury Society, 16 Kingston Road, London SW19 1JZ.
   Tel: 0181 239 5555.

See also Agencies sections in other chapters.

Books

Steve Chalke and Sir Cliff Richard, *Get Up and Give*
   (HarperCollins, 1998)
Michael Fanstone, *The Sheep that Got Away* (Marc, 1993)
John Finney, *Finding Faith Today* (Bible Society, 1994)
Michael Green, *After Alpha* (Kingsway, 1998)
Michael Green, *Evangelism for Amateurs* (Hodder & Stoughton,
   1998)
Mike Hill, *Reaching the Unchurched* (Alpha 1994)
Simon Jones, *Struggling to Believe* (IVP 1998)

See also Books sections in other chapters.

9 We Will Help You Discover for Yourself God's Love, Acceptance and Forgiveness

Preface by Archbishop George Carey and Faith Forster

Archbishop George Carey on discovering God's love and acceptance

This can only come from human acceptance of others. I recall a man in Durham in the University. He came to see me one day and said: 'I've been going to church for years, but I feel so unworthy. How do I know that God loves me? How can I be sure?'

As I got to know him, I found out that he was an only child of an ambitious mother. From his earliest years she'd drummed into him her own anxiety, and in order to get him to excel used to say: 'You're not good enough. You're not trying. You're useless!' So, as a man of 45, now a lecturer in biology, he felt unworthy, useless and unloved. It was only in the context of an accepting and loving Christian fellowship that he found the love of God and began to enjoy what he already knew deep down.

However, the statement above assumes one very true thing – that ordinary people are capable of going deeper into their spiritual natures. Work from the assumption that everyone is made in the image and likeness of God ... but we really need these days to become less churchy, less clerical, less overtly religious. So simple ways of expressing Christian truth are needed.

Faith Forster on discovering God's forgiveness

As human beings we quickly feel a sense of guilt. We're aware of right and wrong. So often we come to God, seeking forgiveness, weighed down by guilt. But we need to remember that our confession is of *faith* as well as *sin*.

If we look at the Lord's Prayer, we see it starts with the confession of faith. We come to 'Our Father', we depend upon him daily for our needs. Then comes the confession of sin. How often do we get the order the wrong way round?

After Nehemiah had rebuilt the city walls of Jerusalem, Ezra led the Israelites in prayers of commitment to God. They looked back over God's faithfulness and provision *before* admitting their own failings and those of previous generations. Their prayers and worship then focused again on the faithfulness of God.

When we acknowledge God and who he is, it gives us the power and the understanding to know that our sins – no matter how big or small – really are forgiven. But in being forgiven, we're called to forgive others. So, as we're forgiven, we're empowered and released to forgive others – whatever they may have done.

Rather than holding on to a memory of our sin, we need to develop a knowledge and understanding of God and who he is – to discover for ourselves God's love, acceptance and forgiveness.

We Will Help You Discover for Yourself God's Love, Acceptance and Forgiveness

Darren and Jackie had been married for 30 years. They seemed like the 'golden couple'. He was a successful businessman at the peak of his profession, she was an attractive wife, mother and grandmother. They lived in a beautiful home, and they were active and popular members of their local church. In short, they 'had it all'. So when people discovered that Darren, an attractive and charismatic man, had been having an affair with a work colleague for five years, they were stunned. Jackie had known about the relationship. There'd been many angry scenes and fights, including one incident when she'd picked up the TV set and hurled it at Darren. But once outside their front door, they presented themselves to the world in general as the perfect, loving, united couple.

Once news of Darren's affair broke, he felt it was only fair to leave Jackie and the church. He didn't want to be seen as hypocritical. He knew he'd made life very tough for Jackie and the family. He knew he was in the wrong, but he'd never actively planned for any of this to happen. An acrimonious separation followed. His children wouldn't talk to him, nor would they let him see his grandchildren. When his affair petered out, Darren didn't go 'back home' – it was too late for that. Over the next couple of years relations with Jackie became less acrimonious and his children gradually made contact with him again.

Then Jackie was diagnosed as having inoperable, terminal cancer. The whole family was devastated. Darren and Jackie's frosty relationship gradually thawed, spurred on by Jackie's determination not to die angry with Darren. They talked about their marriage, and where they'd allowed it to go wrong. They recognized the faults which had led to the breakdown of their relationship. Slowly, a new friendship and respect developed between them. Though they knew they couldn't live together again as husband and wife, Darren moved back into the family home to look after

Jackie. Before she died, they asked each other for forgiveness for the pain they'd caused. Reconciliation at a price, but Jackie died in peace.

> Forgiveness is a catalyst creating the atmosphere necessary for a fresh start and a new beginning.
> *Martin Luther King*

If Only...

We live in a materialistic world of consumables: a society that propounds a philosophy of money, ambition, greed and success. It's a philosophy that feeds our cravings for money, power and sex – cravings that are frequently confused with our three basic needs as human beings: security, significance and love.

At 16, Jane Eyre (no relation to the fictional character) was a tall, slim, pretty and bright teenager. At 25, she'd undergone three breast-enlargement operations, bleached her brown hair peroxide blonde, and changed her name to Ashley Bond. What triggered off her transformation into 'a living Barbie doll'? 'I knew I could earn lots of money fast while I was still young,' she told *Daily Mail* reporters in 1998. She was given some 'fabulous opportunities' modelling for men's magazines, was 'invited onto Fergie's Chat Show, and I'll be starring in other shows, too – isn't that every girl's dream?' Fame and wealth, it seems, are to be achieved at all costs. But why?

The truth is, we're vulnerable. We tend to think that people will only like or love us when we do well, when we succeed, when we've earned the right to be loved. We think love is conditional, like the child who offers to be your best friend ... so long as you give them your last Rolo. Or the expensive gifts you shower on the kids because you only see them every other weekend. We feel we have to earn love. It stems from the same childhood fear and insecurity that whispers on the playground, 'Please pick me to be in your team. Don't reject me.'

When Jeremy started to climb the merchant-banking ladder, his ambition was to buy his own flat in an exclusive part of the city. Three years later, he drew up in his Porsche to his new three-bedroom apartment overlooking the river. 'So, you've got your Porsche, your job and your Docklands flat,' said Gemma, who'd known Jeremy at university. 'What's next?' Without a moment's hesitation, Jeremy replied, 'To earn a million by the time I'm 40. Then I'll settle down, take it easy and be happy.' A knowing smile flickered across Gemma's lips. 'No, Jeremy,' she said. 'Once you earn a million, you'll want another. And then another. Don't delude yourself.'

Gemma had met Jeremy's father, a hugely successful entrepreneur before his untimely death from a heart attack at the age of 47. She knew that a large part of Jeremy's drive to succeed came from a deep-seated need to prove himself to his dad, to earn his love and respect even though he was gone. And she knew that, in all probability, he'd fail, because he'd never reach the point where he could hear his father whispering in his ear, 'It's okay, son. You've done enough. I love you now.' Of course, Jeremy's father had loved him *anyway*, but he'd never been good at showing it. As a result, Jeremy had grown up feeling he had to *do* something in order to win his dad's love and approval.

For Jeremy, the need to feel loved and accepted had set him on the treadmill towards success, and having tasted the fruits of that success, he was hooked. As the ancient Greek philosopher Epicurus put it, 'Nothing is enough for the person for whom "enough" is too little.' But most of us are on one treadmill or another, desperately looking for love and acceptance yet unable to accept it when it comes. Everything becomes 'if only'. If only I were thin, people would love me. If only I were beautiful, people would love me. If only I were clever, people would love me. If only I were successful, people would love me. If only I were good at sport, people would love me...

It never works like this, of course. If we *do* get thin or success-ful, then we're still not satisfied. Our achievement has a hollow ring to it, like climbing a hill and seeing when we get to the top, not only that it *wasn't* as steep and difficult a climb as we'd ini-tially thought, but that there's another hill behind it, and probably another one as well behind that. We never feel that we've *really* made it. Instead, we find another reason why we think people can't love us, and focus our 'if only' sentiments on that. Pretty soon, this swings around, and we start to feel that if we lose what we've done or become, people will stop loving us.

Love takes off the masks that we fear we cannot live without and know we cannot live within.
American novelist James Baldwin

No Strings Attached?

People simply want to be loved ... and loved simply. But for many of us, love comes with strings attached. People seem to love us only for what we can do for them. Sadly, we see the scars and the debris littered all around us: greed, power, promiscuity, the need to please, emotional and physical abuse, lack of self-esteem, con-cern for self-image, eating disorders, etc.

Sarah was trying to get into broadcasting. She'd just given up her job and was doing temporary secretarial work to give her the freedom to do the rounds of meetings with TV and radio produ-cers and occasional media work. When she told this to various people at an annual Christmas drinks party hosted by her friends Tom and Zoe, however, she found that they virtually ignored her. She discovered that 'temping' was a bit of a conversation stopper, and her self-confidence took a rapid nose dive. For the rest of the evening, she was treated as a pariah. But the following year, having landed a job in TV at the BBC, she found that the same people who'd avoided her like the plague before were swarming round her like bees, wanting to know about all the celebrities she worked with. Sarah was shocked at how fickle and shallow it all seemed, and thanked God that at least Tom and Zoe weren't like their 'fair-weather friends'.

At heart, perhaps, motivated by greed, we do form some of our friendships on the basis of what other people can do for us, and then imagine that they'll only love us on the same self-interested basis. But virtually all of us have loved someone unconditionally at some point in our lives, even if we haven't done it very faithfully or very well. And most of us, if we thought about it, could suggest at least one person who loves us with no – or at least very few – strings attached. But still, accepting that people love us for who we are, without preconditions, can be immensely hard.

We've all been hurt, and most of us have therefore built defence mechanisms against the possibility of being hurt in the future. The most basic of these mechanisms is the refusal to believe that other people love us unconditionally. The logic of this is simple: if we never allow ourselves to believe that someone loves us for who we *really* are, then when they let us down we can at least console ourselves with the knowledge that, since they never *loved* the 'real' us, they never *rejected* the 'real' us either. But it's a bit of a booby prize.

What's more, it's a crippling vicious circle. The more we refuse to believe that others *do* love us unconditionally, the harder it becomes for us to believe that others *could* love us unconditionally. At some point everyone lets us down. It's not surprising, really: after all, none of us is perfect. But strangely enough, when they *do* let us down, we tend to assume that the fault lies with *us*, not *them*. We harbour a deep, dark suspicion that, when other people fail us and reject us, it's because we deserve to be failed and rejected. And that just makes it even harder for us to believe that anyone could love us unconditionally.

Our feelings of inadequacy – that we don't deserve love – are reinforced by the images that bombard us from newspapers, magazines, advertising hoardings, TV programmes and the like. We're surrounded by subliminal, and often deliberate, attempts to make us aspire to the perfect shape, perfect looks and perfect lifestyle.

In contrast to these highly conditional forms of love, the gospel blows in like a cool, refreshing summer breeze.

> **Don't go changing to try and please me – you never let me down before**
> **Don't imagine you're too familiar and I don't see you anymore.**
> **Billy Joel, 'Just the Way You Are'**

Just the Way You Are

Tony Campolo tells the story of how he once sat in Business Class on an internal flight in the USA across the aisle from a 10-year-old girl on her way home alone from boarding school. Though he was meant to be catching up on some work, he found himself constantly being distracted by the girl's behaviour. She seemed to be eating and drinking everything that was put in front of her, then demanding more from the flight attendants. Tony, recognizing it was probably her first solo flight, grew a little concerned. As they came to land, he saw that she was looking decidedly green. And as she disembarked, sure enough, she was sick all down the front of her dress. Being a preacher, Tony filed the story away in his memory under 'what goes down must come up', and thought nothing more of it. As the poor flight attendants tried their best to clean her up, he concentrated on getting to the terminal.

But as he was heading towards the terminal building, he noticed a man in an expensive white suit running towards the plane, a big grin on his face. He knew at once this was the girl's father, and watched with curiosity to see what he'd do next. To his amazement, though he could see that her dress was soiled, the father flung his arms round his daughter and picked her up, enfolding her in a great big hug. Tony smiled as father and daughter walked back to the terminal building, the immaculate white suit now permanently stained. Looking into the dad's eyes, all Tony could see was his pure delight at having his daughter back with him again. *That's* unconditional love. And *that's* how God loves us. We're made in his image and he knows us and accepts us exactly as we are: warts and all. We're not manufactured from the latest identikit. As the psalmist (Psalm 139:13–17) wrote:

> It was you who formed my inward parts; you knit me together in my mother's womb. I praise you, for I am fearfully and wonderfully made. Wonderful are your works; that I know very well. My frame was not hidden from you, when I was being made in secret, intricately woven in the depths of the earth. Your eyes beheld my unformed substance. In your book were written all the days that were formed for me, when none of them as yet existed. How weighty to me are your thoughts, O God! How vast is the sum of them.

In other words, God knows us inside out. The *real* us. Not the 'us' we project to people, consciously or not. And not the 'us' we'd like to be. But the 'us' we hide away just in case people don't like us. The 'us' we fear, in the deepest recesses of our hearts, is fundamentally unlovable. God knows us *and* loves us. Not conditional love. Not 'if-only' love. Not 'fair-weather' love. But full, unashamed, all-the-way, can't-help-yourself kind of love. As John puts it (1 John 4:10), 'In this is love, not that we loved God but that he loved us and sent his Son to be the atoning sacrifice for our sins.'

The realization that the Lord loves us and the acceptance of the unmerited gift of the Lord's love are the deepest source of the joy of those who live by God's word.
Peruvian theologian Gustavo Gutierrez

Free Love

But although this kind of love is what we're all after, it's incredibly hard to accept ... even for Christians. A great many Christians, whilst feeling sure of *their* love for God, lack the assurance of God's love for *them*. As a result, they find themselves working tirelessly for God, reading and praying, but all the while feeling a need to earn his love.

In his book *What They Didn't Teach Me in Sunday School*, Rob Parsons tells of a time when, though he'd been a Christian for many years, he used to live 'as though God was constantly looking over the balcony of heaven just waiting for me to prove myself to him'. On days when he'd prayed, made an effort to be nice to the man in the office next to his, and attended an evening church meeting, he fell into bed exhausted. He didn't feel at all liberated – it was just one long, hard slog. On days when he didn't pray, he felt guilty and not good enough to be labelled a Christian. And then, one day, someone told him something that totally revolutionized his life: 'God is *for* you! He's for you when you succeed and when you fail. He's for you when your heart is filled with certainty and your head is filled with doubt. He's for you when you share the faith with thousands and when you deny him.' Rob suddenly realized that God really was on *his* side!

Of course, because this runs completely counter to everything society seems to tell us, it can be a pretty difficult thing to take on board. Many of us can identify with Robert de Niro's character in the Robert Bolt scripted film, *The Mission*, who can't forgive himself for killing his brother in a fit of jealous rage. As an act of penance, he accompanies a small group of Jesuit missionaries to a mission station in the upper reaches of the Amazon, but insists on dragging a full suit of armour with him the whole way. Trussed up in a rope bag, the armour symbolizes everything wrong with his life – all his sins – and even though he desperately wants to be rid of them, he can't bring himself to accept forgiveness and sever the cord. When one of the Jesuits tries to cut it for him, during a particularly treacherous ascent up a waterfall, he climbs back down and ties the armour bag back on himself. He feels the full weight of his sins, and is unable to accept forgiveness because it would seem to make light of them. In the end, he only accepts forgiveness when it's given by someone he feels has the authority to bestow it – neither himself nor a priest, but one of the Guarani Indians he used to hunt and kill or enslave for a living.

Our churches are full of people who have equal difficulty in accepting God's forgiveness. Though they may have been through all the right moves of 'conversion', they still hold onto some of the weight of their guilt because, like de Niro, they feel that being forgiven is too easy. It seems to make light of their sins. But the truth is, of course, that it's refusing to let go of your sins and accept forgiveness, rather than holding onto them, that makes light of their importance.

We usually refuse to accept God's free gift of forgiveness in the misguided belief that there's something we ourselves can do to atone, at least in part, for what we've done wrong. But this is to underestimate the severity of our wrongdoing. In fact, our sins are so grave that even *trying* to atone for them ourselves is not only a waste of time, but in some ways actually offensive. Nothing we can do can even begin to make up for the havoc we wreak in other people's lives, and the pain this causes God as a loving Father. As Paul suggests (Romans 6:23), 'The wages of sin is death.' It's that serious. So if we're offered forgiveness – and by God's undeserved, unconditional love we are – the only thing we can really do is accept it gratefully.

Trapped under a mound of rubble, Gordon Wilson held onto his daughter Marie's hand. They'd been attending a Remembrance Day service in Enniskillen, Northern Ireland, to honour those who'd died in two World Wars when, without warning, a terrorist bomb had exploded, killing Marie and eight other civilians. A few hours later, he told reporters, 'I have lost my daughter, and we shall miss her. But I bear no ill will. I bear no grudge.'

The newspaper headlines the next day read 'Forgiveness'. Millions felt a deep admiration for Gordon's brave decision to forgive his daughter's killers; but millions more felt angry that, 'blinded' or 'brainwashed' by his Christian faith, he could even think of forgiving the perpetrators of so heinous a crime. Wouldn't forgiving them suggest that what they'd done was in some way acceptable? they asked. But Gordon knew what the angry millions, and even the IRA terrorists responsible for the murder, didn't: that nothing they could do, and nothing that could be done to them, could atone for killing Marie. He chose to forgive the IRA killers because he knew that they could never even *begin* to make amends for their crime. And he knew this not only because of the depth of his love for her, but also because, as a Christian, he himself had experienced what it was like to be forgiven for something he could never hope to atone for in his own strength.

> **Grace is, by definition, freely given. Yet both materially and spiritually, Christians act as if we had to earn our way in.**
> *Australian biker minister John Smith*

A Leap of Faith

Our task as churches is to help people discover God's unconditional love – his 'amazing grace' – for themselves, whatever stage they're at in their journey. The discovery may be a sudden revelation or part of a gradual process.

Chrissie had problems accepting God's love. A committed Christian, she could accept it all intellectually and give all the right responses, and her faith was entirely genuine. But somehow, the full assimilation of God's love, acceptance and forgiveness had never made the difficult journey from her head to her heart. At the same time, and not coincidentally, she had trouble accepting the idea that her friends really could love her. She'd joined her church youth group a year or so before, having left another church because she was about the only 16-year-old in the congregation, and had found herself being almost instantly accepted by the other young people. But deep down she harboured a suspicion that it was all a polite pretence, and the moment she left the room they all breathed a sigh of relief and said things like, 'Thank goodness she's gone! I really can't stand her, can you?'

One night, walking home from youth group, and wondering as she always did whether the others genuinely liked her or not, she started chatting out loud to God. She often did this: it was her way of praying, though she suspected it must look strange to passers-by. It made her feel a bit closer to God, though he never seemed to reply in quite the same way. On this occasion, however, as she asked him for the umpteenth time, 'Do you think they really like me?' a thought popped into her head so clearly that she felt as if he were giving an audible response: 'You'll never know.'

At first she found this a depressing prospect – a whole lifetime of never knowing if her friends actually liked her or not. But then it slowly dawned on her that that's not what the reply meant at all. It meant that, because she'd *never* know for sure one way or the other, she was free to make up her own mind. Some people were bound not to like her, just by the law of averages. But the evidence from everyone else would always be open to debate. So she could decide that her friends really liked her, or not, safe in the knowledge that she could *never* be proved wrong. Figuring that she'd probably enjoy life more if she assumed they liked her, she took a step of faith and believed. At first she kept having to tell herself that her friends *did* like her, but after a while she started honestly believing it. She still didn't feel she was particularly *worth* loving; she just came to the conclusion that they liked her anyway. And as she did, she started to realize for the first time what it meant for God to love her unconditionally.

Through biblical teaching, prayer and worship, we should aim to lead people to a similar understanding of God's love. But it shouldn't stop there. Through our love and concern for others, our interdependence and involvement, we can show God's love and forgiveness in ways that people can understand.

Bob Pierce, a young American, was in China in the closing months of the 1947 'War of Liberation'. He was so moved by the plight of some of the Chinese orphans, he gave up his last five dollars to a mission school to look after a little girl, White Jade. Bob returned home vowing to dedicate his life to caring for the White Jades of this world, and set up the international charity World Vision.

From practical deeds in our church and community to simple words of encouragement designed to 'build up each other' (1 Thessalonians 5:11) – catching people 'red handed' doing something right and praising them for it – we can help show God's unconditional love in action.

> **The choice is never between a risk and a sure thing.**
> **It's always a choice between risks. There is never a sure**
> **thing any more than there is ever a free lunch.**
> **American Presbyterian theologian Robert McAfee Brown**

Forgiveness

Our churches' challenge is to be continually pointing people towards an understanding of God's forgiveness in all its fullness. And the starting point is with us, recognizing our own faults and our own need for forgiveness. That may, of course, entail us seeking out people we've knowingly offended, apologizing for those angry words, or picking up the phone and speaking to someone in our family we've not spoken to in years. Through confessing what we've done wrong and asking for forgiveness, we can free ourselves from the past and pave a way for forgiveness, reconciliation and healing.

But we can hardly expect to appreciate the full meaning of forgiveness and acceptance – unconditional love – if we ourselves continue to hold grudges and refuse to 'forgive those who sin against us'. The more we insist on nursing wounds inflicted on us by other people, the more distance we put between ourselves and God. It's not that God will *only* forgive us *if* we forgive other people. That would make a mockery of the unconditional nature of his love. It's that, if we still insist on not forgiving others for the wrong they do against us, we're still harbouring the illusion that they can adequately atone for what they've done.

If it's not important, there's no real reason not to forgive them. And if it *is* important, the chances are that they *won't* be able to atone for it adequately, so we're just kidding ourselves by pretending that they can. And if we're kidding ourselves that they can atone for *their* sins, we're probably kidding ourselves that *we* can atone for *ours* … which inevitably means rejecting God's forgiveness.

In the story Jesus told to illustrate this point (Matthew 18:21–35), he made it very clear that our forgiveness of other people, like God's forgiveness of us, is endless. As Martin Luther King once put it, 'Forgiveness is not an occasional act; it is a permanent attitude.' In the same way, our love of other people, like God's love of us, must be both endless and unconditional. That means, as Gerald Coates is fond of saying, 'Everyone is winnable. We must never write them off.' Having experienced the gratuitous love and forgiveness of God, we're in a unique position to demonstrate that love, acceptance and forgiveness to other people. That means not being so quick to judge people who come to church looking for either love and forgiveness or answers. It means understanding that they'll change slowly, as a full realization of the depth and whole-heartedness of God's love gradually penetrates through their defence mechanisms. It means being patient, loving, accepting and forgiving.

IDEAS

The areas of love, acceptance and forgiveness undoubtedly bring to the fore hurts, anger, questions about self-worth and self-doubt. As churches, we need to be ready to support those in our community who need help, who are broken and hurting. We need to encourage people and love them for who they are, the way God made them. We need to demonstrate God's love, patience and concern in real ways. And we need to forgive.

Discovering God's love...

- Is there something you could do for a neighbour, or someone you know is in need of some practical help and support (e.g. gardening, cooking a meal, baby-sitting, shopping, spending time with them)?
- Cards or postcards are a helpful way of telling people you're thinking of them: birthdays, special anniversaries, exam time, thank-you notes. Even 'Just to say...' cards – when there's no particular occasion – are really appreciated.
- We're not always very good at telling people we love them. When did you last tell your mum, dad, kids, husband, wife, grandchildren, grandparents, best friend, etc., that you loved them? When did you tell them you really appreciate them or care for them? If telling them isn't easy, 'say it with flowers' or a gift (it doesn't have to cost much) instead.
- How often do we thank those on our church leadership team, the coffee rota, the verger or caretaker, the Sunday school teacher, the organist or music group leader, the elderly couple who sit quietly on the back row...?
- In what ways can you show your love in the community?

Think little and large! (Hospital visiting, clearing litter, setting up a soup run for the homeless, building an adventure playground, prison visiting, etc. There are more suggestions in the Ideas sections of other chapters.)

- Get involved in a project that helps people in developing countries. The Big Take, for example, is a fundraising youth project to help street children overseas. Tearfund, World Vision, Voluntary Service Overseas, etc., run projects and offer opportunities for short- or long-term work overseas. Showing you care needn't cost much! For less than 50p a day you can sponsor a child overseas through agencies such as World Vision and Tearfund.

...acceptance...

- Praise and encourage people. We're not always very good at thanking people and getting them to recognize their gifts and skills.
- Home groups are great forums for accepting people. The small group format makes it easier for people to be more honest with themselves and with others. Learn to trust one another, so people will feel valued, and able to share their concerns.
- Teach about self-worth. A lot of people don't believe they're worth very much. Sometimes we need reminding that we're valued by God, and by people around us.
- A personal challenge: how accepting are *you* of others? Who do you find it difficult to accept and why?
- Do you have someone else – other than a busy church leader – looking after the pastoral concerns of the church family and people in your area? Do you set aside times when people can come for pastoring or counselling?
- Offer an opportunity for personal prayer after a service. Some churches have found that a prayer ministry team can be a really effective support. Healing services, or special times of healing, can also be very valuable.

- Preventative measures. Run courses or seminars on areas of life such as: marriage preparation, debt, parenting, unemployment, redundancy, stress, preparing for retirement, growing older, disability awareness, marriage enrichment, singleness, racial injustice, family matters, etc. By facing some of the issues and problems honestly, we may help to avert a crisis situation. Awareness can also lead to greater understanding, tolerance and acceptance.

...and forgiveness

- Forgiveness starts with us. We may need to apologize, to right a past wrong, to forgive a friend, a neighbour, a family member for something we've done. But it may be too late to say sorry to (for example) a dad who died a few years ago. For some people, that may entail pastoral support and counselling. Admitting our mistakes isn't a sign of weakness. It'll let us move forward.
- We'll also need to ask for God's forgiveness. Some people find it helpful to write down their prayer for forgiveness, and then tear up or burn the piece of paper as a physical demonstration of God wiping the slate clean. But we mustn't then keep blaming ourselves and harking back to the mistakes we've made. We can't change yesterday, but tomorrow will be what we make it!
- Although the idea of 'confession' isn't as fashionable is it used to be, it remains a good model of how we can acknowledge and confess our sins to God. Psychologists, it would seem, have taken the place of a spiritual counsellor! We need to be prepared to *accept* forgiveness, too. Sometimes, when we've been really hurt, it's painful to accept an apology and it can lead to bitterness, resentment, etc.
- Dealing with the past – incidents, tensions, pain, family problems, abuse, etc. – may bring up a lot of issues. Pastoral support, prayer and opportunities for counselling are vital.

Some people will need professional help, which may require sensitive handling.

- The small group system – home groups, enquirers groups, youth groups, kids' clubs, etc. – is an important forum for nurturing and dealing with issues to do with forgiveness in a supportive way. Make sure there's time for prayer for everyone in the group. Sensitivity is vital, too, as not everyone will want to share personal issues in a group setting and may prefer a one-to-one or two-to-one opportunity.
- Again, healing services can be very important in the whole area of forgiveness. Allow people opportunities for special moments of healing and prayer.
- Reflect on the good times! Look back at what God has done in your life to get you this far. Thank him for what he's done for you!

RESOURCES

Agencies

Age Concern England, Astral House, 1268 London Road, London SW16 4ER. Tel: 0181 679 8000.

Age Concern Northern Ireland, 3 Lower Crescent, Belfast BT7 1NR. Tel: 01232 245729.

Age Concern Cymru, 4th Floor, 1 Cathedral Road, Cardiff CF1 9SD. Tel: 01222 371566.

Age Concern Scotland, 113 Rose Street, Edinburgh EH2 3DT. Tel: 0131 220 3345.

Association of Christian Counsellors, 173a Wokingham Road, Reading, RG6 1LT. Tel: 0118 9666 2207. ACC run an accreditation system for Christian counsellors.

Big Take Project, 115 Southwark Bridge Road, London SE11 0AX. Tel: 0171 450 9080.

Care for the Family, Garth House, Leon Avenue, Cardiff CF4 7RG. Tel: 01222 811733. Seminars, resources, etc. to support families.

Cruse Bereavement Care, Cruse House, 126 Sheen Road, Richmond, Surrey TW9 1UR. Tel: 0181 940 4818.

Family Alive! 1668 High Street, Knowle, Solihull B93 0LY. Tel: 01564 776133. A ministry of Agape. Residential weekends and local church seminars for couples.

Help the Aged, St James's Walk, Clerkenwell Green, London EC1R 0BE. Tel: 0171 253 0253. Fax: 0171 250 4474.

Marriage Care (formerly Catholic Marriage Advisory Council), Clitherow House, 1 Blythe Mews, Blythe Road, London W14 0NW. Tel: 0171 371 1341.

Relate Marriage Guidance, Herbert Gray College, Little Church Street, Rugby CV21 3AP. Tel: 01788 573241.

The Samaritans (check local phone book for appropriate number).

Tearfund, 100 Church Road, Teddington, Middlesex TW11 8QE. Tel: 0181 977 9144.

Voluntary Service Overseas, 217 Putney Bridge Road, London SW15 2PN. Tel: 0181 780 2266.

Waverley Christian Centre, Waverley Abbey House, Waverley Lane, Farnham GU9 8EP. Tel: 01252 783695. Training in pastoral care and Christian counselling.

World Vision, 599 Avebury Boulevard, Milton Keynes MK9 3PG. Tel: 01908 841010. Counselling, marriage preparation courses, etc.

See also listings under Chapters 1, 2, 3 and 4.

Books

Johann Christoph Arnold, *The Lost Art of Forgiving* (Plough, 1998)

Elias Chacour, *Blood Brothers* (Kingsway, 1985)

Elias Chacour, *We Belong to the Land* (Harper & Row, 1991)

Gary Collins, *Christian Counselling: A Comprehensive Guide* (Word Publishing, 1989)

Richard Genham, *Let My Heart Be Broken* (McGraw-Hill, 1960)

Barbara Johnson, *Stick a Geranium in Your Hat and Be Happy* (Word, 1990)

Henri Nouwen, *The Return of the Prodigal Son* (book) (DLT, 1994)

Henri Nouwen, *The Return of the Prodigal Son* (Lent course) (DLT, 1997)

Henri Nouwen, *The Wounded Healer* (DLT, 1994)

Corrie Ten Boom, *The Hiding Place* (Hodder & Stoughton, 1971)

Derek Tidball, *Skilful Shepherds* (IVP, 1986)

Philip Yancey, *What's So Amazing About Grace?* (Zondervan, 1997)

10 We Will Offer You the Chance to Make a New Start

Preface by Cardinal Basil Hume

*Cardinal Basil Hume was consecrated Archbishop of Westminster in
1976. Born in Newcastle-upon-Tyne in 1923, he entered the Order of
Saint Benedict at Ampleforth Abbey and became the Abbot of
Ampleforth in 1963. He has been President of the Bishops'
Conference of England and Wales since 1979.*

We are all privileged to be living at this special time in human history.
The third millennium is an opportunity for reconciliation with our
neighbour and with God, leading to a fresh start for the individual
and society. But no new beginning is possible unless we first accept
our need as individuals, as a Church, and as a society, for forgiveness
and healing.

Over this last century there have been many astounding achievements.
Science, technology and medicine have brought us untold benefits.
There have been great works of art, music and literature. Many have
enjoyed unparalleled prosperity. We thank God for His gifts. But there is
another side. Over half a million Armenians slaughtered by Turkish

nationalists in 1915; probably millions starved or murdered under Stalin in the 1930s. Nearer our own time we recall the Holocaust, Cambodians murdered by the Khmer Rouge, the genocide in Rwanda in 1994. There have been terrible wars. And there is the scandal of world poverty – often caused by human folly and greed – with 840 million people going hungry every day.

It is vital that we go into the next millennium different people – people intent on justice and peace. But if we are to become different people, then it is essential that we turn away from what is wrong and evil and turn to God. It is a change of heart to which we are constantly being called. We have to become men and women of strong faith, prayerful and of service to each other.

Change must occur in each one of us, if we are to be equipped to play our part in creating a better society. Does this frighten you? Do you find it daunting? I believe that we are being called by Christ to achieve great things for him and his Gospel. Each one of you is being called.

To those who are distanced from the Church, I want to say: 'come back', and to the rest of us: 'make them welcome'. God does not reject you, nor must the Church. God wants you to turn again to him, to learn about his love and to experience it.

We need to ensure the new millennium really will mark a new beginning for our world. Christ is our Way, our Truth, our Life. It is to him that we must turn. After all, the year 2000 is being celebrated to mark his coming into our world – God becoming man, the Incarnation.

We Will Offer You the Chance to Make a New Start

Jim was having a foul day. From the moment he got out of bed, tripped over the cat and hurtled headfirst into the wardrobe door, things hadn't gone according to plan. The kids had argued all over breakfast, he'd lost his car keys and been late for a meeting, the 'hole in the wall' had eaten his cash card, and his mum had slammed down the phone in a huff when he'd told her he was taking the family on holiday this Christmas. Now he was stuck in a massive traffic jam. His hand came down hard on the steering wheel in frustration, and he wished he could wind back the clock and start the day again.

Most people have times in their lives when they'd like to start over, to get a second chance. A failed relationship, vindictive words, unwise decisions, broken promises, failed exams, regrets. 'If only...' are words that constantly ring inside our heads. Yet society doesn't make it very easy for us to start again. Even if we do get an opportunity, we tend to carry a lot of baggage with us in the process. Many of us find it difficult to accept the concepts of forgiveness and unconditional love.

The Church, however, can offer people the chance to start again, because God has given us the opportunity of a new start. Through the torturous death of Jesus on the cross, he has wiped the slate clean for us. Michael Frost illustrates this radical wiping of the slate by telling the story of an American missionary in the Philippines, haunted by a terrible sin he'd committed years before, who encountered a girl said to have visions of the resurrected Jesus. Sceptical, he investigated a little further. What he found was that the girl appeared to be entirely genuine in her claims, though there was no proof whatsoever that they were true. So he set her a little test. He told her that the next time she encountered the risen Lord she should ask him what terrible sin it was he'd committed in his life. The priest had never told anyone about it, having confessed it to Christ and no one else, so he knew that her claims would be genuine if she could relay to him what the sin was. The girl expressed surprise that, having confessed the sin, the priest was still obviously troubled by it, but she agreed to ask Jesus next time she saw him. A few days later she returned.

'Well,' he asked, 'did you ask him what sin it was that I committed all those years ago?'

'Yes,' she replied.

'And what did he say?' the priest continued.

'He said he couldn't remember.'

> **I am not what I might be; I am not what I ought to be; I am not what I wish to be; I am not what I hope to be; but I thank God I am not what I once was, and I can say with the great apostle, 'By the grace of God I am what I am.'**
> *Hymn writer and former slave trader John Newton*

Altar Recall

This can be hard to accept, which is why a great many new Christians make a great many new starts. One just doesn't seem enough. It's like starting to write an important letter and deciding, after just a few lines, that you're not happy with what you've written. Removing the page from your writing pad, you screw the paper up into a ball and toss it into the bin. Then you start again from scratch. The more important the letter, the more of these 'false starts' you're likely to make. In fact, you only *stop* starting again when you've written so much on the sheet of paper that you just can't bear to copy it all out again simply in order to correct one little mistake.

When Michael became a Christian at the age of 14, he felt exactly as if he'd begun a new life. There was an incredible sense of wonder and excitement that lasted almost a full week. And then ... Michael became aware that his new start wasn't quite as 'clean' as he would have liked it to have been. A few weeks later, he was attending a church service designed for people who weren't Christians that ended with an 'altar call': an opportunity, for those who wanted, to commit their lives to faith in Jesus Christ and make a 'new start'. Though he'd already made this commitment and new start, Michael still felt the need to respond. He stood up in his seat as a public gesture of rededication, and felt the same kind of relief and excitement at making a new start that he had the first time.

But a few weeks later, he was back in the doldrums, feeling that he'd blown it again. As if his life were the start of a letter, he wanted to tear off his second 'new start' and begin all over again for a third time. And a couple of weeks later, at another 'altar call', he got the chance to do just that. In fact, for the first six months after initially becoming a Christian, Michael went forward and began all over again at every chance he got.

Of course, Michael's not alone. A great many of us find it hard to begin again, and with good reason: we're under the impression, mistaken though it is, that a 'new' start means a 'perfect' start. It's ironic, really. After all, what brings us to faith in the first place is an admission of our own failings and weakness – imperfections – and our inability to atone for what we've done wrong. Why we should then assume that, just moments after conversion, all our imperfections will have been entirely done away with is anyone's guess.

A perfect faith is nowhere to be found, so it follows that all of us are partly unbelievers. Yet in his kindness, God pardons us and reckons us to be believers upon account of our small portion of faith.
John Calvin

'Born Again'

Though it has been tarnished by its use amongst American tele-
vangelists and right-wing fundamentalist preachers, the Bible presents a wonderful picture of what's involved in this new start:
being 'born again'. What makes it so special is not simply that it
conjures up the image of being able to start from scratch, as if
we're starting out on a brand new life, but that it takes full
account of the fact that our brand new life is a *growing* experience.

Just as no one emerges from their mother's womb fully grown
and clutching a briefcase and a copy of the *Daily Telegraph*, so no
one emerges into what Jesus called 'eternal life' as a mature adult.
Instead, they enter on a steep learning curve, making plenty of
mistakes and entirely dependent on others for the things they
need to survive. The road to maturity and adulthood is a long,
and sometimes painful, one.

It's a little known fact that the whole of Reformation theology,
in many senses, hinges on the translation of a single word: *repentance*. When Martin Luther nailed his infamous 95 Theses to the
door of Castle Church, Wittenberg, on Halloween night, 1517,
he fired the opening salvo in what he hoped would be a serious
churchwide debate about the nature of repentance. In fact, his
first thesis reads, 'When our Lord and Master, Jesus Christ, said
"Repent", He called for the entire life of believers to be one of
penitence.'

Luther had become incensed at the way in which repentance
was being trivialized by the sale of 'indulgences'. Originally
conceived as a symbol of God's forgiveness and grace, an indul-
gence was a kind of pardon. When a person confessed their sins
to a priest, they were required to do an act of penance as a spiritual exercise: a way of focusing on God's grace and thanking
him for his forgiveness. But over the years, people came to see
penance not as a *response* to God's forgiveness, but almost as a
means to *earn* it. Indulgences, a way of writing off some or all

of this penance, were meant to remind people of the unearned nature of God's forgiveness. But as with penance itself, they became corrupted.

By 1517, people had come to see indulgences as a way of reducing the amount of time they or a relative had to spend in the 'refining fire' of purgatory (a kind of clearing house between heaven and hell). More importantly, they were for sale. Pope Leo X used the sale of indulgences as a fundraising exercise for the rebuilding of St Peter's in Rome. Luther was indignant because this turned indulgences into a way of *bribing* God for forgiveness. Turning his attention to the Greek New Testament, long forgotten but recently edited and published by Erasmus, he found that behind the Latin words for 'repent' – *paenitentiam agite*, literally 'do penance' – was a Greek word with a different slant to it: *metanoeite*, literally 'change your understanding'. Luther slowly came to see that repentance was not a one-off act, but an ongoing process of transformation.

In fact, Paul provides us with the model for this transformation in Romans 12:2: 'Do not be conformed to this world, but be transformed by the renewing of your minds, so that you may discern what is the will of God – what is good and acceptable and perfect.' He's clearly not talking about a one-off instance of renewal the moment after conversion. For one thing, he was writing this to people who were *already* Christians, and therefore long past the point when they'd been 'born again'. For another, as Leon Morris points out, 'The force of the present tense should not be overlooked; Paul envisages a continuing process of renewal.' When Paul says 'be transformed' – the Greek verb gives us our word 'metamorphosis', which we normally apply to the total transformation of a caterpillar into a butterfly – he's talking about a life-long experience.

What's more, it's not really something we do – more a process we allow God's *Spirit* to do in us. For Paul, this is the essence of the gospel: God saves us gratuitously through Jesus' death and resurrection, which we accept in faith, and renews us by his Holy

Spirit in the boiling pot we call the Church. (It's no coincidence that the remainder of Romans 12 is concerned with the way individual Christians are members of the whole Body of Christ.)

Immersed in a quick-fix culture, we've tended to focus on those episodes of dramatic, fast-paced transformation that seem to offer us a model of instant perfection, underplaying the slow-but-sure way in which the Holy Spirit habitually works. But behind the scenes, the truth is that even the most flash-in-the-pan transformations are actually more sedate than they first seem. Take the two undisputed 'giants' of the New Testament Church, for example: Peter and Paul.

Peter's transformation at Pentecost is often considered to be a picture of the speed with which the Spirit sometimes operates. Not only did he and others develop instant language skills, but, having denied knowing Jesus only a few weeks before, he preached a blindingly good off-the-cuff sermon about his being the messiah to a crowd of over three thousand loyal Jews. From zero to hero in a little under two months! But this is far from the end of the story, for Paul recalls a run-in with Peter (Galatians 2) in which the 'rock' had gone back to his old tricks and was rapidly back-pedalling from the bold inclusion of Gentiles in the Church which he himself had pioneered (Acts 10). Similarly, after an initial burst of activity following his conversion on the road to Damascus, Paul disappeared off the scene for several years. When he finally emerged from his 'cocoon' as Barnabas' junior partner, his entire way of understanding the world had changed. Hardly quick as a flash.

> **Changed from glory into glory, till in heaven we take our place.**
> *Charles Wesley, 'Love Divine, All Loves Excelling'*

A Work in Progress

In his book *Ordering Your Private World*, Gordon MacDonald recounts the experience he and his family had when they bought an old abandoned farmhouse in New Hampshire. The first challenge they faced was clearing the land round the house in order to turn it into a lawn. Having lain unused for quite a while, it was littered with rocks and stones, some of them quite big. They set about clearing the big rocks first, before turning their attention to the smaller ones. Eventually, having cleared the whole ground of rocks, stones and little pebbles, they were ready to seed the grass. It grew well, and they soon had a lawn around their house to be proud of. But the next year, they noticed that new rocks and stones had begun to appear amongst the blades of grass, having surfaced from beneath ground level.

The MacDonalds discovered that clearing the ground of stones wasn't a one-off event: it needed to be done year after year. Gordon MacDonald compares this in his book with the process of dealing with sin. The things that need transforming in our lives can't be dealt with all in one go: instead, they're dealt with in stages, and some of them don't rise to the surface until after quite a few years have passed.

Not everyone will be at a point where they're ready to make as fresh a start as we might want them to, but we need to remember that we don't set the timescale. The Holy Spirit does. Not everything is dealt with simultaneously. Whatever stage people are at, we need to give them the support, encouragement, opportunity, freedom and space to change at a suitable pace.

Sharon and Derek lived together with their two children on a council estate. Sharon was involved at the local community centre, looking after some of the elderly people, having first made contact with the centre a few years earlier when she used to drop her son Jay into the crèche. The centre was run by one of the local churches, and she and Derek had decided to go along to the family service, to see what it was like. Feeling welcome there, they kept going. The kids enjoyed the 'C Zone Club', and when Derek and Sharon were invited to join the 'Just Looking' Christian basics course the church was running, they felt confident enough to give it a try. It helped them understand a bit more about God and the Church, though they didn't feel ready to make any firm commitments.

After a couple of years of being part of the church, and of having been well supported, both spiritually and practically, Sharon and Derek reached the point where they felt they trusted God enough to become Christians. Quietly, praying with the minister in their front room, they made a commitment of faith. And as that faith grew, and they learned more and more about the depth of God's love for them, they found that they were learning to love and trust each other more as well. Though their relationship had always been good, they both sensed that it was reaching new levels. After about 18 months, they felt they wanted to get married. This was a bold step for them: they'd always shied away from it before, because it had seemed to spell ruin for all their friends' relationships. But now it felt like the right thing to do – the most natural and obvious step to take.

Looking back, they were grateful that the people in the church hadn't made it an issue for them, pushing them into marriage before *they* felt ready for it. No one had ever seemed to mind the fact that they were just living together, they said, and that had spoken volumes to them about God's unconditional love. 'We just figured we'd cross that bridge when we came to it,' the minister replied. 'I admit, one of the church wardens did suggest that I had a "quiet word" with you at one stage, but I felt you had a lot on your plates just coming to grips with some of the basic bits of your new-found faith. I trusted the Holy Spirit would get round to the marriage thing eventually.'

A church will never learn from its mistakes unless it is ready to risk making some.
Former Archbishop of Canterbury Robert Runcie

Believing and Belonging

It's very easy for us to expect people (and ourselves) to change too much too soon. We have to be open instead to the gentle promptings of the Holy Spirit, which may be gradual or may be dramatic. The truth is, there's no blueprint: we're all unique. We need to allow ourselves – and others – to be 'works in progress', allowing God to change us day by day.

As a child, Terri had been a regular churchgoer. She'd had to be: her father was a vicar. But because he found it difficult to talk to his family about his faith, Terri had never really grown much as a Christian. At university she had, along with all her friends, given church the boot, but as she reached her early forties and had a young family of her own, she found herself becoming more and more interested in spiritual things. Since she lived just down the road from the local church, she decided to give it a try. The welcome she received was genuine and enthusiastic, and being an outgoing sort of person she made friends very easily. Having grown up in a similar church, she found it easy to fit in, and to find an opportunity to contribute her artistic and business skills. After a year or so as a regular member of the church, she was asked to join the church leadership council (PCC).

She accepted, but soon realized that a few church members were less than happy about her being on the PCC, as they felt that her faith wasn't yet mature enough. When she drew this to the vicar's attention, wondering if she should resign, he just smiled. 'How mature is "mature enough"?' he asked. 'I don't know. If we had to sit a doctrine exam before we could join the PCC, I don't think any of us would pass, do you? We're all on a journey, learning and maturing the whole time. And we're in good company. Look at the disciples. One of them betrayed Jesus, the rest abandoned him, and none of them really understood him properly until after the resurrection ... and maybe not even then!'

Terri stayed on the PCC. She felt it gave her a sense of self-worth and belonging. It was a forum in which she could contribute her skills. And as she became more and more a *part* of the church, so her understanding of God grew and her faith deepened and matured.

If the church had opted to ask her to stand down, as some of its members wanted, she might never have been given the opportunities she needed to grow in her faith. Trapped in the pews as a consumer, rather than an active participant, her feelings of belonging might well have become feelings of exclusion, and rather than growing in her understanding of God's *unconditional* love, she might have come to see it as being highly *conditional*.

> **I do not seek to understand in order to believe, but rather I believe in order that I may understand.**
> *Former Archbishop of Canterbury St Anselm*

New Era, New Start

The year AD 2000 marks a period of transition. Despite the past two thousand years of civilization and technological advancement, we still haven't found the answers as a society to some of life's most basic questions. Politics, philosophy, materialism – they've all been tried and found decidedly wanting. As we move into the third millennium, many people will be asking questions about our past and becoming concerned for our future. There'll be a lot of heart-searching and reflection, as well as celebration.

But AD 2000 marks something else as well: a measure of time relating to the symbolic birth date of Jesus Christ, when God revealed himself to the world in human form. There were no great public announcements, no royal trappings, no front-page headlines or paparazzi photos. He was born to Mary – a girl who'd become pregnant before she was legally married – and laid in a simple cattle trough in a town whose only real claim to fame had been during its 'Golden Age' a thousand years before. His state execution some 33 years later went by almost without notice. Yet it offered humanity the chance to wipe the slate clean, to make a new start.

Both as individuals and as churches, the new millennium offers us all a chance to renew ourselves afresh to God: spiritually, in our commitment, and practically, in our lives. As a symbolic celebration of God's original 'new start' event, it offers us the chance to begin again – 'to begin at the beginning', as the opening words of Dylan Thomas' *Under Milk Wood* put it. It doesn't matter whether our faith is old, young or as yet non-existent. We need to go back to the moment of incarnation two thousand years ago, when the 'Word' became 'flesh' and, 'though he was in the form of God, did not regard equality with God as something to be exploited, but emptied himself, taking the form of a slave, being born in human likeness. And being found in human form, he humbled himself and became obedient to the point of death – even death on a cross' (Philippians 2:6–8).

The Church's task is the same as it always has been: to glorify God by making him known to each generation. So our churches must be places that are welcoming, relevant and challenging. We need to engage in the community and respond to the people around us at home, in our communities, and in the wider world. For though Jesus was God, he was also human, with ordinary needs, weaknesses and desires. He faced hunger, anguish, fear and suffering. And through his humanity, he responded to people: to their needs, their anxieties, their hopes, their fears and dreams. And he called his followers to do the same.

'At the end of the twentieth century,' said Martin Luther King, 'most of us will not have to repent of the great evils we have done, but simply of the great apathy that stopped us from doing anything.' If we really take on board Jesus' call to follow him, we'll have to be equally committed to both evangelical witness *and* compassionate service, those great 'inseparable twins' of Christian tradition. To quote John Stott again, 'True faith issues in love, and true love issues in service.'

So let's make a new start with God, at home and for the world's poor, by finding ways in which we can realistically make a difference in our own and other people's lives. As Billy Graham once said: 'Every generation is strategic. We are not responsible for the past generation, and we cannot bear the full responsibility for the next one; but we do have *our* generation. God will hold us responsible as to how well we fulfil our responsibilities to this age and take advantage of our opportunities.'

IDEAS

Let's not allow 'the great apathy' to stop us from making the most of the opportunities presented by this strategic era in our history. As we seek to find ways of making a *new start with God*, a *new start at home*, and a *new start for the world's poor*, let's commit ourselves to continually finding ways of making the gospel relevant in our churches and in our communities as we enter the new millennium and beyond.

A new start with God

- Pledge your church to take up these *New Millennium Challenge* goals. Commit yourselves to working through each one, as we look to find ways of making our churches more welcoming, relevant and challenging in our communities. Contact Fanfare for a New Generation for information.
- Find a way that suits you of making a fresh start with God. It may be a simple prayer, it may be a symbolic act, it may be through a more dramatic experience.

- Some people have found writing a letter to God a helpful way of expressing how they feel and saying sorry for all the wrong they've done. They then tear it up in pieces or burn it. If you're creative, you may find art, craft, music, dance, photography, etc. a good way of expressing your feelings.
- A similar exercise with children (and adults!), is to get them to write in thick pen on a balloon, or attach a luggage label to the balloon. You can then let go of it outside and watch it float away. It's really effective with a large number of people.
- You may find holding a special New Start Sunday service a helpful way of encouraging people to make a recommitment to Christ. You may find the first Sunday of 2000 (2 January) a helpful, symbolic time to do that, or around Easter or Pentecost. A number of special prayers are being written for the occasion. Fanfare for a New Generation and the Churches' Millennium Office can help you with further information and resources.
- Consider running some mission or evangelistic events or programmes in the period running up to your New Start Sunday. Organizations preparing specific material include: International Christian Communications (ICC) and Fanfare for a New Generation, with the *Time … to Make a Difference* tapes; March for Jesus with their *Millennium Child* and *Jesus Day* events; Rob Frost team with *Hopes and Dreams* music, drama and community programmes and resources; CPAS/ Agape with *The Jesus Video Project*; Y2000 evangelistic resource material using the 'Y' symbol. Contact Anno Domini for details of more millennium projects, or the Churches Together in England Millennium Office.
- Make sure you have a selection of 'new start' books and booklets for all ages in your church. Try to provide booklets free of charge – a gift – where possible, to those who'd like to know more. You could even get your church to produce its own.

- Do you have a library or bookstall in your foyer or in your church? It's a really helpful resource for people who'd like reading or audio-tape materials to use at home. (See Resources section, Chapter 7 for more ideas.)
- Pray for opportunities in your church and community and pray for the *people*. Prayer cells, all-night prayer vigils, prayer chains, prayer triplets, etc. are all really helpful and effective ways of keeping up the prayer momentum.

A new start at home

- Encourage your church to support your local school, the people who work with and invest in the lives of the young people in your community. *Generation to Generation* is a project aimed at helping you find practical and imaginative ways (big and little) of supporting your young people. Contact Fanfare for a New Generation.
- Find out if your local school is taking part in the *JC2000* arts festival and get involved if you can. Contact JC2000.
- Run some special events or seminars focusing on life choice issues and family values. (See Chapters 2 and 4 for further ideas.)
- What does it mean to be community? In what ways can we help our community better? The Shaftesbury Society, Tearfund and the Evangelical Alliance are running the *Rebuilding Communities* project looking at the whole area of community. Contact the Evangelical Alliance.
- Identify a need in your particular community and work on a special project. Chapter 4 may give you further ideas. Fundraise for a local project or support an organization involved in social action. For plenty of fundraising ideas, check out *Get Up and Give* by Steve Chalke and Sir Cliff Richard.

A new start for the world's poor

- Hold a special service focusing on some of the issues surrounding the world's poor. You could incorporate an after-service lunch, invite a speaker, show a video, show or sell some of the crafts, cards and products produced by developing countries. Agencies such as Tearfund, Oasis Trust, Christian Aid and World Vision are all involved in helping to bring relief to the world's poor in developing countries. Tearfund, World Vision, Jacob's Well and Traidcraft produce useful resource material for churches.
- Get involved in a project (the agencies above will help you with ideas).
- Support a child in a developing country through their education years. A number of charities run child sponsorship programmes including Tearfund and World Vision.
- Get involved in campaigning to help cancel world debt. Jubilee 2000 is a coalition of partner organizations and celebrities, and has produced a number of resources (see Resources section).
- Organize an event on the theme of debt. Discuss debt and the notion of 'Jubilee' (Leviticus 25 and Deuteronomy 15) in home groups, services, Sunday schools and youth clubs.
- Support one of the agencies working to bring relief to the world's poor. Get involved in fundraising, pray for their work, get up to date on the issues and the work they're doing.
- Get your youth group involved in campaigning and raising awareness about major issues in developing countries. The Big Take (a joint Tearfund/Oasis Trust project) can help with this, as well as creating opportunities for the young people to learn media skills.

RESOURCES

Resources

Big Take Video Pack. Video and fundraising ideas for young people, how to learn media skills, plus information about major issues in developing countries. Available from Big Take.

The Debt Cutter's Handbook. Includes a history of the debt crisis, case studies on the impact of debt, and practical ideas to raise awareness about debt. Available from Jubilee 2000.

New Start Pack. Sets out the theology of New Start, details of liturgies, prayers and hymns for services, the Millennium Moment candle and affirmation, a list of useful contacts, plus photocopiable New Start artwork and a disk, for your local publicity. Produced by Churches Together in England.

Generation to Generation Resource Pack. Practical suggestions and ideas for encouraging your local church to support your local school. Available from Fanfare for a New Generation.

The Jesus Video. Film dramatization of Luke's Gospel. Available from Agape.

Y2000 activities, resources, Seeker Service outlines, children's holiday club and youth group material, cell group and discovery course material. Available from Y2000.

Making the Most of the Millennium. Resources, ideas and information for celebrations and mission. Available from CPAS.

CEA (Christian Enquiry Agency) literature. Resources and literature sent through the post for people who want to enquire anonymously about the Christian faith. Available from Christian Enquiry Agency.

Four Corners. Resource material for young people (individuals or groups). Available from World Vision.

World Vision Sunday Resource Pack. Available from World Vision.

Why 2000? A lively illustrated booklet explaining the gospel message to 5–10-year-olds. Available from Hope Designs.

Why Jesus? Booklet by Nicky Gumbel explaining the Christian faith. Available from Alpha.

Agencies

Agape, Fairgate House, King's Road, Tyseley, Birmingham B11
2AA. Tel: 0121 7654404.

Alpha, Holy Trinity Brompton, Brompton Road, London SW7
1JA. Tel: 0171 5818255. Hotline: 0345 581278.

Anno Domini, PO Box 680, Maidenhead, Berks SL6 9ST.
Tel: 07071 202000.

Big Take Project, 115 Southwark Bridge Road, London SE1
0AX. Tel: 0171 4509080.

Christian Aid, PO Box 100, London SE1 7RT. Tel: 0171 620 4444.

Christian Enquiry Agency (CEA), Inter-Church House, 35–41
Lower Marsh, London SE1 7RL. Tel: 0171 523 2123.

Church Pastoral Aid Society (CPAS), Athena Drive, Tachbrook
Park, Warwick, CV34 6NG. Tel: 01926 334242.

Churches Together in England Millennium Office, Church House,
Great Smith Street, London SW1P 3NZ (0171 340 0250).

Evangelical Alliance, Whitefield House, 186 Kennington Park
Road, London SE11 4BT. Tel: 0171 582 0228.

Fanfare for a New Generation, 115 Southwark Bridge Road,
London SE1 0AX. Tel: 0171 450 9070/1. E-mail:
fanfare@btconnect.com

Hope Designs, 18 Portsmouth Lane, Lindfield, West Sussex
RH16 1SJ. Tel/fax: 01444 410949.

International Christian Communications (ICC), Silverdale Road,
Eastbourne, East Sussex BN20 7AB. Tel: 01323 643341.

Jacob's Well, 23 Mount Street, Manchester M4 4DE. Tel: 0171
953 4039.

JC2000, 4–5 Hazlitt Mews, London W14 0JZ. Tel: 0171 371 3716.

Jubilee 2000, PO Box 100, London SE1 7RT. Tel: 0171 401 9999.

March for Jesus, Wellington House, New Zealand Avenue,
Walton on Thames, KT12 1PY. Tel: 01932 232345.

Oasis Trust, 115 Southwark Bridge Road, London SE1 0AX. Tel:
0171 450 9000.

Rob Frost Team, The Methodist Church, Tolverne Road, Raines
Park, London SW20 8RA. Tel: 0181 288 1961.

The Shaftesbury Society, 16 Kingston Road, London SW19 1JZ. Tel: 0181 239 5555.

Tearfund, 100 Church Road, Teddington, Middlesex TW11 8QE. Tel: 0181 977 9144.

Traidcraft, Kingsway, Gateshead, Tyne and Wear NE11 0NE. Tel: 0191 491 0591.

World Vision, 599 Avebury Boulevard, Milton Keynes, MK9 3PG. Tel: 01908 841010.

Y2000, PO Box 94, Chessington, Surrey KT9 2YJ. Tel: 0181 287 3147.

Books

P. Butler and G. Piper, *Following Jesus* (Scripture Union, 1993)

Steve Chalke and Sir Cliff Richard, *Get Up and Give* (HarperCollins, 1998)

A Chance to Start Again: Marking the Millennium (Churches Together in England)

Nicky Cruz, *Run Baby Run* (Hodder & Stoughton, 1968)

Mark Elsdon-Dew (ed.), *The God who Changes Lives* (Holy Trinity Brompton, 1995)

Stephen Gaukroger, *It Makes Sense* (Scripture Union, 1996)

Billy Graham, *Just as I am* (Marshall Pickering, 1998)

Michael Green, *My God* (Eagle, 1992)

Michael Green, *Ten Myths about Christianity* (Lion, 1998)

Nicky Gumbel, *Questions of Life* (Kingsway, 1993)

Paul Little, *How to Give Away Your Faith* (IVP, 1988)

Gordon MacDonald, *Ordering Your Private World* (Highland Books, 1984)

Sue Mummery, *Why 2000?* (Hope Designs, 1998)

Sue Page, *Away with Words* (Lynx, 1998)

Nick Pollard, *Evangelism Made Slightly Less Difficult* (IVP, 1997)

See also other chapters for more book suggestions.

■ About Fanfare for a New Generation

Fanfare for a New Generation is a Christian charity committed to putting Jesus Christ centre stage of the millennial celebrations.

Fanfare for a New Generation has been created to encourage local churches and Christians grasp the opportunities to share their faith at home, at work, among friends and in the community.

NEW MILLENNIUM SUNDAY, 2 January 2000

A UK-wide initiative, celebrating the **first Sunday** of the new millennium, aiming to:

- Challenge people to go to church on that day, giving them the opportunity to make a new start spiritually for the new millennium.
- Challenge each local church to be ready for its visitors/newcomers, ensuring that, as a community, they continue to be welcoming, relevant and challenging.

Pledge your church to be millennium friendly by 2 January 2000 and beyond!

Send off for your free *Making Sunday Best* 'health check' resource pack.

GENERATION TO GENERATION

A practical, ongoing project encouraging and equipping your local church to support and help resource your local school and the young people in your community.

For details about *Fanfare for a New Generation*, the free *Making Sunday Best* 'health check', and the *Generation to Generation Churches Resource Pack*, ring: 0171 450 9070/1.   E-mail: fanfare@btconnect.com

Fanfare for a New Generation is a Registered Charity (1064817) and a Private Limited Company (3398569).